OXFORD REVISE

EDEXCEL GCSE

MATHS

Foundation

COMPLETE REVISION AND PRACTICE

Naomi Bartholomew-Millar

Paul Hunt

Victoria Trumper

OXFORD
UNIVERSITY PRESS

Contents

 Shade in each level of the circle as you feel more confident and ready for your exam.

How to use this book

This book uses a three-step approach to revision: **Knowledge**, **Retrieval**, and **Practice**.
It is important that you do all three; they work together to make your revision effective.

 **Knowledge**

Knowledge comes first. Each chapter starts with a **Knowledge Organiser**. These are clear easy-to-understand, concise summaries of the content that you need to know for your exam. The information is organised to show how one idea flows into the next so you can learn how everything is tied together, rather than lots of disconnected facts.

Worked example

Worked examples offer step by step guidance on working through a question, to a solution.

REVISION TIP

Revision tips offer you helpful advice and guidance to aid your revision and help you to understand key concepts and remember them.

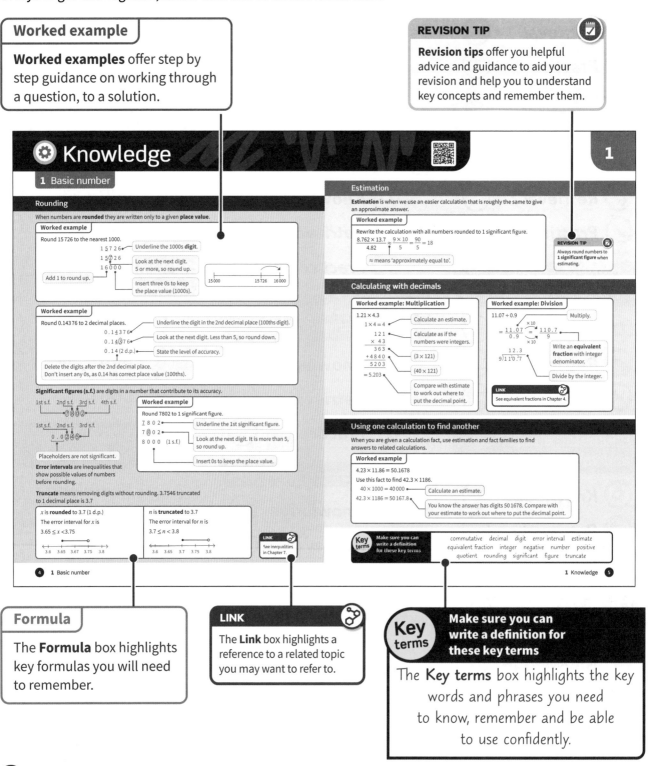

Formula

The **Formula** box highlights key formulas you will need to remember.

LINK

The **Link** box highlights a reference to a related topic you may want to refer to.

Key terms — Make sure you can write a definition for these key terms

The **Key terms** box highlights the key words and phrases you need to know, remember and be able to use confidently.

 Retrieval

The **Retrieval questions** help you learn and quickly recall the information you've acquired. These are short questions and answers about the content in the Knowledge Organiser you have just reviewed. Cover up the answers with some paper and write down as many answers as you can from memory. Check back to the Knowledge Organiser for any you got wrong, then cover the answers and attempt all the questions again until you can answer *all* the questions correctly.

Make sure you revisit the retrieval questions on different days to help them stick in your memory. You need to write down the answers each time, or say them out loud, otherwise it won't work.

Previous Questions

Each chapter also has some **Retrieval questions** from **previous chapters**. Answer these to see if you can remember the content from the earlier chapters. If you get the answers wrong, go back and do the Retrieval questions for the earlier chapters again.

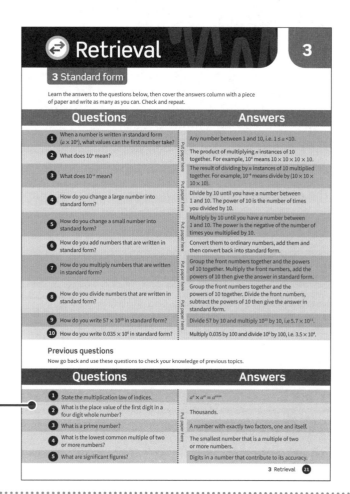

 Practice

Once you think you know the Knowledge Organiser and Retrieval answers really well, you can move on to the final stage: **Practice**.

Each chapter has **exam-style questions**, including some questions from previous chapters, to help you apply all the knowledge you have learnt and can retrieve.

Answers and Glossary

You can scan the QR code at any time to access the sample answers and mark schemes for all the exam-style questions, glossary containing definitions of the key terms, as well as further revision support. Visit go.oup.com/OR/GCSE/Ed/Maths/F

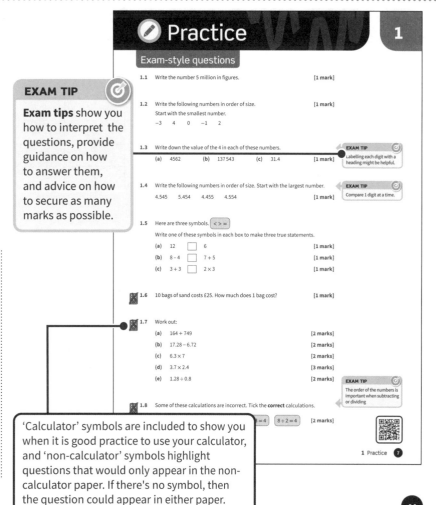

⚙ Knowledge

1 Basic number

Definitions

An **integer** is a whole **number**, such as 1, 73, 946, −17.

The **product** is the result when you multiply numbers.

The **sum** is the result when you add numbers.

The **quotient** is the result when you divide one number by another.

Commutative means that the calculation can be done in any order. For example, addition and multiplication are commutative:

$7 + 4 = 4 + 7$ $8 \times 2 = 2 \times 8$

But subtraction and division are not:

$7 - 4 \neq 4 - 7$ $8 \div 2 \neq 2 \div 8$

Order of operations (BIDMAS)

Use BIDMAS to help you do calculations in the correct order.

Brackets ( )

Indices (powers and roots)

Division and **M**ultplication

Addition and **S**ubtraction

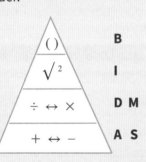

( )	B
$\sqrt{}\ ^2$	I
$\div \leftrightarrow \times$	D M
$+ \leftrightarrow -$	A S

Worked example

1. $43 - 9 \times 4 + 5$ $43 - \underline{9 \times 4} + 5$ ← BIDMAS Multiplication first.

    $= \underline{43 - 36} + 5$ ← BIDMAS Addition and Subtraction.

    $= 7 + 5 = 12$

2. $32 - 6^2 \div 2$ $32 - \underline{6^2} \div 2$ ← BIDMAS Indices (powers) first.

    $= 32 - \underline{36 \div 2}$ ← BIDMAS Division.

    $= 32 - 18 = 14$

Place value

Th	H	T	O	t	h	th
		2	7	1		
	2	7	1			
2	7	1	0			
			2	7	1	
			0	2	7	1

Fill gaps before the decimal point with 0

27.1×10 the numbers move 1 place left.

27.1×100 the numbers move 2 places left.

$27.1 \div 10$ the numbers move 1 place right.

$27.1 \div 100$ the numbers move 2 places right.

Ordering numbers

Worked example

Which is larger, 1.3 or 1.105?

    1 . 3 **0 0**
    1 . 1 0 5 ← Write in columns, then write in 0s so both numbers have the same number of decimal places.

1.3 > 1.105

Inequality symbols

The small end points to the small number.

  $2 < 6$

  $6 > 2$

Negative numbers

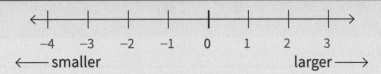

Rules for adding and subtracting negative numbers

Adding a positive number.

$5 + 2$

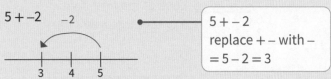

Adding a negative number is the same as subtracting.

$5 + -2$

$5 + -2$
replace $+ -$ with $-$
$= 5 - 2 = 3$

Subtracting a positive number.

$-4 - 3$

Subtracting a negative number is the same as adding.

$-4 - -3$

$-4 - -3$
replace $- -$ with $+$
$-4 + 3 = -1$

Worked example

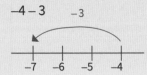

$1 - 3 - -6$

$1 - 3 - -6$ — Replace $- -$ with $+$

$= 1 - 3 + 6$

$= -2 + 6$

$= 4$

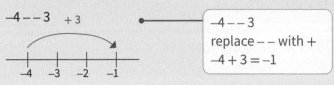

Rules for multiplying and dividing negative numbers

positive $\times$ or $\div$ positive $=$ positive

positive $\times$ or $\div$ negative $=$ negative

negative $\times$ or $\div$ positive $=$ negative

negative $\times$ or $\div$ negative $=$ positive

Worked example

1. $4 \times (-2) = -8$ — positive $\times$ negative $=$ negative

2. $(-3) \times 5 = -15$ — negative $\times$ positive $=$ negative

3. $(-3) \times (-4) = 12$ — negative $\times$ negative $=$ positive

4. $6 \div (-2) = -3$ — positive $\div$ negative $=$ negative

5. $(-8) \div (-2) = 4$ — negative $\div$ negative $=$ positive

⚙ Knowledge

1 Basic number

Rounding

When numbers are **rounded** they are written only to a given **place value**.

Worked example

Round 15 726 to the nearest 1000.

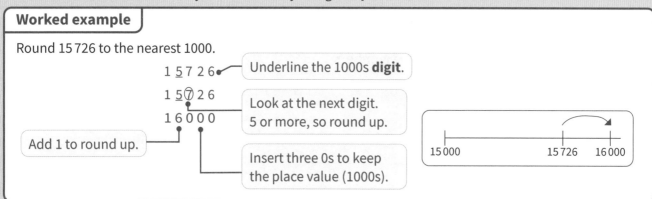

1 5 7 2 6 — Underline the 1000s **digit**.

1 5 7 2 6 — Look at the next digit. 5 or more, so round up.

1 6 0 0 0 — Add 1 to round up.

Insert three 0s to keep the place value (1000s).

Worked example

Round 0.143 76 to 2 decimal places.

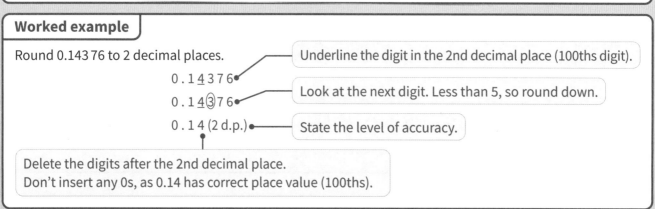

0 . 1 4 3 7 6 — Underline the digit in the 2nd decimal place (100ths digit).

0 . 1 4 3 7 6 — Look at the next digit. Less than 5, so round down.

0 . 1 4 (2 d.p.) — State the level of accuracy.

Delete the digits after the 2nd decimal place.
Don't insert any 0s, as 0.14 has correct place value (100ths).

Significant figures (s.f.) are digits in a number that contribute to its accuracy.

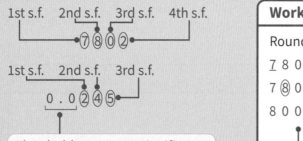

1st s.f.   2nd s.f.   3rd s.f.   4th s.f.

7 8 0 2

1st s.f.   2nd s.f.   3rd s.f.

0 . 0 2 4 5

Placeholders are not significant.

Error intervals are inequalities that show possible values of numbers before rounding.

Worked example

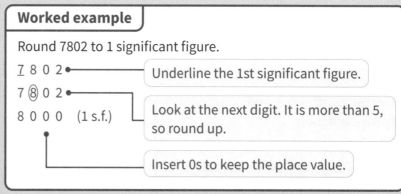

Round 7802 to 1 significant figure.

7 8 0 2 — Underline the 1st significant figure.

7 8 0 2 — Look at the next digit. It is more than 5, so round up.

8 0 0 0   (1 s.f.)

Insert 0s to keep the place value.

Truncate means removing digits without rounding. 3.7546 truncated to 1 decimal place is 3.7

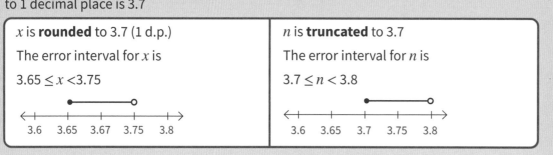

x is **rounded** to 3.7 (1 d.p.)	n is **truncated** to 3.7
The error interval for x is	The error interval for n is
$3.65 \leq x < 3.75$	$3.7 \leq n < 3.8$

LINK

See inequalities in Chapter 7.

Estimation

Estimation is when we use an easier calculation that is roughly the same to give an approximate answer.

Worked example

Rewrite the calculation with all numbers rounded to 1 significant figure.

$$\frac{8.762 \times 13.7}{4.82} \approx \frac{9 \times 10}{5} = \frac{90}{5} = 18$$

$\approx$ means 'approximately equal to'.

> **REVISION TIP**
>
> Always round numbers to **1 significant figure** when estimating.

Calculating with decimals

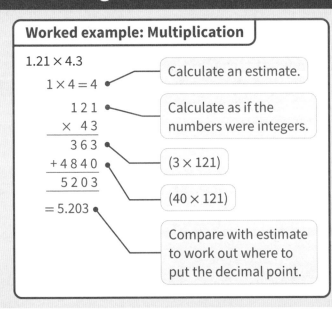

Worked example: Multiplication

1.21×4.3

$1 \times 4 = 4$ — Calculate an estimate.

$$\begin{array}{r} 1\,2\,1 \\ \times\ \ 4\,3 \\ \hline 3\,6\,3 \\ +4\,8\,4\,0 \\ \hline 5\,2\,0\,3 \end{array}$$

$= 5.203$

- Calculate as if the numbers were integers.
- (3×121)
- (40×121)
- Compare with estimate to work out where to put the decimal point.

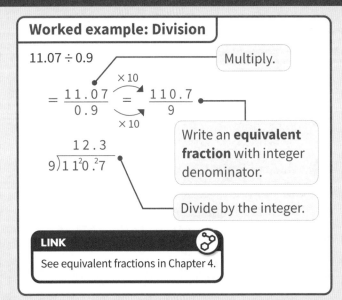

Worked example: Division

$11.07 \div 0.9$ — Multiply.

$$= \frac{11.07}{0.9} \xlongequal[\times 10]{\times 10} \frac{110.7}{9}$$

$$9\overline{)1\,1\,{}^20.{}^27}\ \ 12.3$$

- Write an **equivalent fraction** with integer denominator.
- Divide by the integer.

> **LINK**
>
> See equivalent fractions in Chapter 4.

Using one calculation to find another

When you are given a calculation fact, use estimation and fact families to find answers to related calculations.

Worked example

$4.23 \times 11.86 = 50.1678$

Use this fact to find 42.3×1186.

$40 \times 1000 = 40\,000$ — Calculate an estimate.

$42.3 \times 1186 = 50\,167.8$ — You know the answer has digits 50 1678. Compare with your estimate to work out where to put the decimal point.

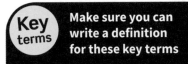

Key terms Make sure you can write a definition for these key terms

commutative   decimal   digit   error interval   estimate
equivalent fraction   integer   negative   number   positive
quotient   rounding   significant figure   truncate

 # Retrieval

1 Basic number

Learn the answers to the questions below, then cover the answers column with a piece of paper and write as many as you can. Check and repeat.

Questions	Answers
1 What do the letters of BIDMAS stand for?	Brackets, indices, division, multiplication, addition, and subtraction.
2 Which part of the following calculation would you do first? $24 - 3 \times 8$	3×8
3 $a > b$ Which is the larger number?	a
4 What can you use to help you order all types of numbers?	A number line.
5 What can you do to make ordering decimal numbers easier?	Write all the numbers to the same number of decimal places.
6 What does the second number after the decimal point count?	Hundredths.
7 When you round to the nearest thousand, which number do you need to look at to decide whether to round up or down?	The hundreds.
8 When you round a number to 1 decimal place, which number do you need to look at to decide whether to round up or down?	The second decimal place.
9 What are error intervals used to measure?	The accuracy of a number after it has been rounded.
10 When you multiply a number by a power of 10, in which direction does the number move on a place value chart?	Left.
11 When you divide a number by a power of 10, in which direction does the number move on a place value chart?	Right.
12 When you round a number to two significant figures, which number do you need to look at to decide whether to round up or down?	The third significant figure.
13 For numbers less than 1, do you count the leading zeroes when rounding to a given number of significant figures?	No.
14 What is the first significant figure?	The first non-zero digit, counting from the left.
15 When rounding 2459 to 2 s.f., what is this the same as rounding to?	The nearest hundred.
16 When you are asked to estimate the value of a calculation, what should you round each number to?	1 significant figure.

Put paper here

Exam-style questions

1.1 Write the number 5 million in figures.   [1 mark]

1.2 Write the following numbers in order of size.   [1 mark]

Start with the smallest number.

−3   4   0   −1   2

1.3 Write down the value of the 4 in each of these numbers.

EXAM TIP
Labelling each digit with a heading might be helpful.

(a)   4562   (b)   137 543   (c)   31.4   [1 mark]

1.4 Write the following numbers in order of size. Start with the largest number.

EXAM TIP
Compare 1 digit at a time.

4.545   5.454   4.455   4.554   [1 mark]

1.5 Here are three symbols.   < > =

Write one of these symbols in each box to make three true statements.

(a)   12   ☐   6   [1 mark]

(b)   8 − 4   ☐   7 + 5   [1 mark]

(c)   3 + 3   ☐   2 × 3   [1 mark]

 1.6 10 bags of sand costs £25. How much does 1 bag cost?   [1 mark]

1.7 Work out:

(a)   164 + 749   [2 marks]

(b)   17.28 − 6.72   [2 marks]

(c)   6.3 × 7   [2 marks]

(d)   3.7 × 2.4   [3 marks]

(e)   1.28 ÷ 0.8   [2 marks]

EXAM TIP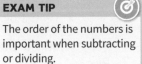
The order of the numbers is important when subtracting or dividing.

 1.8 Some of these calculations are incorrect. Tick the **correct** calculations.

170 − 230 = 60   230 − 170 = 60   2 ÷ 8 = 4   8 ÷ 2 = 4   [2 marks]

Exam-style questions

 1.9 Work out:

    (a) $4 + 5 \times 6$ **[1 mark]**

    (b) $16 \div (2 \times 4)$ **[1 mark]**

    (c) $\dfrac{13 - 4 + 6}{4 - 1}$ **[1 mark]**

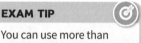
EXAM TIP
Remember the order to calculate in.

 1.10 Given that $670 \times 400 = 268\,000$

    find the value of:

    (a) 670×40 **[1 mark]**

    (b) 67×4 **[1 mark]**

    (c) $268\,000 \div 670$ **[1 mark]**

    (d) $2680 \div 0.4$ **[1 mark]**

1.11 Write brackets ( ) in each statement to make it correct.

    $34 - 20 - 17 = 31$ **[1 mark]**

    $4 + 5 \times 3 - 1 = 18$ **[1 mark]**

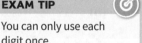
EXAM TIP
You can use more than 1 pair of brackets.

 1.12 A netball team sold 2354 tickets for the Friday netball match.

    They sold 5672 tickets for the Saturday netball match.

    They sold 967 tickets for the Sunday netball match.

    (a) How many tickets did they sell in total for the netball matches?   **[2 marks]**

    (b) They sold more tickets on Saturday than on Friday. How many more?   **[2 marks]**

 1.13 Here are four digits.

    2   6   3   9

    (a) Write one of the digits in each box to make the smallest possible number.   **[1 mark]**

    ☐☐ + ☐☐

    (b) Write one of the digits in each box to make the biggest possible number.   **[1 mark]**

    ☐☐ + ☐☐

    (c) Work out the total of your two numbers from parts (a) and (b).   **[1 mark]**

    (d) Write your answer to part (c) to the nearest 10.   **[1 mark]**

EXAM TIP
You can only use each digit once.

1.14 Work out:

    (a) $6 + -3$ **[1 mark]**

    (b) $-7 - -4$ **[1 mark]**

    (c) -8×-6 **[1 mark]**

    (d) $-12 \div 2$ **[1 mark]**

    (e) $\dfrac{-6 + -3 \times 3}{-1 - 4}$ **[1 mark]**

> **EXAM TIP**
>
> Remember the order of operations.

1.15 Truncate 562.48   **[1 mark]**

1.16 **(a)**   Write 26.345 to 1 decimal place.   **[1 mark]**

      (b)   Write 26.345 to 2 significant figures.   **[1 mark]**

      (c)   Work out an estimate for $312 + \dfrac{47.6}{0.48}$ **[2 marks]**

1.16 George recorded the temperature outside his house on the same day each month for six consecutive months. His results are in the table.

Month	October	November	December	January	February	March
Temperature °C	-1	-4	-5	3	2	8

    (a)   Which month had the lowest temperature?   **[1 mark]**

    (b)   Which month had the highest temperature?   **[1 mark]**

    (c)   Work out the difference between the highest and lowest temperatures.   **[1 mark]**

1.17 The length, L cm, of a rectangle is 14 cm to the nearest centimetre. Complete the error interval for L.

     …. $\leq L <$ ….   **[2 marks]**

1.18 The average length, l seconds, of a chart song is 250 seconds to 2 significant figures. Complete the error interval for l.

     …. $< l \leq$ ….   **[2 marks]**

> **EXAM TIP**
>
> Remember to use the correct inequality symbols: minimum $\leq x <$ maximum.

1.19 A piece of wood has a length, l, of 2.4 m to the nearest cm. Write the error interval for the length, l, of the piece of wood.   **[2 marks]**

⚙ Knowledge

2 Indices, Powers and Roots, Factors, Multiples, Primes

Bases and indices

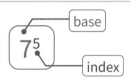

7^5

base

index

Remember, we don't write the power of 1.

So, $5^1 = 5$

Squared means 'multiplied by itself'.

For example, $5^2 = 5 \times 5 = 25$

This square has an area of 25 units^2.

Cubed means 'multiplied by itself and then by itself again'.

For example, $5^3 = 5 \times 5 \times 5 = 125$

This cube has a volume of 125 units^3.

The other indices (or **powers**) don't have 'special' names but the process for calculating them is the same.

$5^4 = 5 \times 5 \times 5 \times 5 = 625$

$5^7 = 5 \times 5 \times 5 \times 5 \times 5 \times 5 \times 5 = 78\,125$

You can also raise a negative number to a power:

$(-5)^2 = (-5) \times (-5) = 5 \times 5 = 25$

If $x^2 = 25$, then $x = \pm 5$.

Roots are the **inverse** of powers.

$\sqrt{25} = 5$

$\sqrt[3]{(-8)} = -2$

LINK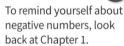

To remind yourself about negative numbers, look back at Chapter 1.

Formula

You need to know these square numbers:

$1^1 = 1$	$6^2 = 36$	$11^2 = 121$
$2^2 = 4$	$7^2 = 49$	$12^2 = 144$
$3^2 = 9$	$8^2 = 64$	$13^2 = 169$
$4^2 = 16$	$9^2 = 81$	$14^2 = 196$
$5^2 = 25$	$10^2 = 100$	$15^2 = 225$

And these cube numbers:

$1^3 = 1$	$2^3 = 8$	$3^3 = 27$
$4^3 = 64$	$5^3 = 125$	

Index laws

$a^0 = 1$	$a^n \times a^m = a^{n+m}$	$a^n \div a^m = a^{n-m}$	$\left(a^n\right)^m = a^{n \times m}$	$a^{-1} = \dfrac{1}{a}$
Example:	Example:	Example:	Example:	Example:
$7^0 = 1$	$3^2 \times 3^4 = 3^{2+4} = 3^6$	$5^7 \div 5^3 = 5^{7-3} = 5^4$	$(4^3)^5 = 4^{3 \times 5} = 4^{15}$	$2^{-1} = \dfrac{1}{2}$
Any number (or letter) raised to the power of 0 is 1.	To multiply numbers with the same base, add the powers.	To divide numbers with the same base, subtract the powers.	To raise a power by another power, multiply the powers.	A number raised to the power of −1 gives the reciprocal of the number.

Index laws

Worked example

Simplify:

1. $5^8 \times 5$ $= 5^8 \times 5^1$

$= 5^{8+1}$

$= 5^9$

2. $\left(5^4\right)^6$ $= 5^{4 \times 6}$

$= 5^{24}$

3. $5^2 \div 5^3$ $= 5^{2-3}$

$= 5^{-1}$

EXAM TIP

The command word is 'simplify', so only simplify the powers.

Worked example

Simplify:

$\left(5^2 \div 5^{-4}\right)^2$ $= \left(5^{2-(-4)}\right)^2$

$= \left(5^{2+4}\right)^2$

$= \left(5^6\right)^2$

$= 5^{6 \times 2}$

$= 5^{12}$

REVISION TIP

Questions about indices usually ask you to **work out** (find the numerical answer) or **simplify** (write the expression in the simplest possible way; you do not need to find the numerical answer).

Worked example

Work out:

1. $\left(\dfrac{2}{3}\right)^2$ $= \dfrac{2^2}{3^2}$

$= \dfrac{4}{9}$

2. 5^{-2} $= \dfrac{1}{5^2}$

$= \dfrac{1}{25}$

EXAM TIP

The command word is 'work out' so you need to find the numerical answer.

Indices on your calculator

The symbols on different calculators vary slightly, but often look like this:

Cube root: Cube: $\boxed{x^3}$ Any root: $\boxed{\sqrt[y]{x}}$

Square root: $\boxed{\sqrt{\blacksquare}}$ Square: $\boxed{x^2}$ Any power: $\boxed{x^y}$

Factors, multiples, and primes

A **factor** is an **integer** that divides exactly into a number.

3 and 4 are factors of 12.

A multiple is the result obtained when one integer is multiplied by another.

12 is a **multiple** of both 3 and 4.

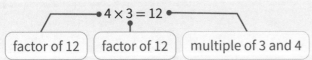

$$4 \times 3 = 12$$

| factor of 12 | factor of 12 | multiple of 3 and 4 |

For example, multiples of 5 are:

$1 \times 5 = 5$

$2 \times 5 = 10$

$3 \times 5 = 15...$ and so on

The **highest common factor** (**HCF**) of two numbers is the *biggest* number that is a factor of both of the numbers.

The **lowest common multiple** (**LCM**) of two numbers is the *smallest* number that is a multiple of both of the numbers.

⚙ Knowledge

2 Indices, Powers and Roots, Factors, Multiples, Primes

Factors, multiples, and primes

Worked example

1. What is the HCF of 18 and 12?

   Factors of 18: ①②③⑥9 18

   Factors of 12: ①②③4⑥12 •————

   The HCF of 18 and 12 is 6.

   > Circle the numbers that appear in both lists. The biggest circled number is 6.

2. What is the LCM of 8 and 20?

   Multiples of 20: 20 ㊵ 60 …

   Multiples of 8: 8 16 24 32 ㊵ … •————

   The LCM of 8 and 20 is 40.

   > You can now stop looking for multiples of 8 because 40 is in both lists.

A **prime** number is a number with exactly two factors.
The first six prime numbers are 2, 3, 5, 7, 11 and 13.
1 is NOT a prime number as it has only one factor.
A **prime factor** is a factor that is also a prime number.

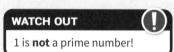

WATCH OUT

1 is **not** a prime number!

For large numbers we can use **prime factor decomposition** to help us find the HCF and LCM.

Worked example

Find the prime factors of 36.

$36 = 2 \times 2 \times 3 \times 3$ •————

$\quad = 2^2 \times 3^3$ •——— Index form

> Use a prime factor tree to write a number as a product of its prime factors.

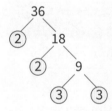

> Note, any correct factor pairs will give the same answer.

Many scientific calculators will find the prime factor decomposition for you.
Look for a FACT button or ask your teacher.

Factors, multiples, and primes

Worked example

$45 = 3^2 \times 5$

Find the LCM and HCF of 36 and 45.

Method 1

$36 = 2 \times 2 \times 3 \times 3$ ●————— Prime factors of 36

$45 = 3 \times 3 \times 5$ ●————— Prime factors of 45.

Draw a Venn diagram with one circle representing factors of 36 and one circle representing factors of 45.

Put the remaining factors of 36 in this section.

Put the common factors in the intersection of the circles.

The HCF is the product of numbers in the intersection = $3 \times 3 = 9$
The LCM is the product of all numbers = $2 \times 2 \times 3 \times 3 \times 5 = 180$

Put the remaining factors of 45 in this section.

Method 2

$36 = 2 \times 2 \times 3 \times 3$

$45 = 3 \times 3 \times 5$

HCF of 36 and 45 = $3 \times 3 = 9$

LCM = $9 \times 2 \times 2 \times 5$

$\quad = 18 \times 10$

$\quad = 180$

Prime factors of 36.

Prime factors of 45.

Compare the prime factors.
3×3 is in both.

LCM = HCF × all the remaining numbers from both lists.

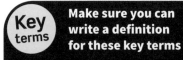

Make sure you can write a definition for these key terms

calculate   cubed   factor   highest common factor (HCF)
integer   inverse   lowest common multiple (LCM)
multiple   power   prime factor decomposition
prime   root   simplify   squared

⇄ Retrieval

2 Indices, Powers and Roots, Factors, Multiples, Primes

Learn the answers to the questions below, then cover the answers column with a piece of paper and write as many as you can. Check and repeat.

	Questions		Answers
1	What is a square number?		A number multiplied by itself.
2	What is the value of any number raised to the power of zero?		One.
3	State the index law for multiplication.		$a^n \times a^m = a^{n+m}$
4	State the index law for division.		$a^n \div a^m = a^{n-m}$
5	What is a factor?		A positive **integer** that divides exactly into a number.
6	What is a multiple?		A multiple of a is $n \times a$, where n is any other integer.
7	How do you make sure that you have listed all the factors of a number?		List factors in pairs.
8	What does HCF stand for?		Highest Common Factor.
9	What does LCM stand for?		Lowest Common Multiple.
10	What is a prime number?		A number with exactly two factors, 1 and itself.
11	How do you find the prime factor decomposition of a number?		Use a prime factor tree or write the number as a product of prime factors.
12	How do you find the HCF of two numbers?		List all the factors of both numbers and then find the highest number common to both lists.

Put paper here (between Questions and Answers columns)

Previous questions

Now go back and use these questions to check your knowledge of previous topics.

	Questions		Answers
1	When you multiply by a power of 10, which way do the numbers move on a place value chart?		Left.
2	What does the letter I in BIDMAS stand for?		Indices.
3	Why do we estimate?		To see if the answer is sensible or to get a rough answer.
4	When you are asked to estimate, what should you round each number to?		One significant figure.

Put paper here (between Questions and Answers columns)

Practice

Exam-style questions

 2.1 Write down the answer to each of these calculations:

(a) 4^2 [1 mark]

(b) 2^3 [1 mark]

(c) $\sqrt{49}$ [1 mark]

(d) $\sqrt[3]{27}$ [1 mark]

 2.2 Work out:

(a) $2 \times \sqrt{9 + 16} + 6^2$ [3 marks]

(b) $3^4 - 6 \times \sqrt[3]{8} + 50 \div 5^2$ [3 marks]

> **EXAM TIP**
> Don't forget to use BIDMAS.

 2.3 The area of a square is 121 cm². Find its perimeter.

> **EXAM TIP**
> Think how the side length of a square relates to its area and perimeter.

$$121 \text{ cm}^2$$

[2 marks]

2.4 (a) Find the value of $\dfrac{\sqrt[3]{3.6^2 + 91 \times 3.7}}{\sqrt{6.25} + 1.8^3}$

Write down all the figures on your calculator display. [1 mark]

(b) Write your answer to part (a) rounded to 3 significant figures. [1 mark]

2.5 Peter says that $2^3 \times 5^2$ simplifies to 10^5. Peter is wrong. What mistake has he made? Include the correct value in your answer. [1 mark]

 2.6 Simplify:

(a) $7^2 \times 7^5$ [1 mark]

(b) $9^{10} \div 9^4$ [1 mark]

(c) $2^5 \times 2^{-3}$ [1 mark]

(d) $7^{-2} \div 7^{-6}$ [1 mark]

(e) $(3^4)^4$ [1 mark]

Exam-style questions

 2.7 Simplify:

     (a) $(8^2)^{-5}$ **[1 mark]**

     (b) $\dfrac{9^3}{9^2 \times 9^4}$ **[2 marks]**

     (c) $(2^7 \times 2^4)^{-1}$ **[2 marks]**

 2.8 Work out the area of this rectangle. Give your answer as a power of 10.

10^3 cm

10^2 cm

[2 marks]

 2.9 Work out:

     (a) 13^0 **[1 mark]**

     (b) 8^{-1} **[1 mark]**

     (c) $\left(\dfrac{2}{5}\right)^3$ **[1 mark]**

     (d) $\left(\dfrac{1}{4}\right)^{-2}$ **[2 marks]**

2.10 Here is a list of numbers:

     3   6   8   10   18   24   30   36

From the list, write down:

     (a)   a factor of 12   **[1 mark]**

     (b)   a multiple of 9   **[1 mark]**

     (c)   a number which is both a multiple of 12 and a multiple of 4   **[1 mark]**

     (d)   a number which is both a factor of 24 and a factor of 16   **[1 mark]**

     (e)   two numbers with a common factor of 5   **[1 mark]**

     (f)   two numbers with a common multiple of 60.   **[1 mark]**

> **EXAM TIP**
> Make sure you know the difference between a factor and a multiple.

 2.11 Find the lowest common multiple (LCM) of 9 and 12.   **[2 marks]**

 2.12 Find the highest common factor (HCF) of 18 and 12.   **[2 marks]**

> 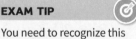 **EXAM TIP**
> You need to recognize this as an LCM question.

 2.13 Alarm A beeps every 6 minutes.
       Alarm B beeps every 5 minutes.
       Alarm C beeps every 15 minutes.
       They all beep together at 9am.
       What time do they next all beep together?   **[2 marks]**

2.14 **(a)** Write 540 as a product of prime factors.
Give your answer in index form. **[2 marks]**

(b) By looking at its prime factors, explain why 540 is
divisible by 15. **[1 mark]**

 2.15 A number is a multiple of 4, 5 and 6. Write the prime factor
decomposition of the smallest number it could be. **[2 marks]**

 2.16 **(a)** Write 160 as a product of prime factors. **[2 marks]**

(b) Find the highest common factor (HCF) of 160
and 280. **[2 marks]**

(c) Find the lowest common multiple (LCM) of 160
and 280. **[2 marks]**

Questions referring to previous content

 2.17 Work out:

(a) $-8 + -4$ **[1 mark]**

(b) $8 - -4$ **[1 mark]**

(c) -8×-4 **[1 mark]**

(d) $8 \div -4$ **[1 mark]**

 2.18 Given that $450 \times 300 = 135\,000$
find the value of:

(a) 45×300 **[1 mark]**

(b) $135\,000 \div 300$ **[1 mark]**

(c) 4500×30 **[1 mark]**

(d) $135 \div 4.5$ **[1 mark]**

# Knowledge

3 Standard form

Standard form: The basics

Standard form is when a power of 10 is used to rewrite a very large or very small number.

Standard form is written in this way:

| between 1 and 10 i.e. $1 \leq a < 10$ | ←── $(a) \times 10^{n}$ ──→ | positive or negative integer |

LINK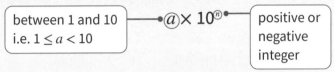
- To remind yourself about multiplying and dividing by powers of 10, look back at Chapter 1.
- To remind yourself about indices, look back at Chapter 2.

These numbers are not written in standard form.

| This number needs to lie in the interval $1 \leq a < 10$ | ←── 16×10^{7} |

$2.4 \times 10^{0.5}$ ●─── | This number needs to be an integer |

Converting from standard form to ordinary number

If n is negative, such as 1.6×10^{-2}:

Divide a by 10 n times.

$1.6 \div 10 \div 10 = 0.016$

which is an ordinary number

If n in positive, such as 1.6×10^{2}:

Multiply a by 10 n times.

$1.6 \times 10 \times 10 = 160$

which is an ordinary number

Worked example

Write these as ordinary numbers.

1. 5.06×10^{5}

   $= 5.06 \times 10 \times 10 \times 10 \times 10 \times 10$

   $= 5.06 \times 100\,000$ ●─── | Multiply by 10 five times. |

   $= 506\,000$

2. 1.7×10^{-3}

   $= 1.7 \div 10 \div 10 \div 10$

   $= 1.7 \div 1000$ ●─── | Divide by 10 three times. |

   $= 0.0017$

Converting from ordinary number to standard form

If a number is smaller than 1, such as 0.016:

Multiply by 10 until it is between 1 and 10.

$0.016 \times 10 \times 10 = 1.6$

Write in the form $a \times 10^{-n}$

n is the number of times you divided by ten.

$0.016 = 1.6 \times 10^{-2}$

If number is larger than 10, such as 160:

Divide by 10 until it is between 1 and 10.

$160 \div 10 \div 10 = 1.6$

Write in the form $a \times 10^{n}$

n is the number of times you divided by ten.

$160 = 1.6 \times 10^{2}$

Worked example

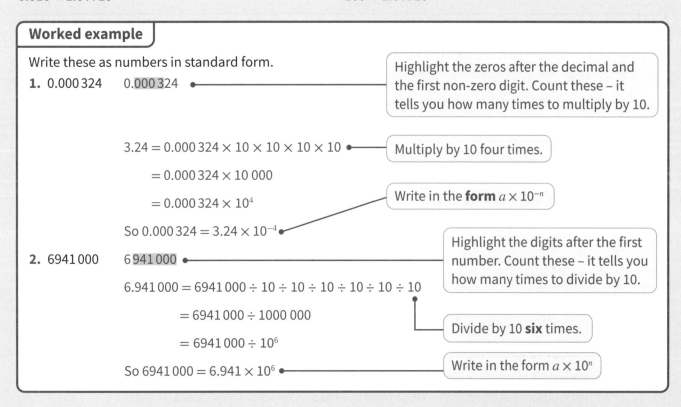

Write these as numbers in standard form.

1. 0.000 324   0.000 324 ●——————

> Highlight the zeros after the decimal and the first non-zero digit. Count these – it tells you how many times to multiply by 10.

$3.24 = 0.000\,324 \times 10 \times 10 \times 10 \times 10$ ●——

> Multiply by 10 four times.

$= 0.000\,324 \times 10\,000$

$= 0.000\,324 \times 10^{4}$

> Write in the **form** $a \times 10^{-n}$

So $0.000\,324 = 3.24 \times 10^{-4}$ ●

> Highlight the digits after the first number. Count these – it tells you how many times to divide by 10.

2. 6 941 000   6 941 000 ●——————

$6.941\,000 = 6\,941\,000 \div 10 \div 10 \div 10 \div 10 \div 10 \div 10$

$= 6\,941\,000 \div 1\,000\,000$

> Divide by 10 **six** times.

$= 6\,941\,000 \div 10^{6}$

So $6\,941\,000 = 6.941 \times 10^{6}$ ●——————

> Write in the form $a \times 10^{n}$

Adding or subtracting numbers in standard form

To add or subtract numbers in standard form, convert them to ordinary numbers first.

Worked example

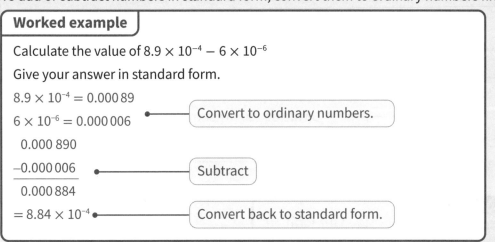

Calculate the value of $8.9 \times 10^{-4} - 6 \times 10^{-6}$

Give your answer in standard form.

$8.9 \times 10^{-4} = 0.000\,89$

$6 \times 10^{-6} = 0.000\,006$

> Convert to ordinary numbers.

$0.000\,890$

$\underline{-0.000\,006}$

$0.000\,884$

> Subtract

$= 8.84 \times 10^{-4}$ ●——————

> Convert back to standard form.

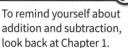

LINK

To remind yourself about addition and subtraction, look back at Chapter 1.

 # Knowledge

3 Standard form

Multiplying or dividing numbers in standard form

To multiply or divide numbers in standard form, you need to use these two laws of indices:

1. $a^n \times a^m = a^{n+m}$ If you multiply numbers with the same base, you add the powers.

2. $a^n \div a^m = a^{n-m}$ If you divide numbers with the same base, you subtract the powers.

> **LINK**
>
> To remind yourself about laws of indices, look back at Chapter 2.

Worked example

Given that $a = 6 \times 10^5$ and $b = 3 \times 10^{-2}$, work out the value of:

1. $a \times b = (6 \times 10^5) \times (3 \times 10^{-2})$

$= (6 \times 3) \times (10^5 \times 10^{-2})$ ← Group ordinary numbers on one side.

$= 18 \times 10^{5+(-2)}$ ← Use $a^n \times a^m = a^{n+m}$ to simplify the indices.

$= 18 \times 10^3$

$= 1.8 \times 10^4$ ← Write your answer in standard form.

2. $a \div b = (6 \times 10^5) \div (3 \times 10^{-2})$

$= \dfrac{6 \times 10^5}{3 \times 10^{-2}}$ ← Write as a fraction.

$= \dfrac{6}{3} \times \dfrac{10^5}{10^{-2}}$ ← Group ordinary numbers and powers of 10.

$= 2 \times 10^{-5-(-2)}$ ← Use $a^n \div a^m = a^{n-m}$

$= 2 \times 10^7$ ← Write your answer in standard form.

In the previous Worked example, part 1, you saw that 18×10^3 is **not** in standard form.
To make the first number between 1 and 10, you must divide 18 by 10 and multiply 10^3 by 10.

Worked example

Write these numbers in standard form.

1. 23×10^4

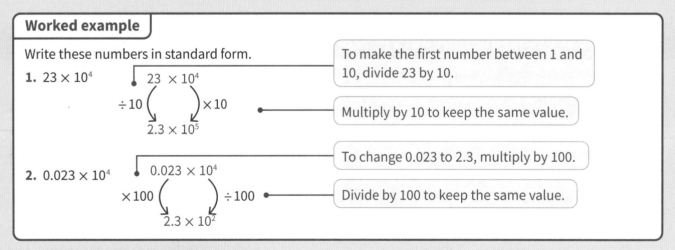

23×10^4

$\div 10 \quad \times 10$

2.3×10^5

To make the first number between 1 and 10, divide 23 by 10.

Multiply by 10 to keep the same value.

2. 0.023×10^4

0.023×10^4

$\times 100 \quad \div 100$

2.3×10^2

To change 0.023 to 2.3, multiply by 100.

Divide by 100 to keep the same value.

> **Key terms** — Make sure you can write a definition for these key terms
>
> standard form

3 Standard form

Learn the answers to the questions below, then cover the answers column with a piece of paper and write as many as you can. Check and repeat.

Questions	Answers
1 When a number is written in standard form $(a \times 10^n)$, what values can the first number take?	Any number between 1 and 10, i.e. $1 \le a < 10$.
2 What does 10^n mean?	The product of multiplying n instances of 10 together. For example, 10^4 means $10 \times 10 \times 10 \times 10$.
3 What does 10^{-n} mean?	The result of dividing by n instances of 10 multiplied together. For example, 10^{-4} means divide by $(10 \times 10 \times 10 \times 10)$.
4 How do you change a large number into standard form?	Divide by 10 until you have a number between 1 and 10. The power of 10 is the number of times you divided by 10.
5 How do you change a small number into standard form?	Multiply by 10 until you have a number between 1 and 10. The power is the negative of the number of times you multiplied by 10.
6 How do you add numbers that are written in standard form?	Convert them to ordinary numbers, add them and then convert back into standard form.
7 How do you multiply numbers that are written in standard form?	Group the front numbers together and the powers of 10 together. Multiply the front numbers, add the powers of 10 then give the answer in standard form.
8 How do you divide numbers that are written in standard form?	Group the front numbers together and the powers of 10 together. Divide the front numbers, subtract the powers of 10 then give the answer in standard form.
9 How do you write 57×10^{10} in standard form?	Divide 57 by 10 and multiply 10^{10} by 10, i.e 5.7×10^{11}.
10 How do you write 0.035×10^6 in standard form?	Multiply 0.035 by 100 and divide 10^6 by 100, i.e. 3.5×10^4.

Put paper here

Previous questions

Now go back and use these questions to check your knowledge of previous topics.

Questions	Answers
1 State the multiplication law of indices.	$a^n \times a^m = a^{n+m}$
2 What is the place value of the first digit in a four digit whole number?	Thousands.
3 What is a prime number?	A number with exactly two factors, one and itself.
4 What is the lowest common multiple of two or more numbers?	The smallest number that is a multiple of two or more numbers.
5 What are significant figures?	Digits in a number that contribute to its accuracy.

Put paper here

Practice

 3.1 Write these as ordinary numbers.

    (a) 1.56×10^8 **[1 mark]**

    (b) 8.02×10^{-3} **[1 mark]**

 3.2 Write these numbers in standard form.

    (a) 48 000 000 000   **[1 mark]**

    (b) 0.000 0703   **[1 mark]**

    (c) 95×10^6 **[1 mark]**

    (d) 0.68×10^{-4} **[1 mark]**

 3.3 The distance from the Sun to Earth is approximately 150 000 000 km.
Write 150 000 000 in standard form.   **[1 mark]**

 3.4 Write these numbers in order of size.
Start with the greatest.

    2.1×10^4 2.3×10^5 0.21×10^4 2200   **[3 marks]**

> **EXAM TIP**
> Write all the numbers in the same form.

 3.5 The length of a bacteria cell is 4×10^{-7} m.
The length of a virus is 0.000 000 05 m.
Which is shorter, the bacteria cell or the virus?   **[2 marks]**

 3.6 Work out the value of each expression.
Write your answers in standard form.

    (a) $2 \times (3 \times 10^2)$ **[1 mark]**

    (b) $(4 \times 10^{-4}) \div 2$ **[1 mark]**

    (c) $(3 \times 10^{-2}) + (5 \times 10^{-2})$ **[1 mark]**

    (d) $(9 \times 10^7) - (3 \times 10^7)$ **[1 mark]**

 3.7 Everly says that $6 \times (3 \times 10^6)$ is written as 18×10^6 in standard form.
Is Everly correct? Show working to support your answer.   **[1 mark]**

3.8 Work out $7 \times 10^{-2} \times 30\,000$.
Give your answer in standard form.   **[2 marks]**

3.9 Work out the value of each expression.
Write your answers in standard form.

(a) $(5 \times 10^4) + (6 \times 10^5)$ [2 marks]

(b) $(9 \times 10^{-3}) - (3 \times 10^{-4})$ [2 marks]

(c) $(2.1 \times 10^8) \times (3 \times 10^{-5})$ [2 marks]

(d) $(8.2 \times 10^3) \div (4.1 \times 10^7)$ [2 marks]

 3.10 Write each number in standard form.

(a) 60×10^4 [1 mark]

(b) 0.3×10^6 [1 mark]

(c) 650×10^{-5} [1 mark]

(d) 0.0035×10^{-7} [1 mark]

 3.11 Simplify $(2 \times 10^4) \times (2 \times 10^2)^2$.
Give your answer in standard form. [2 marks]

 3.12 The diameter of Earth is 12 742 000 m.
The diameter of Jupiter is $1.429\,84 \times 10^8$ m.
Ayesha says, "The diameter of Jupiter is more than 1000 times greater than the diameter of Earth."
Is Ayesha correct?
You must show how you get your answer. [3 marks]

 3.13 $z = \dfrac{xy}{x + y}$

$x = 2.5 \times 10^8$

$y = 4 \times 10^7$

Work out the value of z.
Give your answer in standard form to 3 significant figures. [4 marks]

Questions referring to previous content

3.14 Brad says that 1 is a prime number. Is Brad correct? Give a reason for your answer. [1 mark]

3.15 Work out

(a) 4^{-2} [1 mark] **(c)** $\left(\dfrac{3}{2}\right)^3$ [1 mark]

(b) y^0 [1 mark] **(d)** $\sqrt{\dfrac{9}{16}}$ [1 mark]

⚙ Knowledge

4 Fractions, decimals, percentages

Getting started

$\frac{3}{5}$ ⟵ the **numerator** is the top number in a fraction.

⟵ the **denominator** is the bottom number in a fraction.

$\frac{15}{7}$ is an **improper fraction** because the numerator (15) is larger than the denominator (7).

$2\frac{1}{3}$ is a **mixed number** because it has a whole part (2) and a fraction part $\left(\frac{1}{3}\right)$.

The **reciprocal** of a is $\frac{1}{a}$. For example, the reciprocal of 4 is $\frac{1}{4}$. Any number multiplied by its reciprocal is 1.

When dealing with fractions of amounts, '**of**' means multiply (×). For example:

$\frac{2}{3}$ of $12 = \frac{2}{3} \times 12 = 8$

Simplest form is when the numerator and the denominator have no common factors.

Changing between improper fractions and mixed numbers

To change a mixed number to an improper fraction, multiply the whole number by the denominator and add it to the numerator.

For example:

$4\frac{3}{7} = \frac{(4 \times 7) + 3}{7} = \frac{31}{7}$

To change an improper fraction to a mixed number, divide the numerator by the denominator.

For example:

$\frac{17}{6} = 2$ remainder $5 = 2\frac{5}{6}$

Equivalent fractions

You can find **equivalent fractions** if you multiply or divide both the numerator and the denominator by a common factor. You use this method when simplifying fractions. For example,

$\frac{9}{5} = \frac{(3 \times 3)}{(5 \times 3)} = \frac{9}{15}$

$\frac{6}{10} = \frac{(6 \div 2)}{(10 \div 2)} = \frac{3}{5}$

$\frac{3}{5} = \frac{(3 \times 100)}{(5 \times 100)} = \frac{300}{500}$

$\frac{72}{120} = \frac{(72 \div 24)}{(120 \div 24)} = \frac{3}{5}$

Ordering fractions

Use equivalent fractions to compare the size of fractions. Use common denominators or common numerators to make it easy to compare. Remember: the bigger the denominator, the smaller the fraction.

> **Worked example**
>
> Put these fractions in ascending order.
>
> $\frac{2}{3}, \frac{5}{12}, \frac{5}{8}$ — Ascending means increasing size.
>
> **Method 1**
>
> $\frac{2}{3} = \frac{16}{24}; \frac{5}{12} = \frac{10}{24}; \frac{5}{8} = \frac{15}{24}$ — Write the fractions with a common denominator.
>
> $\frac{10}{24}, \frac{15}{24}, \frac{16}{24}$ — Order by numerators in ascending order.
>
> $\frac{5}{12}, \frac{5}{8}, \frac{2}{3}$ — Answer the question using the original fractions given.

> **EXAM TIP** ◎
>
> Look at which method is more efficient for the question you are answering.

Ordering fractions

Method 2

$\frac{2}{3} = \frac{10}{15}$; $\frac{5}{12} = \frac{10}{24}$; $\frac{2}{3} = \frac{10}{16}$ •——— Write the fractions with a common numerator.

$\frac{10}{24}$, $\frac{10}{16}$, $\frac{10}{15}$ •——— Order by denominators in ascending order.

$\frac{5}{12}$, $\frac{5}{8}$, $\frac{2}{3}$ •——— Answer the question using the original fractions given.

LINK

To remind yourself about HFC and LCM, look back at Chapter 2.

Four operations with fractions

Worked example: Multiplying fractions

$\frac{4}{5} \times \frac{2}{3} = \frac{4 \times 2}{5 \times 3}$ •——— Multiply the numerators.

•——— Multiply the denominators.

$= \frac{8}{15}$

REVISION TIP

If you have a mixed number, change it into an improper fraction. Always try to simplify your answer if you can, using equivalent fractions.

Worked example: Subtracting fractions

A jug contains $\frac{7}{8}$ litre of lemonade.

How much lemonade is left in the jug after $\frac{1}{6}$ litre is poured out?

$\frac{7}{8} - \frac{1}{6} = \frac{7 \times 3}{24} - \frac{1 \times 4}{24}$ •——— Write both fractions with a common denominator.

$= \frac{21}{24} - \frac{4}{24}$ •——— Subtract the numerators once the denominators are the same.

$= \frac{17}{24}$ litre •——— The amount of lemonade is left in the jug.

Worked example: Dividing fractions

$\frac{4}{5} \div \frac{2}{3} = \frac{4}{5} \times \frac{3}{2}$ •——— Multiply by the reciprocal of $2\frac{2}{3}$.

$= \frac{4 \times 3}{5 \times 2}$ •——— Multiply the numerators.

$= \frac{12}{10}$ •——— Multiply the denominators.

$= \frac{6}{5}$ •——— Simplify

Worked example: Adding fractions

$\frac{4}{5} + \frac{2}{3}$

$= \frac{12}{15} + \frac{10}{15}$ •——— Write both fractions with a common denominator.

$= \frac{22}{15}$

Worked example: Finding a fraction of an amount

Find $\frac{3}{5}$ of 35

$\frac{3}{5}$ of $35 = \frac{3}{5} \times 35$

$= \frac{3 \times 35}{5 \times 1} = \frac{105}{5} = 21$

An alternative method is:

$\frac{1}{\cancel{5}} \times \frac{\cancel{35}^{7}}{1} = 21$

4 Fractions, decimals, percentages

Fractions, decimals, and percentages

Percent means 'out of 100'.

Percentages are fractions with a denominator of 100.

To write a percentage as a fraction, use 100 as the denominator and simplify if necessary.

$$54\% = \frac{54}{100}$$

To write a fraction as a decimal, find an equivalent fraction with denominator 100.

$$\frac{2}{5} = \frac{40}{100} = 40\%$$

To convert from a percentage to a decimal, divide by 100.

$$35\% = 0.35$$

To write a decimal as a percentage, multiply by 100.

$$0.782 = 78.2\%$$

You should learn these common fractions, decimals and percentages:

$$\frac{1}{2} = 0.5 = 50\%$$

$$\frac{1}{4} = 0.25 = 25\%$$

$$\frac{1}{8} = 0.125 = 12.5\%$$

$$\frac{1}{5} = 0.2 = 20\%$$

$$\frac{1}{10} = 0.1 = 10\%$$

$$\frac{1}{3} = 0.\dot{3} = 33.\dot{3}\%$$

$0.\dot{3}$ means 0.3333333... and is called a **recurring decimal** which means it repeats forever.

Worked example

I have some money.

I spend $\frac{2}{5}$ of the money on shoes, and 35% on clothes.

What fraction of the original amount do I have left?

$$35 = \frac{35}{100}$$ ——— Convert 35% to a fraction.

$$\frac{2}{5} = \frac{40}{100}$$ ——— Write $\frac{2}{5}$ as an equivalent fraction with denominator 100.

$$\frac{35}{100} + \frac{40}{100} = \frac{75}{100}$$ has been spent. ——— Add the fractions to find the total amount spent.

$$1 - \frac{75}{100} = \frac{100}{100} - \frac{75}{100} = \frac{25}{100} = \frac{1}{4}$$ ——— Subtract the fraction spent from 1 to find the fraction that is left.

I have $\frac{1}{4}$ left.

Key terms — Make sure you can write a definition for these key terms

decimal   denominator   equivalent fractions
improper fraction   mixed number   numerator
percent   percentage   reciprocal   recurring decimal

4 Fractions, decimals, percentages

Learn the answers to the questions below, then cover the answers column with a piece of paper and write as many as you can. Check and repeat.

Questions | Answers

Put paper here

#	Question	Answer
1	What is an improper fraction?	A fraction where the numerator is larger than the denominator.
2	What is a mixed number?	A number that has a whole number and a fraction.
3	What is the reciprocal of a number?	The reciprocal of a number is $1 \div$ the number, i.e the reciprocal of a is $\frac{1}{a}$.
4	How do you know if two fractions are equivalent?	You can multiply the numerator and denominator of one of the fractions by the same number to get the other fraction.
5	What is the bottom number in a fraction called?	The denominator.
6	How do you divide by a fraction?	Multiply by its reciprocal.
7	How do you add/subtract fractions?	Write all the fractions with common denominators, then add/subtract the numerators.
8	What form should you leave a fractional answer in?	As a fully simplified proper fraction or mixed number.
9	How can you find a fraction of an amount?	Multiply the fraction by the amount.
10	How do you convert a percentage into a decimal?	Divide the percentage by 100.
11	How would you add a fraction and a decimal together?	Change one of them so that both are either fractions or decimals.

Previous questions

Now go back and use these questions to check your knowledge of previous topics.

Questions | Answers

Put paper here

#	Question	Answer
1	How many places to the left on the place value chart would a number move when multiplied by 1000?	Three.
2	What is a prime number?	A number with exactly two factors, one and itself.
3	How do you simplify $3^5 \times 3^4$?	Add the powers.
4	How do you multiply two decimal numbers together?	Ignore the decimal point, multiply the whole numbers and then decide where the decimal point should go.
5	How does estimation help you when dividing by a decimal?	Estimation helps you check your answer is approximately correct and that the decimal point is in the correct place.

Practice

4.1 Work out which of these fractions is larger.

$\frac{1}{5}$ or $\frac{1}{4}$

You **must** show how you get your answer. **[1 mark]**

4.2 Write these fractions in order of size.

Start with the smallest fraction.

$\frac{3}{4}$ $\frac{2}{3}$ $\frac{5}{8}$ $\frac{7}{12}$ **[2 marks]**

4.3 **(a)** Write each mixed number as an improper fraction.

Give your answer in its simplest form.

(i) $1\frac{2}{5}$ **[1 mark]**

(ii) $3\frac{3}{4}$ **[1 mark]**

(b) Write each improper fraction as a mixed number.

Give your answer in its simplest form.

(i) $\frac{17}{9}$ **[1 mark]**

(ii) $\frac{92}{40}$ **[2 marks]**

4.4 After a party,

Rhodri has $2\frac{1}{3}$ bottles of cola left.

Lizzie has $\frac{19}{8}$ bottles left.

Who has the most cola?

You **must** show how you get your answer. **[3 mark]**

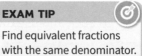
EXAM TIP
Find equivalent fractions with the same denominator.

4.5 Which of these is the value of the reciprocal of 0.25? **[1 mark]**

$\frac{1}{25}$ $\frac{1}{4}$ 4 $\frac{2}{5}$

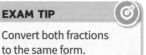
EXAM TIP
Convert both fractions to the same form.

4.6 Work out each calculation.

Give each answer as a fraction in its simplest form.

(a) $\frac{1}{3} \times \frac{2}{5}$ **[1 mark]**

(b) $\frac{3}{7} \times \frac{14}{9}$ **[2 marks]**

4.7 Work out each calculation.

Give each answer as a fraction in its simplest form.

(a) $\dfrac{3}{4} \div \dfrac{1}{11}$ [2 marks]

(b) $\dfrac{6}{5} \div \dfrac{7}{10}$ [2 marks]

 4.8 A café uses $\dfrac{2}{3}$ of a box of coffee beans every day.

The café has 16 full boxes of coffee beans.

How many days will it take for the café to use 16 full boxes of coffee beans? [2 marks]

4.9 In a model village, everything is built at a size of $\dfrac{1}{9}$ of the original size.

In real life a street is 30 m long.

Work out the length of this street in the model village.

Give your answer as a fraction in its simplest form. [2 marks]

 4.10 Raf saves $\dfrac{3}{10}$ of his wages to pay his bills.

He spends $\dfrac{1}{4}$ of his saved wages on electricity.

What fraction of his wages does he spend on electricity? [2 marks]

EXAM TIP

What calculation does the word 'of' represent?

 4.11 This triangle has base length $1\dfrac{1}{5}$ cm and perpendicular height $\dfrac{6}{5}$ cm.

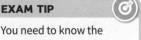

EXAM TIP

You need to know the formula for the area of a triangle.

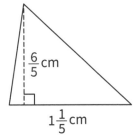

$\dfrac{6}{5}$ cm

$1\dfrac{1}{5}$ cm

This rectangle has the same area as the triangle.

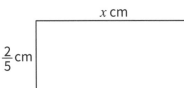

x cm

$\dfrac{2}{5}$ cm

Find the value of x.

Give your answer as a fraction in its simplest form. [3 marks]

4.12 Work out each calculation.

Give each answer as a fraction in its simplest form.

(a) $\frac{1}{3} + \frac{1}{5}$ [2 marks]

(b) $\frac{2}{9} + \frac{5}{6}$ [2 marks]

(c) $1\frac{7}{8} + 2\frac{3}{4}$ [3 marks]

4.13 Work out each calculation.

Give each answer as a fraction in its simplest form.

(a) $\frac{7}{9} - \frac{1}{2}$ [2 marks]

(b) $3\frac{1}{6} - 2\frac{3}{4}$ [3 marks]

4.14 Midori says that $\frac{2}{5} + \frac{4}{5} = \frac{6}{10}$.

Is Midori correct? You **must** show how you get your answer. [1 mark]

4.15 In a class:

$\frac{1}{8}$ of the students in a class drive to school.

$\frac{2}{3}$ of the students walk to school.

The rest take the bus.

What fraction of the students take the bus? [3 marks]

EXAM TIP

The whole class is represented by the number 1.

4.16 Daisy has $2\frac{4}{5}$ metres of model train track.

She takes out a piece of track which is $\frac{7}{8}$ m long. She puts in a piece of track which is $1\frac{1}{20}$ m long.

Work out the **total** length of the track now. [3 marks]

4.17 Max reads a book on an e-reader. When he starts reading one day he is already $\frac{1}{3}$ of the way through.

When he finishes reading that day he is $\frac{3}{4}$ of the way through.

What fraction of the book did he read that day? [2 marks]

4.18 **(a)** Write 0.4 as a fraction in its simplest form. [1 mark]

(b) Write 6% as a decimal. [1 mark]

(c) Write $\frac{1}{8}$ as a percentage. [1 mark]

 4.19 **(a)** Write $\frac{6}{5}$ as a percentage. [1 mark]

(b) Write 0.035 as a fraction in its simplest form. [1 mark]

(c) Write 3.6% as a decimal. [1 mark]

 4.20 Put these numbers in order.

Start with the smallest.

34%   0.3 $\frac{1}{3}$ $\frac{16}{50}$ [3 marks]

 4.21 A music streaming service finds that

$\frac{7}{20}$ of users listen to its daily mix,

$\frac{1}{5}$ of users listen to their own playlist,

and the rest listen to an album.

What percentage of users listen to an album? [3 marks]

> **EXAM TIP**
>
> Convert the fractions to decimals first.

Questions referring to previous content

4.22 Write down a prime number that is between 20 and 30. [1 mark]

 4.23 Write the correct sign < or > in the box to make a true statement.

(a) $\frac{1}{5}$ ☐ $\frac{1}{4}$ [1 mark]

(b) $\frac{2}{3}$ ☐ $\frac{3}{4}$ [1 mark]

(c) $\frac{1}{12}$ ☐ 8% [1 mark]

(d) 0.375 ☐ $\frac{7}{18}$ [1 mark]

Knowledge

5 Percentages

Calculating percentages of amounts without a calculator

To find:

50%, divide by 2   25%, divide by 4   10%, divide by 10   1%, divide by 100

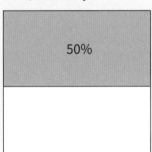

Worked example

Calculate these percentages without using a calculator.

1. 30% of 62

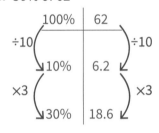

2. 26% of 16

100% of $16 = 16$

25% of $16 = 16 \div 4$

$\qquad = 4$

1% of $16 = 16 \div 100$

$\qquad = 0.16$

$26\% = 25\% + 1\%$

$\qquad = 4 + 0.16$

$\qquad = 4.16$

Worked example

Decrease £76 by 9% without using a calculator.

10% of £76 $=$ £7.60

1% of £76 $=$ £0.76

9% of £76 $= 10\% - 1\%$

$\qquad = £7.60 - £0.76$

$\qquad = £6.84$

£76 $-$ £6.84 $=$ £69.16 ●——— Decrease means make smaller.

Calculating percentages of amounts with a calculator

You can calculate percentages of amounts using **multipliers**.

Worked example

Calculate 63% of 576.

$63\% = \dfrac{63}{100} = 0.63$ — Find the decimal equivalent of 63% (this is the multiplier).

63% of $576 = 0.63 \times 576$ — Multiply 576 by 0.63

$= 362.88$

Formula box

original amount × multiplier = new amount

LINK

To remind yourself about further decimals and percentages, look back at Chapter 1.

To remind yourself about place value, look back at Chapter 1.

Percentage increase

If a value has been **increased** by 10% ...

you now have 110%

| original 100% | 10% |

Worked example

Increase 75 by 8%

$100\% + 8\% = 108\%$ — Add the percentage to 100.

$108\% = \dfrac{108}{100} = 1.08$ — Find the multiplier.

$1.08 \times 75 = 81$ — Multiply by the original amount.

Percentage decrease

If a value has been **decreased** by 10% ...

original 100%

| you now have 90% | 10% |

Worked example

Decrease 75 by 8%

$100\% - 8\% = 92\%$ — Subtract the percentage from 100.

$92 = \dfrac{92}{100} = 0.92$ — Find the multiplier.

$0.92 \times 75 = 69$ — Multiply by the original amount.

Express one quantity as a percentage of another

First write the numbers as a fraction, then convert this to a percentage.

Worked example

Write 6 as a percentage of 30.

$\dfrac{6}{30}$ — Write as a fraction.

$\dfrac{6}{30} = \dfrac{2}{10} = \dfrac{20}{100}$ — Convert so denominator is 100.

$\dfrac{20}{100} = 20\%$

Worked example

There are 24 adults and 16 children in a club. What percentage are children?

$16 + 24 = 40$ — Find the total.

$\dfrac{16}{40} = \dfrac{4}{10} = \dfrac{40}{100}$ — Convert so the denominator is 100.

$\dfrac{40}{100} = 40\%$

⚙ Knowledge

5 Percentages

Compound and simple interest

Simple interest is calculated only on the original amount deposited.

Compound interest is calculated on both the original amount deposited and any previous interest payments made.

Worked example

Natalie keeps 3500 in a savings account for 2 years. The account pays 4% interest each year. Calculate the amount of interest earned if:

1. Natalie takes the interest out of the account each year.

This is **simple** interest.

4% of 3500 = £140

Total interest for two years = £140 × 2 = £280

2. Natalie leaves the interest in the account next year.

This is **compound** interest.

Total in account after one year = £3500 × 1.04
$$= £3640$$

Total after two years = £3640 × 1.04 = £3785.60

So, interest = £3785.60 − £3500 = £285.60

Finding percentage increase/decrease

Formula box

$$\text{percentage (\%) increase} = \left(\frac{\text{actual increase}}{\text{original amount}}\right) \times 100$$

$$\text{percentage (\%) decrease} = \left(\frac{\text{actual decrease}}{\text{original amount}}\right) \times 100$$

You can use these formulae, or use multipliers, to solve a percentage increase or decrease problem.

Worked example

The height of a plant increases from 64 cm to 87.04 cm.

Calculate the percentage increase in the height of the plant.

Method 1: Using the formula

Actual increase = 87.04 − 64
$$= 23.04 \text{ cm}$$

$$\text{\% increase} = \frac{23.04}{64} \times 100$$
$$= 0.36 \times 100 = 36\%$$

Method 2: Using multipliers

$$64x = 87.04$$
$$x = \frac{87.04}{64}$$
$$x = 1.36$$

Let the multiplier be x.
original amount × multiplier = new amount

Percentage increase in height was 36%.

Finding percentage increase/decrease

Exam questions may tell you the percentage increase or decrease and ask you to calculate the original amount.

Worked example

A pair of shoes were discounted by 16% and now cost £52.08.

Find the original price of the shoes.

Method 1: Using multipliers

The original price of the shoes was discounted by 16%, so the shoes now cost 100% – 16% = 84% of their original price.

If the original price was £y, then 84% of y = 52.08

As a multiplier, 84% = 0.84

$y \times 0.84 = 52.08$ original amount × multiplier = new amount

$$y = \frac{52.08}{0.84}$$

$$y = 62$$

The original price was £62.00

WATCH OUT !

After you finish your calculations, make sure you answer the original question. Here, if you finished your answer at '$y = 62$', you would not score the final mark. You must write 'The original price was £62.00'

Method 2: Using bars

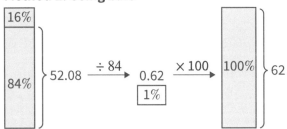

The original price was £62.00

You could draw a different diagram to show the same thing:

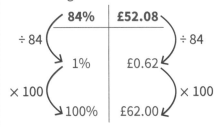

Key terms — Make sure you can write a definition for these key terms

compound interest   percentage decrease   percentage increase
multiplier   percentage   simple interest

⇄ Retrieval

5 Percentages

Learn the answers to the questions below, then cover the answers column with a piece of paper and write as many as you can. Check and repeat.

Questions	Answers
1 How do you find 50% of a number?	Divide by 2.
2 How do you find 10% of a number?	Divide by 10.
3 How do you find 1% of a number?	Divide by 100.
4 How do you convert a percentage to a decimal?	Divide by 100.
5 What is a multiplier?	A number, usually a decimal, which is used to calculate a percentage of an amount.
6 What is the formula for percentage change?	Original amount × multiplier = new amount.
7 What multiplier would you use to find an increase of 13%?	1.13
8 What multiplier would you use to find a decrease of 67%?	0.33
9 What is simple interest?	A fixed amount of interest calculated as a percentage of the original amount invested, that is added to a bank account each year.
10 Given that interest is paid at the end of each year, will simple interest give the same amount of money as compound interest at the end of year 2?	No, because the simple interest for year 2 is based on the initial sum invested, whereas the compound interest for year 2 is based on the initial sum invested plus the interest earned in the first year.

Previous questions

Now go back and use these questions to check your knowledge of previous topics.

Questions	Answers
1 How do you subtract two fractions?	Write both fractions with common denominators then subtract the numerators.
2 What is the reciprocal of a number?	The reciprocal of a number is 1 ÷ the number, i.e the reciprocal of a is $\frac{1}{a}$.
3 What is a square number?	A number multiplied by itself.
4 What is the general form of a number written in standard form?	$a \times 10^n$ where $1 \le a < 10$.

Exam-style questions

5.1 Work out:

    (a)   30% of 220   **[2 marks]**

    (b)   54% of 50   **[2 marks]**

    (c)   27% of 720   **[2 marks]**

    (d)   10.5% of 18   **[2 marks]**

5.2 Every month Faizal gets a bonus.

His bonus is 15% of what he earns that month.

In April, Faizal earns £2460.

Work out his bonus for April.   **[2 marks]**

5.3 Here are three symbols. $< \, > \, =$

Write one of these symbols in the box to make a true statement.

110% of 90 ⬜ $\frac{8}{7}$ of 84

You must show how you get your answer.   **[2 marks]**

5.4 Increase £50 000 by 3%.   **[2 marks]**

5.5 The volume of water in a puddle is 4 litres.

At the end of the day of the volume of water in the puddle is 2.5 litres.

Work out the percentage decrease in the volume of the puddle.   **[2 marks]**

5.6 Akeem draws a square with area 16 cm².

He enlarges his square so it has area 25 cm².

Work out the percentage increase in the side length of the square.   **[2 marks]**

> **EXAM TIP** ◎
>
> area of square
> = length × length

5.7 The table shows Kenny's weekly test scores in English and Maths.

	Week 1	Week 2	Week 3	Week 4
Maths	50	62	78	90
English	58	58	57	

The total of Kenny's English scores is 15% lower than the total of his Maths scores.

Work out the missing English score in the table.   **[4 marks]**

Exam-style questions

 5.8 At the age of 10, the mass of Talia's dog was 20 kg.
Between the ages of 10 and 12, the dog's mass increases by the same percentage as its age.

What is the mass of Talia's dog at age 12? **[2 marks]**

> **EXAM TIP**
> percentage increase = actual increase ÷ original value × 100%

 5.9 A length is multiplied by 1.4.

Work out the percentage increase in the length. **[1 mark]**

> **EXAM TIP**
> Work out what percentage of the original you have and then divide by this percentage.

 5.10 (a) Increase 50 by 10%. **[2 marks]**

(b) Decrease 40 by 55%. **[2 marks]**

 5.11 Moyra bowls a cricket ball at 90 miles per hour.

The second ball she bowls is 7% slower.

Work out the speed of the second ball. **[2 marks]**

 5.12 (a) Lucy invests £2450 in a savings account for 2 years.
The account pays simple interest at a rate of 6% per annum.

Calculate the total amount of interest Lucy will get at the end of 2 years. **[3 marks]**

(b) Yin invests £2450 in a savings account for 2 years.
The account pays compound interest at a rate of 6% per annum.

Calculate the total amount of interest Yin will get at the end of 2 years. **[3 marks]**

> **EXAM TIP**
> Compound interest is when interest also earns interest.

 5.13 A population of mayflies is decreasing at a rate of 4% per year.

At the start of 2023 the population is 3 000 000.

Work out the expected population after 2 years.

You **must** show your working. **[3 marks]**

5.14 In a sale, a shop reduces its prices by 30%.

The sale price of a pair of jeans is £28.

Work out the original price of the jeans. **[3 marks]**

> **EXAM TIP**
> Work out what percentage of the original you have and then divide by this percentage.

5.15 Sara ran 23 miles today.

This distance is 15% further than she ran yesterday.

Work out the distance she ran yesterday. **[3 marks]**

 5.16 After 20% VAT has been added, a tablet costs £92.40.

Work out the cost of the tablet before VAT is added. **[3 marks]**

 5.17 When its shell has been removed, an egg weighs 44.5 grams.

Find the weight of the egg before its shell was removed. **[3 marks]**

 5.18 Gemma chooses a number and increases it by 20%.

She then writes down the answer and decreases it by 20%.

Ben says that Gemma's final answer is wrong because it isn't the same as the original number.

Is Ben correct? Show working to support your answer. **[3 marks]**

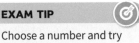
EXAM TIP
Choose a number and try Gemma's calculations.

Questions referring to previous content

5.19 Work out each calculation.

Give each answer as a fraction in its simplest form.

(a) $\frac{3}{7} \times \frac{5}{6}$ **[2 marks]**

(b) $\frac{2}{5} \div \frac{3}{10}$ **[3 marks]**

 5.20 Write 144 as a product of prime factors. **[2 marks]**

⚙ Knowledge

6 Algebra and expressions

Algebra terminology

Expression: A collection of letters and numbers which cannot be solved (no equals sign).

$$3x - \frac{1}{2}y + 2ab^2 - 3$$

Term: Part of an expression separated by a + or −

$3x, -\frac{1}{2}y, +2ab^2, -3$ are all terms.

Coefficient: The number before a letter.

The coefficient of $-\frac{1}{2}y$ is $-\frac{1}{2}$

Like terms: Terms which have the same letters and powers of letters. Coefficients do not matter.

$2x^2, -4x^2$ and $7x^2$ are like terms.

Notation: The symbols and conventions used.

$3x \times x$ is written as $3x^2$

$3 \div x$ is written as $\dfrac{3}{x}$

$1x$ is written as x

$x \times x$ is written as x^2

> **LINK** ⚙
> To remind yourself about indices, look back at Chapter 2.

Simplifying expressions

To **simplify** an **expression**, you may need to collect **like terms**.

> **Worked example**
>
> Remember to check whether you are adding, subtracting or multiplying.
>
> 1. Simplify $3x - 6y + 3x + 2y + 7$
>
> $3x - 6y + 3x + 2y + 7$ ●——[Collect like terms.]
>
> $= 3x + 3x - 6y + 2y + 7$
>
> $= 6x - 4y + 7$
>
> 2. Simplify $3x \times 4xy$
>
> $3x \times 4xy$ ●—————[Multiply numbers together and letters together.]
>
> $= 3 \times 4 \times x \times x \times y$
>
> $= 12 \times x^2 \times y$
>
> $= 12x^2 y$ ●————[Remember to use the correct **notation**.]

Expanding and factorising

To **expand** a single bracket, multiply each **term** inside the bracket by the term in front of the bracket.

> **Worked example**
>
> 1. Expand $3x(x + 7)$
>
>   [Remember: this means $3x \times (x + 7)$]
>
>   **Method 1:** Use an area model
>
> $3x(x + 7)$
>
> | × | x | $+7$ |
> |-----|--------|--------|
> | $3x$ | $3x^2$ | $+21x$ |
>
> $= 3x^2 + 21x$
>
>   **Method 2**
>
> $3x(x + 7)$
>
> $= 3x^2 + 21x$

Expanding and factorising

To **factorise**, find the highest common factor (HCF) of the terms and put this outside the bracket. (The HCF can be numbers and/or letters.) Then work out what needs to go inside the brackets.

Worked example

1. Fully factorise $12x^2y + 16xy^2$

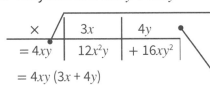

$$= 4xy$$
$$= 4xy(3x + 4y)$$

The HCF of $12x^2y$ and $16xy^2$ is $4xy$. This will go outside the brackets.

To work out what needs to go in the brackets divide $12x^2y$ and $16xy^2$ by $4xy$.

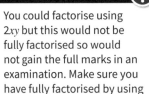

WATCH OUT

You could factorise using $2xy$ but this would not be fully factorised so would not gain the full marks in an examination. Make sure you have fully factorised by using the highest common factor.

Expanding and factorising are opposites of one another.

$$4xy(3x + 4y) \xleftarrow[\text{factorise}]{\text{expand}} 12x^2y + 16xy^2$$

Worked example

Write an <u>expression</u> for the <u>perimeter</u> of this shape.

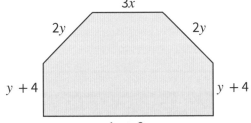

Start by underlining key words so you know exactly what the question is asking you to do. In this case, be careful to note if area or perimeter is needed.

Perimeter $= (3x) + (2y) + (y) + (4) + (4x) + (6) + (y) + (4) + (2y)$

Highlight or circle like terms in the same colour.

$$= \underbrace{3x + 4x}_{\text{terms in } x} + \underbrace{2y + y + y + 2y}_{\text{terms in } y} + \underbrace{4 + 6 + 4}_{\text{numbers}}$$

Collect like terms.

$$= 7x + 6y + 14$$

Simplify your expression.

⚙ Knowledge

6 Algebra and expressions

Substitution

Substitution is replacing a letter in an expression with a particular value.

Worked example

Find the value of each of these expressions when $a = -4$, $b = 5$ and $c = 2$

1. $2a + 10$

$2a + 10 = 2 \times (-4) + 10$ — Replace a with (-4). Write it in brackets so you multiply -4 by 2.

$= -8 + 10$

$= 2$ — Remember $2a$ means $2 \times a$.

2. $ab^2 + c$

$ab^2 + c = -4 \times 5^2 + 2$ — Indices first.

$= -4 \times 25 + 2$ — Multiplication next.

$= -100 + 2$

$= -98$

3. $abc + a^2$

$abc + a^2 = -4 \times 5 \times 2 + (-4)^2$

$= -4 \times 5 \times 2 + 16$ — Squaring a negative gives a positive.

$= -4 \times 10 + 16$

$= -40 + 16$

$= -24$

Identities

An **identity** is an equation that is always true, no matter what the value of the variable is.

If two expressions are equivalent, then you can show they form an identity if you can rearrange the left hand side to make it the same as the right-hand side.

Worked example

Show that $3(a + 2b) - 4a \equiv -a + 6b$ — The 'three-line' symbol ($\equiv$) tells you that this is an identity. It is true no matter what the value of a and b.

$\text{LHS} \equiv 3(a + 2b) - 4a$

$\equiv 3a + 6b - 4a$ — Start with one side (usually the most complicated).

$\equiv -a + 6b$ — Expand the bracket.

$\equiv \text{RHS}$ — Collect like terms.

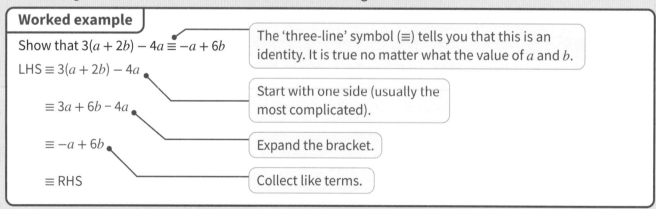

Key terms Make sure you can write a definition for these key terms

coefficient   expand   expression   factorise   identity
like terms   notation   simplify   substitution   term

6 Algebra and expressions

Learn the answers to the questions below, then cover the answers column with a piece of paper and write as many as you can. Check and repeat.

Questions	Answers
1 In algebra, what is a term?	A single number or variable, or numbers and variables multiplied together. For example, 2, x, $5y$ are all examples of terms.
2 How do you factorise an expression?	First find the highest common factor (HCF) of all the terms and put this outside the bracket. Then work out what needs to go inside the brackets.
3 What is the opposite of factorising?	Expanding.
4 What does it mean to expand a single bracket?	To multiply each term inside the bracket by the term in front of the bracket.
5 What is an expression?	A collection of letters and numbers which cannot be solved (no equals or inequality sign).
6 What is a coefficient	The number before a letter. For example, the coefficient of $6m$ is 6.
7 What is a variable?	A letter used to represent an unknown numerical value.
8 What do you have to do if you are asked to substitute a given value for a variable into an expression?	Replace the variable with the given value, then calculate the expression.
9 What does a^2 mean?	a multiplied by a.
10 What does it mean to factorise fully?	To make sure that you have used the highest common factor, not just a common factor.
11 In algebra, what does $\frac{3}{x}$ mean?	3 divided by x.
12 How can you check that you have factorised an expression correctly?	Expand the brackets and check you get the original expression.

Put paper here

Previous questions

Now go back and use these questions to check your knowledge of previous topics.

Questions	Answers
1 What does the B in BIDMAS mean?	Brackets.
2 What is an improper fraction?	A fraction where the numerator is larger than the denominator.
3 How do you find the HCF of two numbers?	List all the factors of each number then find the highest number common to both lists.

Put paper here

Practice

Exam-style questions

6.1 Simplify:

    (a) $2x + 3x - x$ **[1 mark]**

    (b) $3p - 5q + 7q - 2q + 4p$ **[2 marks]**

    (c) $7 + 5t - 2 - 9t$ **[2 marks]**

6.2 Simplify:

    (a) $x^2 + 4x + 3x^2 - 6x + 1$ **[2 marks]**

    (b) $9mn - 2m^2 + 7nm + 11m^2$ **[2 marks]**

6.3 Football cards cost £2 per pack. Athletics cards cost £3 per pack.

Mia buys x packs of football cards and y packs of athletics cards.

Write an expression for the **total** cost.   **[2 marks]**

6.4 Write an expression for the perimeter of this triangle.

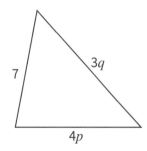

> **EXAM TIP**
>
> The perimeter is the distance around the edges of a shape.

                                                 [1 mark]

6.5 Write an expression for the perimeter of this quadrilateral.

Give your answer in its simplest form.   **[2 marks]**

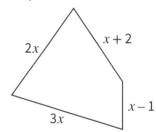

6.6   Niki has x pens. Gabi has twice as many pens as Niki.

Paulo has three more pens than Niki and Gabi have together.

Write an expression for the **total** number of pens.

Give your answer in its simplest form.   **[3 marks]**

6.7   Palesa repairs pianos.

She uses this formula to work out the cost of a repair.

$$\text{cost} = 80 + \text{number of hours worked} \times 15$$

(a)   A repair takes 5 hours. Work out the cost of this repair.   **[2 marks]**

(b)   Another repair costs £275. Work out the number of
hours worked.   **[2 marks]**

6.8   Work out the value for each expression when $a = 5$, $b = 2$ and $c = -4$.

   (a) $2a + 3b$ **[2 marks]**

   (b) $10 - c$ **[2 marks]**

   (c) $\dfrac{8a}{c}$ **[2 marks]**

   (d) $ac + b$ **[2 marks]**

6.9   For each formula, work out the value of d when $c = 4$.

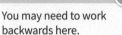

EXAM TIP
You may need to work
backwards here.

   (a) $d = \dfrac{c + 5}{2}$ **[2 marks]**

   (b) $d = c^2 - 3c$ **[2 marks]**

   (c) $c = 2d - 12$ **[3 marks]**

6.10   The acceleration, a, of a car is given by the formula $a = \dfrac{v - u}{t}$

where,

u is its starting speed

v is its final speed

t is the time it travels for.

Work out the acceleration of a car that goes from 0 m/s to 24 m/s in
8 seconds.   **[2 marks]**

Exam-style questions

6.11 Expand:

    (a) $5(x + 3)$ **[1 mark]**

    (b) $2x(3x - y)$ **[1 mark]**

6.12 Expand and simplify:

    (a) $2(x + 4) + 3(x - 8)$ **[2 marks]**

    (b) $9(x + 2) - 4(2x - 1)$ **[2 marks]**

    (c) $4(y + 3) - (y + 2)$ **[2 marks]**

> **EXAM TIP** 🎯
>
> Expand each bracket separately and be careful when subtracting.

6.13 Write an expression for the area of this triangle.   **[2 marks]**

6.14 Grant says that the difference between the area of this square and the area of this rectangle is $7x^2 + 8x$.

    Show that Grant is correct.   **[2 marks]**

6.15 Factorise fully:

    (a) $4x + 6y$ **[1 mark]**

    (b) $6a + 15b$ **[1 mark]**

    (c) $pq - 2p$ **[1 mark]**

6.16 Factorise fully:

> **EXAM TIP** 🎯
>
> Fully factorising requires you to take out the HCF from the brackets.

    (a) $20x^2 - 5x$ **[2 marks]**

    (b) $16x + 12xy$ **[2 marks]**

    (c) $x^2y + y^2x$ **[2 marks]**

    (d) $8p - 4p^2q + 6pq$ **[2 marks]**

6.17 James is n years old. Lily is two years younger than James. Katie is eleven years older than Lily.

Write an expression for:

(a) Lily's age [1 mark]

(b) Katie's age. [1 mark]

6.18 Mykhail has g games. Nisha has three times as many games as Mykhail.

Write an expression for the number of games Mykhail has. [1 mark]

Questions referring to previous content

 6.19 Here is a calculation:

$$4.5 \times 192 = 864$$

You can use the calculation to help answer the following questions.

(a) 4.5×19.2 [1 mark]

(b) 450×0.0192 [1 mark]

(c) $8.64 \div 0.45$ [1 mark]

6.20 Work out $6 \times 10^4 - 3.5 \times 10^3$. Write your answer in standard form. [3 marks]

⚙ Knowledge

7 Solving equations and inequalities

Function machines

This is a function machine for the **equation**

$y = 6x - 4$

input → | × 6 | → | − 4 | → output

If the input is $x = 3$, then the output, y is:

$(3 \times 6) - 4 = 18 - 4 = 14$

To work backwards, use the **inverse operations**.

input ← | ÷ 6 | ← | + 4 | ← output

If the output is $y = 20$, then the input, x is:

$(20 + 4) \div 6 = 24 \div 6 = 4$

Equations terminology

Expression: A collection of letters and numbers with no equals sign.

Equation: Two expressions which are equal in value and connected by an equals sign.

Unknown: A variable; a letter in an expression or equation.

Identity: An equation that is always true, no matter what the value of the variable is.

Formula: An equation which links different variables in a real-life relationship.

Solve: To solve an equation, you need to find the value of the unknown.

Inverse operations: an operation that reverses the effect of another operation, such as + and −.

Solving equations

To solve an equation, you must use inverse operations. Remember: do exactly the same thing to both sides of the equation. This keeps the equation balanced.

To **solve** the equation $3x + 1 = 7$:

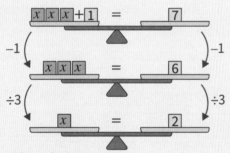

The solution is $x = 2$

To solve the equation $2x + 5 = 8 + x$:

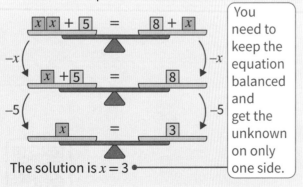

You need to keep the equation balanced and get the unknown on only one side.

The solution is $x = 3$

Solving equations

Worked example

1. $b - 12 = -2$

   $b - 12 + 12 = -2 + 12$ — Add 12 to both sides.

   $b = 9$

2. $5c + 17 = 32$

   $5c + 17 - 17 = 32 - 17$ — Subtract 17 from both sides.

   $5c = 15$

   $\dfrac{5c}{5} = \dfrac{15}{5}$ — Divide both sides by 5.

   $c = 3$

You can check your solution by substituting back into the original equation

$5 \times 3 + 17 = 15 + 17 = 32$ ✓

REVISION TIP

You need to look at the equation and choose the correct inverse operations to use each time.

Solving equations with fractions

Worked example

Solve

1. $\dfrac{8-2x}{2} = x$

> Get rid of the denominator by multiplying both sides by 2.

$\dfrac{8-2x}{2} \times 2 = x \times 2$

$8 - 2x = 2x$

$8 - 2x + 2x = 2x + 2x$

> Add $2x$ to both sides so that x only appears on one side.

$8 = 4x$

$\dfrac{8}{4} = \dfrac{4x}{4}$

> Divide both sides by 4.

$2 = x$

2. $\dfrac{3x}{2} + 4 = 12$

> Use inverse operations to get the fraction on its own.

$\dfrac{3x}{2} + 4 - 4 = 12 - 4$

$\dfrac{3x}{2} = 8$

$\dfrac{3x}{2} \times 2 = 8 \times 2$

> Get rid of the denominator by multiplying both sides by 2.

$3x = 16$

$\dfrac{3x}{3} = \dfrac{16}{3}$

> Divide both sides by 3.

$x = \dfrac{16}{3}$

$x = 5\dfrac{1}{3}$

> Simplify

Solving equations with brackets

Worked example

Solve $\dfrac{2(x+3)}{3} = x - 1$

> Get rid of the denominator by multiplying.

$\dfrac{2(x+3)}{3} \times 3 = (x-1) \times 3$

$2(x+3) = 3(x-1)$

$2x + 6 = 3x - 3$

> Expand the brackets.

$2x + 6 - 2x = 3x - 3 - 2x$

> Use inverse operations to get x on one side of the equation.

$6 = x - 3$

$6 + 3 = x - 3 + 3$

> Use inverse operations to get x on its own.

$9 = x$

REVISION TIP

In a linear equation, the highest power of the **variable** is always 1.

$x + 5 = 7x$ is linear but $x^2 + 2 = 3x$ is not linear.

Forming and solving equations

Worked example

1. A workshop produces two types of toy: model <u>cars</u> and model <u>boats</u>. In one hour, it produces <u>4</u> model cars and <u>x</u> model boats. If it produces <u>72</u> toys <u>total</u> in an <u>8-hour</u> day, <u>form an equation</u> and find the number of <u>model boats</u> it makes in one hour.

> Underline key words that will help you form an equation.

2. The square and the triangle have the same perimeter.

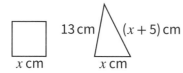

13 cm $(x+5)$ cm

x cm x cm

Form an equation and solve it to find the value of x.

The workshop produces 4 cars + x boats in 1 hour, so in 8 hours it produces:

$(8 \times 4) + (8 \times x) = 72$ toys

$32 + 8x = 72$

> Simplify the equation.

$8x = 40$

> Subtract 32 from both sides.

$x = 5$

> Divide both sides by 8.

So, it makes 5 model boats in one hour.

Perimeter of square $= 4x$

Perimeter of triangle $= x + (x+5) + 13 = 2x + 18$

The equation is $4x = 2x + 18$

$4x - 2x = 2x - 2x + 18$

> Subtract $2x$.

$2x = 18$

$\dfrac{2x}{2} = \dfrac{18}{2}$

> Divide by 2.

$x = 9$

⚙ Knowledge

7 Solving equations and inequalities

Forming and solving equations

Sometimes, you will need to use inverse operations to rearrange **formulae** to change the subject.

> **Worked example**
>
> 1. The formula for the area of a circle is $A = \pi r^2$
>   Rearrange the formula to make r the subject.
>
> $A = \pi r^2$
>
> $\dfrac{A}{\pi} = r^2$ ●——— Divide both sides by π.
>
> $\sqrt{\dfrac{A}{\pi}} = r$ ●——— Take the square root of both sides.
>
> 2. The area of a circle is 28.27 cm². Find the radius of this circle correct to 1 d.p.
>
> $r = \sqrt{\dfrac{28.27}{\pi}}$
>
> $= 3.0 \text{ cm (1 d.p.)}$
>
> > **LINK** ⚛
> >
> > You will revise area and circumference in Chapters 20 and 21.

Solving inequalities

When two **expressions** are not equal, you can use an inequality to show which is bigger.

For example, $5 < 9$ and $15 > 6$

When an inequality contains an unknown x, you can solve to find the values of x that satisfy the inequality.

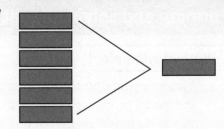

> **Worked example**
>
> Solve $2x + 13 \geq 25$
>
> $2x + 13 \geq 25$
>
> $2x + 13 - 13 \geq 25 - 13$ ●——— Subtract 13 from both sides.
>
> $\qquad 2x \geq 12$
>
> $\qquad \dfrac{2x}{2} \geq \dfrac{12}{2}$ ●——— Divide both sides by 2.
>
> $x \geq 6$
>
> > **WATCH OUT** ⚠
> >
> > As with equations, make sure you do the same operation to both sides of the inequality.

Solving inequalities

You can use a number line to represent the values of x which are included in the solution to the inequality.

A hollow circle shows that the number is **not** included.	A filled-in circle shows that the number **is** included.

If you multiply or divide both sides of an inequality by a negative number, the direction of the inequality changes. See Method 1, in the following Worked example.

Worked example

Solve $-2x + 13 \geq 25$

Method 1

$$-2x + 13 \geq 25$$
$$-2x + 13 - 13 \geq 25 - 13 \quad \bullet\!\!-\!\!\!-\!\!\!- \text{ Use inverse operations.}$$
$$-2x \geq 12$$
$$\frac{-2x}{-2} \geq \frac{12}{-2} \quad \bullet\!\!-\!\!\!-\!\!\!- \text{ Divide both sides by } -2.$$
$$x \leq -6$$

Notice how the inequality has changed direction when dividing by (-2).

Method 2

$$-2x + 13 \geq 25$$
$$-2x + 13 - 13 \geq 25 - 13 \quad \bullet\!\!-\!\!\!- \text{ Use inverse operations.}$$
$$-2x \geq 12$$
$$-2x + 2x \geq 12 + 2x \quad \bullet\!\!-\!\!\!- \text{ Add } 2x \text{ to get rid of the negative.}$$
$$0 \geq 12 + 2x$$
$$0 - 12 \geq 12 + 2x - 12 \quad \bullet\!\!-\!\!\!- \text{ Subtract 12.}$$
$$-12 \geq 2x$$
$$\frac{-12}{2} \geq \frac{2x}{2} \quad \bullet\!\!-\!\!\!- \text{ Divide by 2.}$$
$$-6 \geq x$$

Sometimes you will be given two inequalities and be asked to find values of x which satisfy both inequalities.

Worked example

1. Find the integer values of x which satisfy both:

$$2x + 1 > 7 \text{ and } x - 4 \leq 5$$

$$2x + 1 > 7 \qquad x - 4 \leq 5 \quad \bullet\!\!-\!\!\!- \text{ Solve each inequality separately.}$$
$$2x > 6 \qquad x \leq 9$$
$$x > 3$$
$$3 < x \leq 9 \quad \bullet\!\!-\!\!\!- \text{ Combine the inequalities.}$$

So, $x = 4, 5, 6, 7, 8, 9$

2. Represent your solution to Worked example 1 on a number line

Always draw number lines from smallest to largest.

Key terms Make sure you can write a definition for these key terms

equation   expression   formula   identity
inverse operations   solve   unknown

7 Solving equations and inequalities

Learn the answers to the questions below, then cover the answers column with a piece of paper and write as many as you can. Check and repeat.

Questions | Answers

	Questions		Answers
1	What is an expression?	Put paper here	A collection of letters and numbers with no equals sign.
2	What is an equation?		Two expressions which are equal in value and connected by an equals sign.
3	What is an inequality?		A relationship between two expressions which are not equal to each other.
4	When you need to solve an equation where one side is a fraction, what should you do first?	Put paper here	Remove the denominator by multiplying.
5	What is a formula?		An equation which links different variables in a real-life relationship.
6	How do you represent an inequality on a number line where the value is included?	Put paper here	Draw a solid circle.
7	How do you represent an inequality on a number line where the value is not included?		Draw an open circle.
8	What is the difference between an equation and an identity?	Put paper here	An identity is true for all values of the variable.
9	What is a 'linear' equation?		An equation with no power higher than one.
10	What should you do when you multiply or divide an inequality by a negative number?		Change the direction of the inequality symbol.

Previous questions

Now go back and use these questions to check your knowledge of previous topics.

Questions | Answers

	Questions		Answers
1	How do you convert a decimal into a percentage?	Put paper here	Multiply by 100.
2	How do you find 25% of a number?		Divide by 4 or multiply by 0.25.
3	What is the reciprocal of x?		$\frac{1}{x}$
4	How can you compare the size of any two fractions?		Write them both with either common numerators or common denominators.
5	How do you multiply fractions?		Multiply the numerators and multiply the denominators.

Exam-style questions

7.1 Here is a function machine.

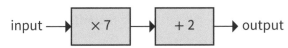

input → × 7 → + 2 → output

EXAM TIP

Read the question carefully. You might be given the input or output.

(a) Work out the output when the input is 5. [1 mark]

(b) Work out the input when the output is 23. [1 mark]

 7.2 Here is a function machine.

input → − 5 → ÷ 2 → + 4 → output

(c) Work out the output when the input is 5. [1 mark]

(d) Work out the input when the output is −1. [2 marks]

(e) Write an expression for the output when the input is h. [2 marks]

7.3 Rearrange each formula to make p the subject.

(a) $q = p + 3r$ [1 mark]

(b) $r = 3p + 2$ [2 marks]

(c) $q = p^2$ [1 mark]

(d) $\dfrac{q + p}{6} = r$ [2 marks]

 7.4 Solve:

(a) $4t = 28$ [1 mark]

(b) $w + 6 = 15$ [1 mark]

(c) $15 - p = 8$ [1 mark]

(d) $\dfrac{b}{5} = 10$ [1 mark]

Exam-style questions

7.5   Solve:

    (a) $\dfrac{a}{4} - 1 = 10$ **[2 marks]**

    (b) $\dfrac{2k + 1}{3} = -4$ **[2 marks]**

    (c) $5p + 3 = 3p + 7$ **[2 marks]**

    (d) $3 + p = 4p - 6$ **[2 marks]**

    (e) $9 - 6p = 4 - 11p$ **[2 marks]**

7.6   In a netball game:

Sarah scores n goals

Ewan scores 5 fewer goals than Sarah.

Cameron scores twice as many goals as Sarah.

They score 35 goals in total.

Write and solve an equation to work out how many goals Sarah scores.

                                                                                   [3 marks]

7.7   Here is a rectangle.

y cm

$(2x - 1)$ cm $(x + 3)$ cm

    (a)   Write and solve an equation to find the value of x.   **[3 marks]**

    (b)   Given that the perimeter of the rectangle is 34 cm,
           find the area of the rectangle.   **[4 marks]**

7.8   Show each inequality on the given number line.

> **EXAM TIP** 🎯
>
> Remember to show if an end point on a number line is included in the inequality.

    (a) $x > 7$

                                                                 [1 mark]

    (b) $x \leq -4$

                                                                 [1 mark]

(c) $-2 \le x < 5$

[2 marks]

(d) $1 \le x$

[1 mark]

7.9 n is an integer and $-1 \le n < 5$.
List all the possible values of n. [2 marks]

7.10 n is an integer and $-6 < 2n \le 8$.
List all the possible values of n. [2 marks]

7.11 Solve:

(a) $2x \ge 5$ [2 marks]

(b) $2x - 1 < 5$ [3 marks]

(c) $3x + 5 > 2$ [3 marks]

(d) $3x + 6 > 5x + 15$ [3 marks]

Questions referring to previous content

 7.12 A bag contains 180 g of flour. Mohammed uses $\frac{2}{3}$ of the flour in a recipe.
How much of the flour does Mohammed use? [2 marks]

7.13 Decide whether each statement is an expression, formula, equation or identity.
The first one has been done for you.

(a) $2x + 3 = 5$

(b) $S = \left(\dfrac{u + v}{2}\right) t$

(c) $x^2 = 9$

(d) $3x + 5x - 2x = 6x$

(e) $4k - 2$

(f) $V = IR$

(g) $y^2 - 9y + 20$

(h) $6p^2 - 4p + 2p^2 + 3p = 8p^2 - p$ [7 marks]

⚙ Knowledge

8 Straight line graphs

Graph terminology

A **coordinate grid** is a grid and a set of **axes** that you can plot points (called **coordinates**) and lines on.

The x-axis is a horizontal scale on the coordinate grid. The x-**intercept** is a point where a **graph** cuts the x-axis. In this graph, it is at $x = 3$.

The y-axis is the vertical scale. The y-intercept is a point where a graph cuts the y-axis. In this graph, it is at $y = 2$.

The **origin** is the point with coordinates $(0, 0)$.

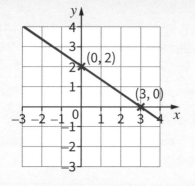

Linear graphs

A **linear** graph is a set of coordinates that make a straight line when plotted. This line can be horizontal, vertical or sloping.

$y = 3$ is a horizontal line

$y = 3$
goes through
the y-axis at $(0, 3)$

$x = 3$ is a vertical line

$x = 3$
goes through
the x-axis at $(3, 0)$

All lines of the form $y = a$ are horizontal for any value of a.

All lines of the form $x = a$ are vertical for any value of a.

Gradients

The **gradient** is a measure used to describe how steep a line graph is. It is how many units up (or down) the line goes for every one unit across.

To find the gradient of a line, first find two points on the line where you can read the exact coordinates. Then:

$$\text{gradient} = \frac{\text{change in } y}{\text{change in } x}$$

Which, in this example $= \frac{4}{2} = 2$

A line through the origin with gradient m has equation $y = mx$.

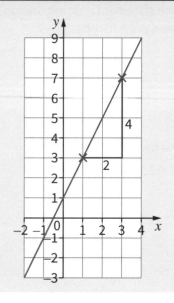

WATCH OUT ❗

A gradient can be positive or negative.

+ve ↗ up   –ve ↘ down

Gradients

Worked example

1. Calculate the gradient of this line.

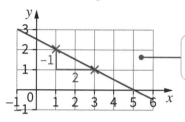

Find two points where you can read the exact coordinates.

$$\text{gradient} = \frac{\text{change in } y}{\text{change in } x} = \frac{-1}{2} = -0.5$$

Equation of a straight line

The **equation of a straight line** is a rule that is true for all points on the straight line. For example, $y = 2x + 5$.

Equations such as $y = x$ and $y = 2x + 5$ are sloping lines.

The **general equation of a straight line** is $y = mx + c$

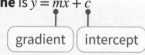

gradient | intercept

A **table of values** is a way of writing down the values that satisfy a **function** or equation. For example:

for $y = 2x$:

x	0	1	2	3
y	0	2	4	6

for $y = 2x + 5$:

x	0	1	2	3
y	5	7	9	11

Remember this...

$$y = mx + c$$

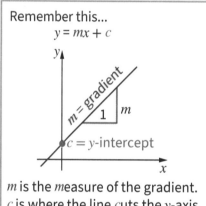

m is the *m*easure of the gradient.
c is where the line *c*uts the y-axis.

Worked example

A straight line has a gradient of 3 and passes through the point $(-2, 7)$.
Find the equation of the line.

$y = mx + c$ — Use the general formula for a straight line.

$m = 3, x = -2, y = 7$

$7 = 3 \times (-2) + c$ — Substitute the values for the gradient and points into the equation.

$7 = -6 + c$ — Rearrange to find c.

$c = 7 - (-6)$

$c = 13$

$y = 3x + 13$ — Write out equation.

⚙ Knowledge

8 Straight line graphs

Equation of a straight line

Worked example

1. Fill in the table of values for the equation
$y = 2x - 3$

x	−2	−1	0	1
y		−5		

$y = 2 \times (-2) - 3 = -7$ •——— Substitute the values of x into the equation to find y

$y = 2 \times 0 - 3 = -3$

$y = 2 \times 1 - 3 = -1$

x	−2	−1	0	1
y	**−7**	**−5**	**−3**	**−1**

2. Draw the graph of $y = 2x - 3$

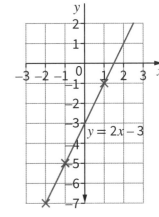

Plot each of the points from the table $(-2, -7), (-1, -5), (0, -3), (1, -1)$

Use a ruler to draw a straight line through all the points.

LINK

To remind yourself about rearranging equations, look back at Chapter 6.

EXAM TIP

When drawing graphs:
- use a ruler
- check the scales on both axes
- the line must go all the way to the edge of the coordinate grid.

Worked example

A line has the equation $2y + 6 = 4x$

Work out the gradient and the y-intercept of the line.

$2y + 6 - 6 = 4x - 6$ •——— Rearrange the equation so it's in the form $y = mx + c$

$2y = 4x - 6$

$\dfrac{2y}{2} = \dfrac{4x - 6}{2}$

$y = 2x - 3$

The gradient (m) is 2 and the y-intercept (c) is −3 •——— Compare to $y = mx + c$

Equation of a straight line

Worked example

Find the equation of the line.

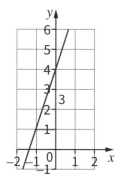

$$\text{gradient } (m) = \frac{\text{change in } y}{\text{change in } x} = \frac{3}{1} = 3$$

y-intercept $(c) = 4$

$$y = mx + c$$

$$y = 3x + 4$$

REVISION TIP

Two lines are **parallel** when they are always the same distance from each other. A pair of parallel lines will have the same gradient. These lines are parallel. They both have a gradient of 3.

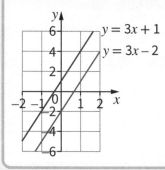

Worked example

A line passes through the coordinates (1, 2) and (4, −7).

Work out the equation of the line.

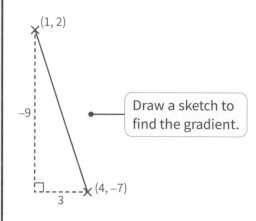

Draw a sketch to find the gradient.

$$\text{gradient } (m) = \frac{\text{change in } y}{\text{change in } x} = \frac{-9}{3} = -3$$

$$y = mx + c \Rightarrow y = -3x + c$$

$$y = -3x + c$$

$$2 = -3 \times 1 + c$$

$$2 = 3 + c$$

$$c = 5$$

To find c, substitute the coordinate pair (1, 2) into the equation (you could also have used the point (4, −7)).

The equation is $y = -3x + 5$

Key terms Make sure you can write a definition for these key terms

axes   coordinate   coordinate grid   equation of a graph   function   general equation of a straight line   graph   gradient   intercept   linear   origin   parallel   table of values

8 Straight line graphs

Learn the answers to the questions below, then cover the answers column with a piece of paper and write as many as you can. Check and repeat.

	Questions		Answers
1	What is a linear graph?	Put paper here	A linear graph is a straight line which can be horizontal, vertical or sloping.
2	What would the line $x = a$ look like?		A vertical line passing through $x = a$.
3	What is the general equation of a straight line?		$y = mx + c$
4	What does the gradient of the line measure?		How steep it is.
5	If a gradient is negative, what do you know about the line?	Put paper here	It goes 'downhill' from left to right.
6	If a gradient is positive, what do you know about the line?		It goes 'uphill' from left to right.
7	How do you calculate the gradient of a line?	Put paper here	$\dfrac{\text{change in } y}{\text{change in } x}$
8	What does m represent in $y = mx + c$?		The gradient.
9	What does c represent in $y = mx + c$?		The y-intercept.
10	What is a table of values for the equation of a line used for?	Put paper here	To generate points that lie on the line.
11	If the equation is of the form $ax + by = c$ (where a, b, c are integers) how do you find the gradient?	Put paper here	Rearrange into the form $y = mx + c$.

Previous questions

Now go back and use these questions to check your knowledge of previous topics.

	Questions		Answers
1	What does 'commutative' mean?	Put paper here	The calculation can be done in any order.
2	What does LCM mean?		Lowest common multiple.
3	What is the reciprocal of a?		$\dfrac{1}{a}$
4	What is the formula for percentage decrease?		percentage decrease $= \dfrac{\text{actual decrease}}{\text{original amount}} \times 100$
5	What does 10^n mean?		The product of multiplying n instances of 10 together. For example, 10^4 means $10 \times 10 \times 10 \times 10$.

Exam-style questions

8.1 Work out the gradient of each line segment.

(a)	(b)	(c)	(d)
		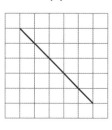	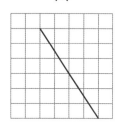

[8 marks]

8.2 **(a)** Complete the table of values for $y = 3x - 1$.

x	−1	0	1	2	3
y			2		8

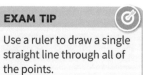

EXAM TIP

Use a ruler to draw a single straight line through all of the points.

[2 marks]

(b) On the grid below, draw the graph of $y = 3x - 1$ for values of x from −1 to 3.

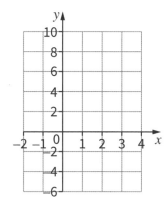

[3 marks]

 8.3 On the grid below, draw the graph of $x + y = 5$ for values of x from −2 to 5.

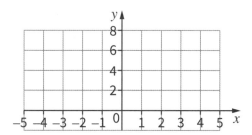

[3 marks]

Exam-style questions

8.4 Draw the graph of $y = 3 - 2x$ for values of x from -2 to 2.

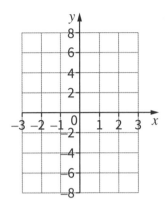

[2 marks]

8.5 The line L is shown on the grid.

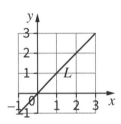

Find an equation for L.

[3 marks]

> **EXAM TIP**
>
> The equation of a line going through $(0, 0)$ is $y = mx$ where m is the gradient.

8.6 The line L is shown on the grid.

> **EXAM TIP**
>
> You may find it helpful to draw on the coordinate axes to help you calculate the gradient.

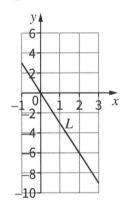

Find an equation for L.

[3 marks]

8.7 Write down the gradient and y-intercept of each of these lines.

(a) $y = 5x + 1$ **[1 mark]**

(b) $y = 3 - 2x$ **[1 mark]**

(c) $2y = x + 6$ **[1 mark]**

(d) $y - x = 10$ **[1 mark]**

(e) $8x + 4y = 3$ **[1 mark]**

8.8 Write the equation of a line parallel to $y = 4x - 8$ [1 mark]

8.9 Find an equation for the line that passes through.

(a) $(0, -1)$ and $(2, 3)$ [3 marks]

(b) $(-3, 5)$ and $(1, 1)$ [3 marks]

8.10 The equation of a straight line L is $y = 4 - 3x$.

The equation of a straight line M is $3x + y = 0$.

Sajid says that line M is parallel to line L.

Is Sajid correct?

You must show how you get your answer. [2 marks]

8.11 The line L is shown on the grid.

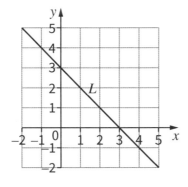

[2 marks]

(a) Find an equation for L. [3 marks]

(b) If the line is extended, will the point with coordinates $(97, -100)$ lie on the line?

You must show how you get your answer. [2 marks]

Questions referring to previous content

 8.12 Olivia is 68 inches tall.

Write 68 inches in feet and inches.

1 foot = 12 inches [2 marks]

 8.13 In Lin's class, 6 out of 25 students read fantasy books.

In Jay's class, 8 out of 32 students read fantasy books.

Lin says the percentage of students who read fantasy books is greater in her class than in Jay's.

Is Lin correct? You **must** show how you get your answer. [2 marks]

Knowledge

9 Real-life graphs

Finding approximate values from a linear graph

Worked example

1. Find the value of x when $y = 2$.

   $x = 2.5$

2. Find the value of y when $x = 1$.

   $y = -1$

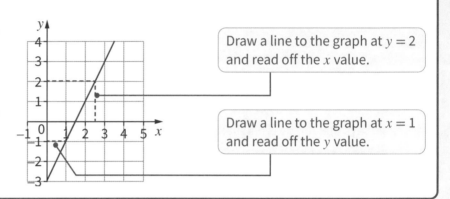

Draw a line to the graph at $y = 2$ and read off the x value.

Draw a line to the graph at $x = 1$ and read off the y value.

Real-life graphs

Real-life graphs are used to represent real-life situations and data. They can be straight lines or curves.

Worked example

This graph shows the cost of Peter's phone contract per month.

1. Explain why the graph starts at (0, 10).

   For 0 hours, Peter pays £10. This is a fixed cost before he makes any calls.

2. One month, Peter makes 40 hours of calls. Work out how much Peter's bill is.

   Look to see where the line is when the x-axis is at 40 hours.

   £30

3. Determine how much a call costs per hour.

   You need to find the **gradient**.

   £5 ÷ 10 hours = £0.50 per hour of calls.

LINK

To remind yourself about gradients, look back at Chapter 8.

Formula box

$$\text{gradient} = \frac{\text{change in } y}{\text{change in } x}$$

WATCH OUT

Always check what each unit on each scale represents.

Distance-time graphs

A distance-time graph shows how the distance changes as time passes.
On a distance-time graph, gradient = **speed**.

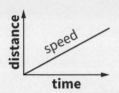

$$\text{gradient} = \frac{\text{distance}}{\text{time}}$$

$$= \textbf{speed}$$

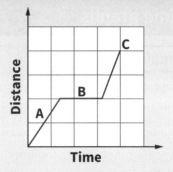

A. Straight sloped line means the speed is constant.

B. Horizontal section means time is passing but the distance isn't changing, so the speed is 0.

C. Steepest section, so the speed was the quickest here.

Worked example

The graph shows the height of a chilli plant at the end of each week.

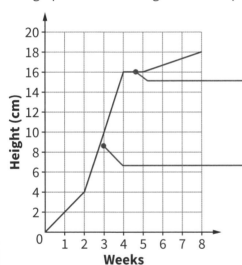

The line is flat between 4 and 5 weeks, which means the plant didn't increase in height in this time.

The line is steepest between 2 and 4 weeks, this means the height was increasing faster than at any other time.

1. How tall was the plant after three weeks?

   It was 10 cm tall.

2. In which week did the plant not grow?

   It did not grow between weeks 4 and 5.

3. When did the plant grow the fastest and what was its speed of growth during this time?

   The fastest increase was between 2 and 4 weeks. The speed of growth was $\frac{12}{2} = 6$ cm/week.

9 Real-life graphs

Distance-time graphs

Worked example

Min-Su drives a total of 14 km to work.

- She travels the first 6 km at a constant speed of 36 km/h.

- She then stops for 5 minutes at roadworks.

- It takes her 15 minutes to complete the rest of the journey at a constant speed.

Draw a distance-time graph of the journey.

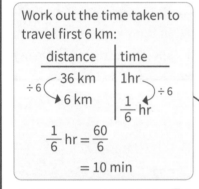

Work out the time taken to travel first 6 km:

distance	time
36 km	1 hr
6 km	$\frac{1}{6}$ hr

÷6 ... ÷6

$\frac{1}{6}$ hr = $\frac{60}{6}$

= 10 min

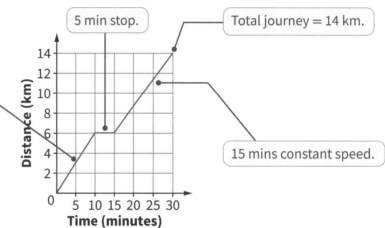

5 min stop.

Total journey = 14 km.

15 mins constant speed.

WATCH OUT ⚠

Be careful of the units – check if the time is given in minutes or hours.

Worked example

The distance-time graph shows how a snail moved one morning.

What was its speed in m/h between 09:00 and 09:30?

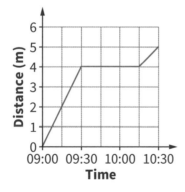

The snail moved 4 m in 0.5 hour.

distance	time
4 m	0.5 hr
8 m	1 hr

×2 ... ×2

speed = 8 m/hr ⟵ Use hours, not minutes here.

Speed–time graphs

A speed-time graph shows how the speed changes as time passes.
The gradient of a speed-time graph is the equal to the **acceleration**.

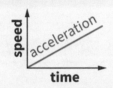

$$\text{gradient} = \frac{\text{speed}}{\text{time}}$$
$$= \textbf{acceleration}$$

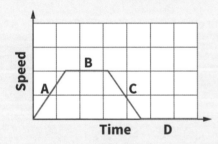

A. Straight sloped lines mean that acceleration is constant.

B. Horizontal section means time is passing but the speed isn't changing, so the speed is constant.

C. Negative gradient, which means deceleration or slowing down.

D. Speed = 0; they have stopped.
The area under the graph represents the distance travelled.

Rates of change

Worked example

These vases are filled with water at a constant rate. Sketch a graph for each to show how the depth of water varies over time.

A. 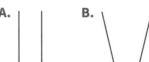   B.   C.

A.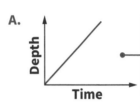
A. Depth of vase increases at constant rate so the graph is a straight line.

B.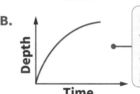
B. Rate of change of vase depth decreases as it gets wider, so the graph is a curve.

C.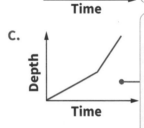
C. Graph has straight lines as the depth of the vase increases at a constant rate in both sections, but fills faster when it is narrower.

LINK
You will revise compound measures in Chapter 14.

Worked example

The graph shows the speed of a runner at the start of a 100 m race.

(a) Find their initial acceleration in m/s.

(b) Find the distance covered by the runner in the first 4 seconds.

(a) 2.5 m/s

The distance travelled is the area under the graph between 0 and 4 seconds.

This is a triangle with a base of length 4 and a height of 10.

Using Area $= \frac{1}{2} \times$ base $\times$ height

Distance covered $= \frac{1}{2} \times 4 \times 10$
$= 20$ m.

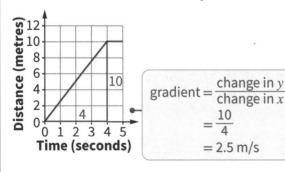

$$\text{gradient} = \frac{\text{change in } y}{\text{change in } x}$$
$$= \frac{10}{4}$$
$$= 2.5 \text{ m/s}$$

Key terms Make sure you can write a definition for these key terms

acceleration
real-life graph   speed

Retrieval

9 Real-life graphs

Learn the answers to the questions below, then cover the answers column with a piece of paper and write as many as you can. Check and repeat.

Questions	Answers
1 When you are given a real-life graph, what should you look for on each axis?	The labels, to find out what each axis represents.
2 What quantity will you find on the vertical axis of a distance-time graph?	Distance.
3 What quantity will you find on the horizontal axis of a distance-time graph?	Time.
4 What might it mean if a graph showing time against cost starts at (0 s, £15)?	The standing charge / fixed cost is £15.
5 What does the gradient represent on a distance-time graph?	Speed.
6 What does the gradient represent on a speed-time graph?	Acceleration.
7 What does a straight, sloping line represent on a distance-time graph?	Constant speed.
8 What does a horizontal section represent on a distance-time graph?	No movement; the speed is 0.
9 What does a horizontal section represent on a speed-time graph?	Constant speed; the acceleration is 0.
10 What does the area under a speed-time graph represent?	The distance travelled.

Put paper here

Previous questions

Now go back and use these questions to check your knowledge of previous topics.

Questions	Answers
1 What is standard form used for?	To make it easier to understand very large or very small numbers.
2 What is $a \times a \times a$ in index notation?	a^3
3 What is a factor?	A positive integer that divides exactly into another integer leaving no remainder.
4 What is the equation for a straight line that passes through the origin?	$y = mx$
5 How many factors does a prime number have?	Exactly two; one and itself.

Put paper here

Exam-style questions

9.1 Kai leaves home at 11:00.

He cycles for $1\frac{1}{2}$ hours.

Here is a distance-time graph of his cycle ride.

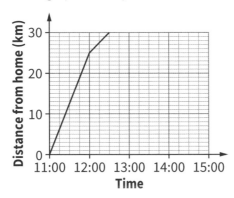

(a) How far did Kai cycle in the first $1\frac{1}{2}$ hours of his ride? **[1 mark]**

(b) Kai cycled at a slower speed.

Explain how the graph shows this. **[1 mark]**

(c) Work out Kai's speed, in km/h, between 12:00 and 12:30. **[2 marks]**

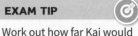

EXAM TIP

Work out how far Kai would travel in 1 hour.

(d) At 12:30 Kai stops for 45 minutes for lunch.

Then he cycles home at a speed of 20 km/h.

Complete the distance-time graph. **[2 marks]**

9.2 Sophie mows her grass every few weeks.

The graph shows the height of her grass over a period of 12 weeks one summer.

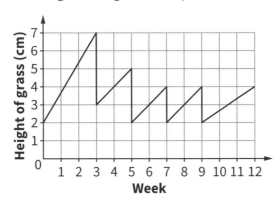

(a) In which weeks does Sophie cut the grass? **[1 mark]**

(b) Between which weeks does the grass grow at the slowest rate? **[1 mark]**

EXAM TIP

The steeper the graph, the faster the rate of change.

(c) What was the rate of growth of the grass, in cm per week, between weeks 5 and 7? **[1 mark]**

9.3 Here are the cross-sections of three swimming pools.

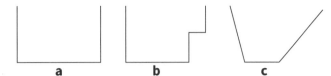

Each pool is filled with water from a hose.

The graphs show the depth of water in the pool as it fills.

Match each pool to the correct graph.

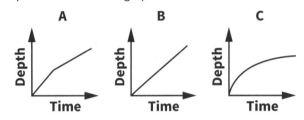

[2 marks]

9.4 You can use this graph to change between pounds and euros.

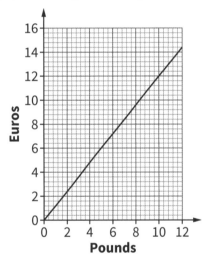

(a) Use the graph to convert 5 Pounds into Euros [1 mark]

(b) Use the graph to convert 14.50 Euros into Pounds. [1 mark]

(c) Convert 200 Pounds into Euros. [2 marks]

9.5 Jesse travels from Amsterdam to Rotterdam.

He stops for one rest on the journey.

Write down the letter of the graph that could represent his journey.

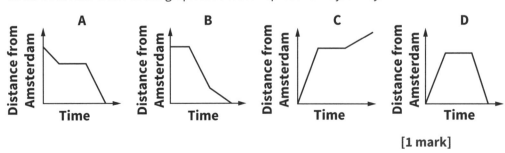

[1 mark]

9.6 The graph shows the cost of a taxi journey for different numbers of km travelled.

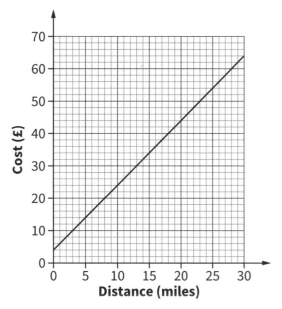

(a) Write down the fixed charge. **[1 mark]**

(b) Work out the charge per mile. **[1 mark]**

(c) Jackie's taxi journey cost £50.

How far did Jackie travel? **[1 mark]**

Questions referring to previous content

9.7 The perimeter of the kite is 38 cm.

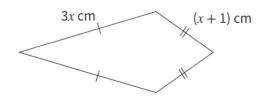

> **EXAM TIP**
>
> Write an expression for the perimeter of the kite and then solve an equation.

Work out the value of x **[3 marks]**

9.8 A straight line passes through the points (1, 3) and (7, 8). Work out the equation of the straight line. **[2 marks]**

Knowledge

10 Solving quadratic equations by factorising

Quadratic expressions

A **quadratic expression** is an expression where the highest power of the variable is 2.

It is of the form $ax^2 + bx + c$, where a, b and c are the **coefficients**.

For example, $x^2 + 5x - 7$ is a quadratic expression, where $a = 1$, $b = 5$, and $c = -7$.

Expanding double brackets

To **expand** (multiply out) a pair of brackets, multiply each term in the first set of brackets by each term in the second pair of brackets.

$(x + 5)(2x - 7) = 2x^2 - 7x + 10x - 35$

$\qquad\qquad\quad = 2x^2 + 3x - 35$ ← Collect like terms.

If you prefer, you can use a multiplication grid.

×	x	5
$2x$	$2x^2$	$10x$
-7	$-7x$	-35

Factorising into double brackets

The opposite of expanding is **factorising**. Some expressions of the form $x^2 + bx + c$ can be factorised into a double set of brackets.

Worked example

Factorise $x^2 + 2x - 3$

$-3 + 1 = -2$ ✗

$+3 - 1 = +2$ ✔

First write out the factor pairs of -3. Find the pair that adds to $+2$. This allows you to split the x-term.

$x^2 + 3x - x - 3$

Rewrite.

×	x	$+3$
x	x^2	$+3x$
-1	$-x$	-3

Put in a grid and factorise each part.

$(x - 1)(x + 3)$ ← Write in double brackets.

Factorising into double brackets

Try not to confuse signs. Look back at the previous worked example. Imagine you had incorrectly written the two numbers as -3 and 1, instead of -1 and 3.

×	x	-3
x	x^2	$-3x$
$+1$	$+x$	-3

or

×	x	$+3$
x	x^2	$3x$
-1	$-x$	-3

This grid gives

$x^2 - 3x + x - 3$

$= x^2 - 2x - 3$ ✗

This grid gives

$x^2 + 3x - x - 3$

$= x^2 + 2x - 3$ ✔

Worked example

Factorise $x^2 - 11x + 24$

$+1 + 24 = 25$ ✗ ← Remember positive and negative factors.

$-1 - 24 = -25$ ✗

$+2 + 12 = +14$ ✗

$-2 - 12 = -14$ ✗

$+3 + 8 = +11$ ✗

$-3 - 8 = -11$ ✔

$(x - 3)(x - 8)$ ← You can put the factors straight into the brackets.

REVISION TIP

It is always worth expanding to see if you factorised correctly.

Key terms Make sure you can write a definition for these key terms

coefficient   difference of two squares
expand   factor   factorising
quadratic expression   solve

Solving equations by factorising

You can **solve** some quadratic equations by factorising.

Worked example

Solve these quadratic equations.

1. $x^2 - 5x + 6 = 0$

$(x - 3)(x - 2) = 0$ — Factorise into double brackets.

$x - 3 = 0$ or $x - 2 = 0$

$x = 3$ or $x = 2$ — Put each factor equal to zero.

2. $3x^2 + 12x = 0$

$3x(x + 4) = 0$ — Notice the common factor in both terms.

$3x = 0$ or $x + 4 = 0$

$x = 0$ or $x = -4$ — Factorise into single brackets.

Put each factor equal to zero.

LINK

To remind yourself about solving linear equations, look back at Chapter 7.

Difference of two squares

The **difference of two squares** is an expression, such as $a^2 - b^2$, which contains one square number minus another square number. For example, $x^2 - 9$ is the difference of two squares.

Formula box

The difference of two squares can be factorised:

$a^2 - b^2 = (a + b)(a - b)$

When you multiply out the brackets, the middle terms $-ab$ and $+ab$ cancel out and leave just $a^2 - b^2$

$\times$	a	$+b$
a	a^2	$+ab$
$-b$	$-ab$	$-b^2$

$a^2 + ab - ab - b^2$
$= a^2 - b^2$

Worked example

Factorise $x^2 - 9$

$9 = 3^2$, so $x^2 - 9 = x^2 - 3^2$

$= (x - 3)(x + 3)$

$(x - 3)(x + 3) = x^2 - 3x + 3x - 9$

$= x^2 - 9$ — Check by multiplying out.

Choosing how to factorise

Worked example

Factorise these expressions fully.

1. $x^2 - 3x + 2$ — Three terms including x^2, so use double brackets.

$(-2) \times (-1) = 2$

$(-2) + (-1) = -3$ — Find two numbers that multiply to give 2 and add to give -3.

$x^2 - 3x + 2 = (x - 2)(x - 1)$

2. $5x^2 - 15x$ — Two terms with common factors, so use single brackets.

$5x^2 - 15x = 5x(x - 3)$

The HCF of $5x^2$ and $15x$ is $5x$

3. $x^2 - 25$

$x^2 - 25 = (x - 5)(x - 5)$

x^2 and 25 are square terms and there's a minus sign, so it is the difference of two squares. The square root of x^2 is x and the square root of 25 is 5.

REVISION TIP

When factorising quadratic expressions, check these things.

1. Are there two terms and do they have a common factor? If yes, use single brackets:

$x^2 + 3x = x(x + 3)$

2. Are there three terms, which include x^2? If yes, use double brackets:

$x^2 + 6x + 5 = (x + 5)(x + 1)$

3. Is it a difference of two squares? If yes, use double brackets with the square roots:

$x^2 - 9 = (x + 3)(x - 3)$

10 Solving quadratic equations by factorising

Learn the answers to the questions below, then cover the answers column with a piece of paper and write as many as you can. Check and repeat.

Questions	Answers
1 What is a quadratic equation?	An equation where the highest power of the variable is 2.
2 What should your first step be if you want to solve $x^2 + x = 12$?	Subtract 12 from both sides so the equation is equal to 0.
3 If you factorise $x^2 + bx + c$, you need to find two numbers which add to give which letter?	b
4 If you factorise $x^2 + bx + c$, you need to find two numbers which multiply to give which letter?	c
5 What is an expression in the form $a^2 - b^2$ called?	The difference of two squares.
6 What does $a^2 - b^2$ factorise to?	$(a+b)(a-b)$
7 What happens when you expand $(a+b)(a-b)$	The $-ab$, $+ab$ will cancel out leaving $a^2 - b^2$.
8 What is the general form of a quadratic expression?	$ax^2 + bx + c$
9 How do you solve a quadratic expression that can be factorised?	Rearrange the equation such that $ax^2 + ax + c = 0$, then factorise. Make each bracket = 0, and solve.
10 In the general form of a quadratic equation what is the coefficient of the x^2 term?	a

Put paper here

Previous questions

Now go back and use these questions to check your knowledge of previous topics.

Questions	Answers
1 What do you have to do if you are asked to substitute a given value for a variable into an expression?	Replace the variable with the given value, then calculate the expression.
2 What does $2a$ mean?	2 multiplied by a.
3 What is a variable?	A letter used to represent an unknown numerical value.
4 What does the gradient of a line tell you about the line?	How steep the line is.
5 What do the letters of BIDMAS stand for?	**B**rackets, **I**ndices, **D**ivision, **M**ultiplication, **A**ddition, **S**ubtraction.

Put paper here

Exam-style questions

10.1 Expand and simplify: [2 marks]

    (a) $(x + 3)(x + 6)$ [2 marks]

    (b) $(b - 3)(b + 4)$ [2 marks]

    (c) $(t - 5)^2$ [2 marks]

10.2 Expand and simplify:

    (a) $(x + 1)(y + 7)$ [1 mark]

    (b) $(x - y)^2$ [2 marks]

    (c) $(3 - 2p)(2p + 9)$ [2 marks]

10.3 Write an expression for the area of the triangle.
Expand any brackets.

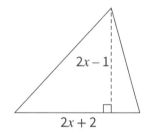

$2x - 1$

$2x + 2$

[3 marks]

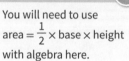

> **EXAM TIP**
>
> You will need to use
> area $= \frac{1}{2} \times$ base $\times$ height
> with algebra here.

10.4 Factorise:

    (a) $x^2 + 5x + 6$ [2 marks]

    (b) $y^2 - 3y + 2$ [2 marks]

    (c) $p^2 - 9p - 36$ [2 marks]

10.5 This rectangle has area $x^2 + 6x - 27$.
Write expressions for the length and width of the rectangle.

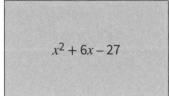

$x^2 + 6x - 27$

[2 marks]

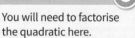

> **EXAM TIP**
>
> You will need to factorise
> the quadratic here.

Exam-style questions

10.6 Factorise fully:

    (a) $y^2 + 16y$ **[1 mark]**

    (b) $x^2 - 16$ **[1 mark]**

    (c) $a + 16a + 64$ **[2 marks]**

 10.7 Solve $2x^2 = 98$ **[2 marks]**

10.8 Solve:

> **EXAM TIP**
>
> Before solving, make sure one side of the equation is zero.

    (a) $x^2 + 9x + 20 = 0$ **[2 marks]**

    (b) $x^2 - 7x - 8 = 0$ **[2 marks]**

    (c) $x^2 + 5x = 0$ **[2 marks]**

    (d) $x^2 - 1 = 0$ **[2 marks]**

    (e) $2x^2 + 6x = 0$ **[2 marks]**

10.9 Here is a rectangle. The area of the rectangle is 12 cm².

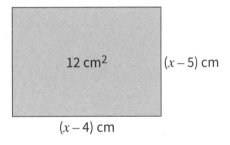

12 cm² $(x - 5)$ cm

$(x - 4)$ cm

    (a)   Show that $x^2 - 9x + 8 = 0$ **[3 marks]**

    (b)   Find the length of the shortest side of the rectangle.   **[3 marks]**

> **EXAM TIP**
>
> Use the information in the diagram to write an equation for the area of the rectangle. Rearrange it into the form given.

10.10 Here is a square divided into sections.

The area of the whole square is 30 cm².

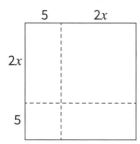

[3 marks]

Show that $4x^2 + 20x = 5$

10.11 Anna tries to solve $(x - 3)(x + 4) = 0$. Here is her working:

$x - 3 = 0$ or $x + 4 = 0$

$x = 3$ or $x = 4$

One of Anna's solutions is wrong.

What mistake has she made?

Include the correct solution in your answer.   [1 mark]

Questions referring to previous content

10.12 (a)   Increase 60 by 5%   [2 marks]

    (b)   Decrease 0.5 by 80%   [2 marks]

10.12 (a)   A number x is rounded to two decimal places. The result is 0.87.
Complete the error interval for x.
$\ldots \leq x < \ldots$ [2 marks]

    (b)   A number y is truncated to a whole number. The result is 7.
Complete the error interval for y.
$\ldots \leq y < \ldots$ [2 marks]

⚙ Knowledge

11 Quadratic, cubic, and reciprocal graphs

Quadratic graphs

A **quadratic graph** is one with the general equation:

$$y = ax^2 + bx + c$$

where a, b, and c are numbers.

Roots are the solutions of $ax^2 + bx + c = 0$.
These are the x-intercepts of the graph.

The maximum or minimum point of the graph is called the **turning point**.

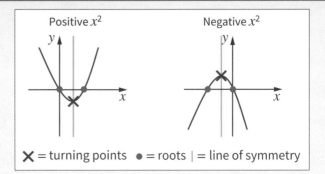

Positive x^2 Negative x^2

✖ = turning points ● = roots | = line of symmetry

All quadratic graphs have a **line of symmetry** through the turning point.

Worked example

Here is the graph $y = x^2 + 2x - 1$

1. Write down the coordinates of the turning point of $y = x^2 + 2x - 1$

   $(-1, -2)$

2. Write down estimates for the roots of $x^2 + 2x - 1 = 0$

   Approximately, $x = 2.4$ and $x = 0.4$

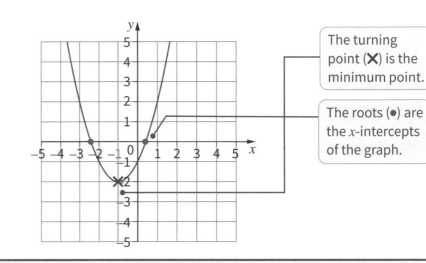

The turning point (✖) is the minimum point.

The roots (●) are the x-intercepts of the graph.

Worked example

1. Complete the table of values for $y = 2x^2 - 4$

x	-2	-1	0	1	2
y	4	-2	-4	-2	4

   Substitute values into equation and complete table. For example, when $x = -2$, $y = 2 \times -2^2 - 4 = 4$

2. Sketch the graph and identify the line of symmetry.

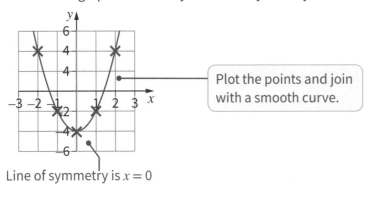

Plot the points and join with a smooth curve.

Line of symmetry is $x = 0$

> **REVISION TIP** ✅
>
> When you square a negative, the answer is positive.

> **LINK** 🔗
>
> To remind yourself about substitution, look back at Chapter 7.

Quadratic graphs

Worked example

The graph shows the speed of an object after t seconds.

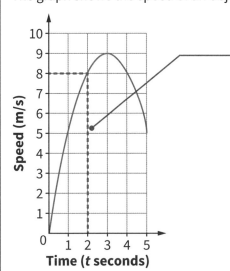

Speed (m/s) vs **Time (t seconds)**

1. Write down the speed of the object after 2 seconds.

> From the graph, you can work out the speed after 2 seconds.

Speed = 8 m/s

2. When does the object start decelerating?

The gradient of the graph is the acceleration. The gradient is negative after 3 seconds. Therefore, the object starts decelerating after 3 seconds.

> Note: negative acceleration is called **deceleration**.

Cubic and reciprocal graphs

A **cubic graph** has an x^3 term in its equation.

For example, $y = x^3 + x^2 + 4x + 7$

The general equation of a cubic graph is:

$y = ax^3 + bx^2 + cx + d$

where a, b, c, and d are constants.

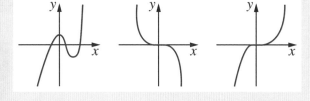

A **reciprocal graph** is of the form $y = \dfrac{a}{x}$, where a is a constant.

When $y = \dfrac{1}{x}$, the value of x cannot be 0, because $\dfrac{1}{0}$ is not a defined value.

The curve will get closer and closer to the axes but will never touch them.

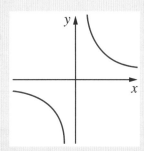

REVISION TIP

An inverse proportion graph is a type of reciprocal graph. You will revise inverse proportion in Chapter 16.

Knowledge

11 Quadratic, cubic, and reciprocal graphs

Cubic and reciprocal graphs

Worked example

Match each graph with a possible equation.

$y = 2x - 1$ $y = 2x^2 - 1$ $y = 2x^3 - 1$ $y = \dfrac{2}{x}$

> **REVISION TIP**
>
> If it's a cubic graph, look for x^3 in the equation.
>
> If it's a quadratic graph, look for x^2 in the equation.

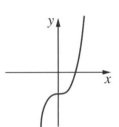

Graph is a cubic
$y = 2x^3 - 1$

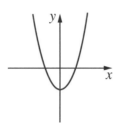

Graph is a quadratic
$y = 2x^2 - 1$

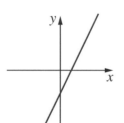

Graph is a straight line
$y = 2x - 1$

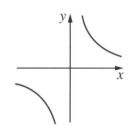

Graph is a reciprocal
$y = \dfrac{2}{x}$

Worked example

1. Complete the table of values for
   $y = x^3 + 1$

x	-2	-1	0	1	2
y	-7	0	1	2	9

2. Draw the graph of $y = x^3 + 1$

   > It is cubic, so we expect a ∿ shape.

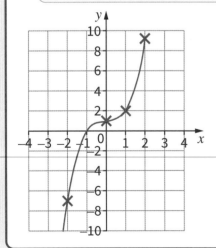

Worked example

The time, t hours, taken to complete a journey at speed v km/h is given by the equation $t = \dfrac{75}{v}$.

1. Find the missing values for t and v.

v (km/h)	1	3	5	$\dfrac{75}{7.5} = 10$
t (hours)	$\dfrac{75}{1} = 75$	25	$\dfrac{75}{5} = 15$	7.5

2. Plot a graph of t against v.

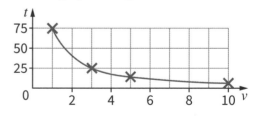

> **REVISION TIP**
>
> Start by drawing a sketch of the type of graph you expect, so that you can check it once you have plotted it.

 Key terms   **Make sure you can write a definition for these key terms**

cubic graph   deceleration   quadratic graph
roots   turning point

11 Quadratic, cubic, and reciprocal graphs

Learn the answers to the questions below, then cover the answers column with a piece of paper and write as many as you can. Check and repeat.

	Questions	Answers
1	What is the general equation of a quadratic graph?	$y = ax^2 + bx + c$
2	What are the roots of a quadratic or cubic equation?	The x-intercepts.
3	How do you find the roots of an equation algebraically?	Set y equal to zero and solve for x.
4	What is a turning point on a graph?	A maximum or minimum point.
5	Describe a quadratic graph with a negative x^2 term.	A smooth ∩-shaped curve.
6	What is a cubic graph?	A graph of an equation with x^3 as the highest power.
7	What is a reciprocal graph?	A graph where the equation has x in the denominator.
8	Where is the line of symmetry on a quadratic graph?	On the vertical line that passes through the turning point.
9	For the graph $y = \frac{1}{x}$, why can $x \neq 0$?	Because $\frac{1}{0}$ is undefined.
10	What is the general equation for a cubic graph?	$y = ax^3 + bx^2 + cx + d$

Put paper here

Previous questions

Now go back and use these questions to check your knowledge of previous topics.

	Questions	Answers
1	What is the equation for speed?	$\text{speed} = \frac{\text{distance}}{\text{time}}$
2	What does the graph of $y = a$ look like?	A horizontal line passing through $y = a$.
3	What is the opposite of expanding brackets?	Factorising.
4	What is negative acceleration called?	Deceleration.
5	What does c represent in $y = mx + c$?	The y-intercept.

Put paper here

Practice

11.1 **(a)** Draw the graph of $y = x^2$ for values of x from −3 to +3.

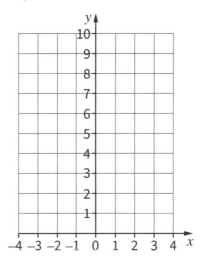

[2 marks]

(b) The graph of $y = x^2$ has one line of symmetry.

Write down the equation of the line of symmetry. [1 mark]

11.2 **(a)** On the grid, draw the graph of $y = x^2 - x - 1$ for values of x from −2 to +3.

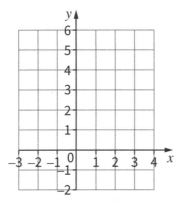

[2 marks]

(b) Write down the coordinates of the turning point of the graph of $y = x^2 - x - 1$. [1 mark]

> **EXAM TIP**
>
> The turning point is the maximum or minimum.

11.3 Here is the graph of $y = 2 - x^2$.

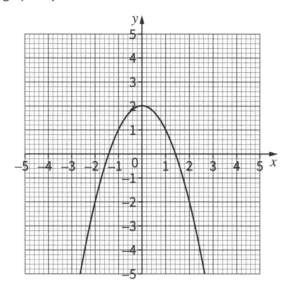

(a) Use the graph to find estimates for the roots of $2 - x^2 = 0$. **[2 marks]**

(b) Write down the coordinates of the turning point of $y = 2 - x^2$. **[1 mark]**

(c) Use the graph to estimate the values of x for which $y = -3$. **[2 marks]**

11.4 The diagram shows four graphs.

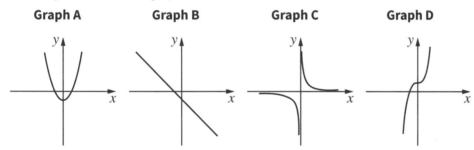

Each of the equations in the table is the equation of one of the graphs.
Complete the table.

Equation	Letter of graph
$y = \dfrac{1}{x}$	
$y = x^3 + 1$	
$y = x^2 - 1$	
$y = -x - 1$	

[3 marks]

Exam-style questions

11.5 wvOn the grid, draw the graph of $y = 2x^3 + 1$ for values of x from -2 to $+2$.

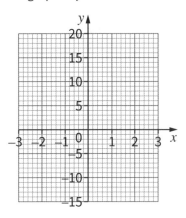

[2 marks]

11.6 On the grid, draw the graph of $y = x^3 + 1$ for values of x from -2 to $+2$.

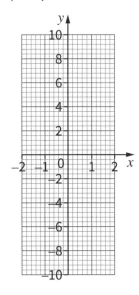

[2 marks]

11.7 (a) Complete the table of values for $y = \dfrac{4}{x}$

x	-4	-2	-1	-0.5	0.5	1	2	4
y		-2			8			

[2 marks]

(b) On the grid, draw the graph of $y = \dfrac{4}{x}$ for values of x from -4 to $+4$.

[2 marks]

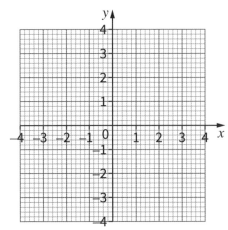

11.8 Which **one** of the following graphs could have an equation of the form
$ax^2 + b$ where $a > 0$ and $b < 0$?

Graph A   **Graph B**   **Graph C**   **Graph D**

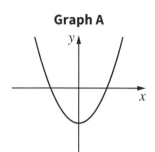 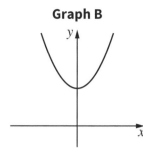 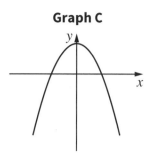 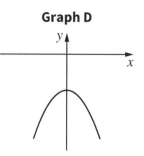

[1 mark]

11.9 Match the following graphs to the descriptions in the table below.

Graph A   **Graph B**   **Graph C**   **Graph D**

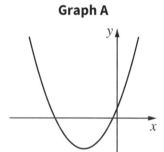 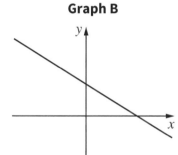 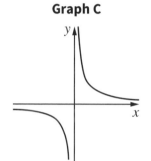 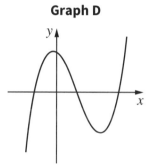

Type of graph	Letter of graph
Linear	
Quadratic	
Cubic	
Reciprocal	

[2 marks]

Questions referring to previous content

 11.10 Simplify $\dfrac{2(x+3)^2}{(x+3)}$ [1 mark]

11.11 Which of these fractions is larger?

$\dfrac{4}{5}$ or $\dfrac{7}{8}$

Show your method clearly. [2 marks]

⚙ Knowledge

12 Simultaneous equations

Equation pairs

Simultaneous equations are equations with the same solutions.

For example, for this pair of simultaneous equations:

$2x + y = 5$ and $x - y = 1$

the values $x = 2$ and $y = 1$ are true for both equations:

$2 \times 2 + 1 = 5$ and $2 - 1 = 1$

The graphical method

Using the **graphical method**, the solution to a pair of simultaneous equations is the point of **intersection** (where the two lines cross) of their graphs.

Look at the graphs of $y = 4 - 2x$ and $y = x + 1$

Their graphs intersect at the point (1, 2). This is the *only* point which lies on both lines.

So $x = 1$, $y = 2$ are the only values which satisfy *both* $y = 4 - 2x$ and $y = x + 1$.

Check:

$2 = 4 - 2 \times 1$ $2 = 1 + 1$
$2 = 4 - 2$ $2 = 2$ ✔
$2 = 2$ ✔

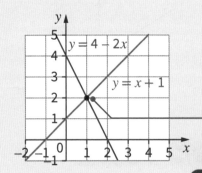

The point of intersection is (1, 2), so the solution to the simultaneous equations is $x = 1$, $y = 2$

LINK

To remind yourself about straight line graphs, look back at Chapter 8.

Worked example

Use a graphical method to find the solutions of the simultaneous equations

$y = 2x + 7$ and $y = -x + 4$

First draw both lines on the same axes.

$y = 2x + 7$ has gradient 2 and y-intercept 7

$y = -x + 4$ has gradient −1 and y-intercept 4

The lines intersect at the point (−1, 5).

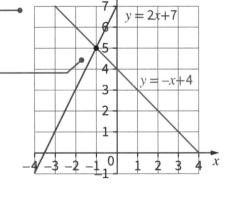

The solution to the simultaneous equations is:

$x = -1$, $y = 5$

Check:

$5 = 2 \times (-1) + 7$ $5 = -1(-1) + 4$
$5 = -2 + 7$ $5 = +1 + 4$
$5 = 5$ ✔ $5 = 5$ ✔

The elimination method

There are two **algebraic methods** to solve simultaneous equations. This means solving them using algebra and not a graph.

In the **elimination method** you add or subtract the two equations to get rid of either x or y.

Worked example

Solve this pair of simultaneous equations: $2x + 3y = 25$ and $6x - 2y = -2$

$2x + 3y = 25$ ①

$6x - 2y = -2$ ②

Number the equations ① and ②.

$(2x + 3y = 25) \times 3 = 6x + 9y = 75$ ③

We need the x or y coefficient to be the same. Here, $6x$ is a multiple of $2x$, so multiply equation ① by 3. Label this equation ③.

$6x + 9y = 75$ ③

$-(6x - 2y = -2)$ ②
_____

$0x + 11y = 77$

$y = 77$

Both equations now have $6x$, so we can **eliminate** x by subtracting equation ② from ③.

Be careful subtracting negatives.

$2x + 3(7) = 25$

$2x + 21 = 25$

$2x = 4$

$x = 2$

Substitute $y = 7$ into equation ① to find x.

Check:

$2(2) + 3(7) = 25$ $6(2) - 2(7) = -2$

$4 + 21 = 25$ $12 - 14 = -2$

$25 = 25$ ✔ $-2 = -2$ ✔

EXAM TIP

If the signs are the same: **Subtract**

$5x \boxed{+ 2y} = 16$ ①

$\ominus (3x \boxed{+ 2y} = 12)$ ②
_____
$2x + 0y = 4$

If the signs are different: **Add**

$5x \boxed{+ 2y} = 16$ ①

$\oplus (3x \boxed{- 2y} = 12)$ ②
_____
$8x + 0y = 28$

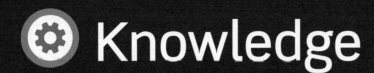 # Knowledge

12 Simultaneous equations

Word-based problems

Sometimes you will be given a **word-based problem** from which you need to form two simultaneous equations.

Worked example

The cost of three adult tickets and two child tickets to a theme park is £155.

The cost of two adult tickets and five child tickets is £195.

1. Form a pair of simultaneous equations to describe this situation.

> Decide what the two variables represent and give them each a letter.

a = cost of adult ticket

c = cost of child ticket.

> Use the information in the question to form two equations using your variables. Number them ① and ② to help with the next part of the question.

$3a + 2c = 155$ ① and $2a + 5c = 195$ ②

2. Solve your equations to find the cost of an adult ticket and the cost of a child ticket.

> Multiply ① by 2: $6a + 4c = 310$ ③
> Multiply ② by 3: $6a + 15c = 585$ ④
> Both of the $6a$ terms are positive, so subtract equation 3 from equation 4.

④ − ③: $11c = 275$

$c = 25$

> Substitute into equation ①: $3a + 50 = 155$

$3a = 105$, so $a = 35$

The cost of an adult ticket is £35 and the cost of a child ticket is £25.

The substitution method

Sometimes, it is easier to **substitute** one variable into another; for example, if one example has a variable as the subject.

Worked example

Find the values of x and y.

$y = x + 2$ ① $2x + 3y = 11$ ②

$2x + 3y = 11$

$2x + 3(x + 2) = 11$

$2x + 3x + 6 = 11$

$5x + 6 = 11$

$5x = 5$

$x = 1$

$y = x + 2$

$y = 1 + 2$

$y = 3$

> Start with the more complicated equation.

> Using ①, substitute $x + 2$ in place of y in equation ②.

> Multiply out the bracket.

> Collect like terms.

> Subtract 6 from both sides.

> Divide by 5 to find the value of x

> Substitute $x = 1$ into equation ① to find y.

REVISION TIP

You can check your answers by substituting $x = 1$, $y = 3$ into equation ②:

$2x + 3y = 2 \times 1 + 3 \times 3 = 2 + 9 = 11$ which is correct.

 Key terms — Make sure you can write a definition for these key terms

algebraic method   elimination method   graphical method
pair of simultaneous equations   substitute   word-based problem

12 Simultaneous equations

Learn the answers to the questions below, then cover the answers column with a piece of paper and write as many as you can. Check and repeat.

Questions	Answers
1 What are simultaneous equations?	A pair of equations in two variables that you solve at the same time.
2 What are the two algebraic methods you can use to solve simultaneous equations?	Elimination and substitution.
3 How can you check your answers to a pair of simultaneous equations?	Substitute your values back into the equations.
4 How would you eliminate x from these equations? $3x + 5y = 1$ ① $\qquad 3x - 2y = 8$ ②	Subtract equation ② from equation ①.
5 How would you eliminate y from these equations? $2x - y = 2$ ① $\qquad 7x + y = 43$ ②	Add the two equations together.
6 What would be your first step to solve these simultaneous equations by substitution? $y = 3 + x$ ① $\qquad 2x + 2y = 22$ ②	Substitute $3 + x$ from equation ① into equation ②: $2x + 2(3 + x) = 22$.
7 If you form and solve simultaneous equations from a word problem, what should your final step be?	Use your solutions to answer the original question in context.

Put paper here

Previous questions

Now go back and use these questions to check your knowledge of previous topics.

Questions	Answers
1 What does $a \geq b$ mean?	a is greater than or equal to b.
2 What is an identity?	An equation that is true for any value of the variable, such as $3x = 4x - x$ and cannot be solved.
3 How do you convert a fraction to a percentage?	Write it as a fraction out of 100.
4 When calculating the error interval from a value that is rounded, what do you do first?	Add and subtract half a unit.
5 What is the general equation of a quadratic graph?	$y = ax^2 + bx + c$

Put paper here

⬤ Practice

Exam-style questions

12.1 The line of $x + 2y = 6$ is shown on the grid.

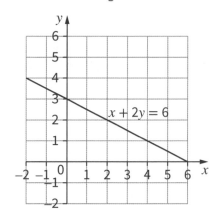

By drawing a suitable line on the graph, solve these simultaneous equations.

$x + 2y = 6$ $y = x$ **[2 marks]**

12.2 Here are the graphs of $y = 2x - 3$ and $x + y = 4$.

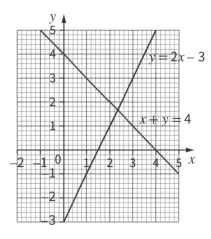

Use the graphs to estimate the solution to these simultaneous equations.

$y = 2x - 3$ $x + y = 4$ **[2 marks]**

12.3 Solve each pair of simultaneous equations.

     (a) $x + y = 14$ $x - y = 8$ **[2 marks]**

     (b) $2x - 2y = 4$ $2x + 3y = 14$ **[2 marks]**

     (c) $4x + 5y = 37$ $2x + y = 11$ **[3 marks]**

     (d) $3x - 2y = 2$ $12x - 4y = 10$ **[3 marks]**

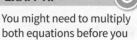

EXAM TIP

You might need to multiply both equations before you can eliminate x or y.

90   **12** Exam-style questions

12.4 Solve each pair of simultaneous equations.

(a) $2x + 5y = 11$ $3x - 2y = -12$ **[3 marks]**

(b) $2x - 7y = 12$ $5x - y = -3$ **[3 marks]**

(c) $3x + 8y = 12$ $2x + 12y = 13$ **[3 marks]**

(d) $6x - 4y = 9$ $5x + 3y = -2$ **[3 marks]**

12.5 At the cinema:

The Smith family buys one adult ticket and three child tickets for £39
The McAllister family buys two adult tickets and four child tickets for £62.

(a)   Write a pair of simultaneous equations for this information.   **[2 marks]**

(b)   Solve your equations to find the cost of an adult ticket and
the cost of a child ticket.   **[3 marks]**

12.6 The mass of 20 apples and 30 satsumas is 4050 g.

The mass of 12 apples and 15 satsumas is 2205 g.

Work out the mass of one apple and the mass of one satsuma.   **[4 marks]**

12.7 Here is a rectangle.

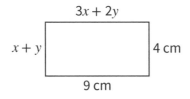

Work out the values of x and y.   **[4 marks]**

> **EXAM TIP**
>
> Start by writing a pair of simultaneous equations to represent the information.

12.8 Solve this pair of simultaneous equations.

$2a - b = 7$ $b = a - 4$ **[3 marks]**

12.9 The sum of two numbers is 120 and their difference is 50. By forming
and solving a pair of simultaneous equations, find the two numbers. **[4 marks]**

12.10 A parallelogram has sides as shown.

The perimeter of the parallelogram is 22.
Work out the values of p and q.   **[5 marks]**

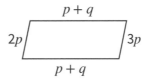

Questions referring to previous content

 12.11 Solve $11 + 2x \geq 5x - 1$.

Show your solution on the number line.   **[3 marks]**

⚙ Knowledge

13 Sequences

Sequences: an overview

A **sequence** is an ordered set of numbers or patterns that follow the same rule.

The numbers in a sequence are called **terms**.
first number = first term
second number = second term
nth number = nth **term**

An **arithmetic sequence** (or linear sequence) is one in which the next term can be found by adding or subtracting the same number each time.

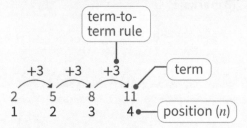

Term-to-term rule

The rule that gets you from one term to the next. This is the same for every term.

Position-to-term rule

A rule that finds the term based on where it is in the sequence. The position to term rule is always written in terms of n. This is called the nth term. In the example above, it is $3n - 1$.

The term-to-term rule

Worked example

The first three patterns in a sequence made from sticks are shown.

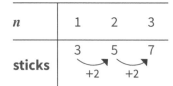

Pattern 1   Pattern 2   Pattern 3

1. Write down the term-to-term rule for this sequence.

   Make a table and count the number of matches for each pattern.

n	1	2	3
sticks	3	5	7

   $+2$ $+2$

   Two more sticks are **added** each time. So this is an **arithmetic** sequence.

   The term-to-term rule is 'add 2'.

2. How many sticks will there be in Pattern 6?

   Continue adding 2.

n	1	2	3	4	5	6
sticks	3	5	7	9	11	13

   $+2$ $+2$ $+2$ $+2$ $+2$

   There are 13 sticks in Pattern 6.

The position-to-term rule

Worked example

The nth term of a sequence is $11 + 3n$.

1. Work out the seventh term of the sequence.

   seventh term
   $= 11 + 3 \times 7 = 32$ ⟵ Substitute $n = 7$

   REVISION TIP ✅

   The question gives you an expression for the nth term, so you know that $11 + 3n$ is the position-to-term rule.

2. Is 81 a term of this sequence? Show how you get your answer.

   $11 + 3n = 81$

   $$\frac{3n}{3} = \frac{70}{3}$$

   $n = 23.\dot{3}$

   70 is not a multiple of 3, so the solution is not an integer. Hence 81 is **not** in the sequence.

Finding the *n*th term

The **nth term** is the position-to-term rule. You can use it to find any term in the sequence.
n is the term number. To find the *n*th term, follow the steps in the worked example.

Worked example

Find the *n*th term of the sequence: 5, 9, 13, 17

5   9   13   17
  +4   +4   +4 •

> Work out the common difference between terms.

Common difference = 4

$4n$:   4   8   12   16 •

> Write out the multiples of the common difference.

$\downarrow+1$ $\downarrow+1$ $\downarrow+1$ $\downarrow+1$
  5   9   13   17

nth term = $4n + 1$

$(4 \times 2) + 1 = 9$

> Work out what to add or subtract to get the original sequence.

> Write out the *n*th term rule.

> Check your answer by substituting in $n = 2$.

Worked example

Find the *n*th term of the sequence 25, 15, 5, −5

25   15   5   −5
  −10   −10   −10 •

> Work out the common difference between terms.

Common difference = −10

$-10n$:   −10   −20   −30   −40 •

> Write out the multiples of the common difference.

$\downarrow+35$ $\downarrow+35$ $\downarrow+35$ $\downarrow+35$
  25   15   5   −5

nth term = $35 - 10n$

$35 - (10 \times 2) = 15$

> Work out what to add or subtract to get the original sequence.

> Write out the *n*th term rule.

> Check your answer by substituting in $n = 2$.

Geometric sequences

In a **geometric sequence**, the next term is found my multiplying or dividing by the same number each time.

For example,

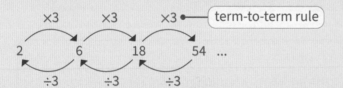

Worked example

Find the next term of the sequence

1.2, 2.4, 4.8, 9.6 •

> Find the term-to-term rule, $\frac{2.4}{1.2} = 2$
> Check: $\frac{4.8}{2.4} = 2$
> So, we need to multiply the previous term by 2

Next term = $9.6 \times 2 = 19.2$

Key terms

Make sure you can write a definition for these key terms

> sequence   arithmetic sequence   cube numbers
> Fibonacci sequence   geometric sequence   *n*th term
> position-to-term rule   square numbers   term
> term-to-term rule   triangular numbers

⚙ Knowledge

13 Sequences

Special sequences

Special sequences do not have a common difference between their terms. They are not arithmetic sequences.

Fibonacci sequences

Any sequence where you add the previous two terms to get the next term is a Fibonacci-*type* sequence. The 'original' **Fibonacci sequence** is:

1, 1, 2, 3, 5, 8, 13, 21 ...

Worked example

The first two terms of a Fibonacci sequence are 2 and 5. What are the next two terms?

$2 + 5 = \mathbf{7}$ ← first term + second term = third term

$7 + 5 = \mathbf{12}$ ← second term + third term = fourth term

Sequence: 2, 5, 7, 12

The first five **square numbers**:

 $2^2 = \mathbf{4}$

 $3^2 = \mathbf{9}$

 $4^2 = \mathbf{16}$

 $5^2 = \mathbf{25}$

 $6^2 = \mathbf{36}$

The first three **cube numbers**:

 $1^3 = \mathbf{1}$

 $2^3 = \mathbf{8}$

 $3^3 = \mathbf{27}$

The first four **triangular numbers**:

1

$1 + 2 = 3$

$1 + 2 + 3 = 6$

$1 + 2 + 3 + 4 = 10$

REVISION TIP ☑

To find the next triangular number, just add on the next positive integer.

Quadratic sequences

In a quadratic sequence, the position-to-term rule includes a squared term.

Worked example

1. Here are the first five terms of a sequence.

1 5 12 22 35

Find the next term of this sequence.

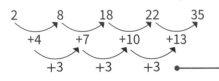

The next difference will be $13 + 3 = 16$

The next term will be $35 + 16 = 51$

2. The nth term of a different sequence is $n^2 - 2n$

What is the third term of the sequence?

$3^2 - 2 \times 3 = 3$ ← To find the third term, substitute $n = 3$.

The difference changes each time, but notice that the differences form an arithmetic sequence with the rule '+3'.

13 Sequences

Learn the answers to the questions below, then cover the answers column with a piece of paper and write as many as you can. Check and repeat.

Questions	Answers
1 An arithmetic sequence increase or decreases by what?	The same amount each time.
2 How do you get to the next term in a geometric sequence?	Multiply or divide by the same number each time.
3 What is the term-to-term rule?	The rule that gets you from one term to the next. This is the same for every term.
4 How would you find the 100th term of a sequence if you know the expression for the nth term?	Substitute $n = 100$ into the expression for the nth term.
5 How do you find the next term in a Fibonacci sequence?	Add the previous two terms to get the next one.
6 What is a cube number?	A number multiplied by itself three times, such as $3 \times 3 \times 3 = 27$.
7 What is the position-to-term rule?	A rule that finds the term based on where it is in the sequence.
8 What is a 'linear' sequence?	A sequence that increases or decreases by the same amount each time.
9 If the nth term of a linear sequence has a negative coefficient of n, what does that tell you about the sequence?	The sequence is decreasing.
10 How would you find the next term in the sequence 10, 8, 6, 4 …?	Subtract 2.

Put paper here

Previous questions

Now go back and use these questions to check your knowledge of previous topics.

Questions	Answers
1 How do you represent an inequality on a number line where the value is not included?	With an open circle.
2 How do you find 50% of a number?	Divide by 2 or multiply by 0.5.
3 What quantity do you find on the vertical axis of a distance-time graph?	Distance.
4 What is the multiplier for a 22% increase?	1.22

Put paper here

Exam-style questions

13.1 Complete the table for each sequence, (a)-(d).

An example has been given.

Sequence	Term-to-term rule	Next term	Seventh term	Type of sequence
2, 6, 10, 14	Add 4	18	26	Arithmetic
(a) 25, 31, 37, 43				
(b) 1, 2, 4, 8				
(c) 20, 10, 5, 2.5				
(d) 20, 17, 14, 11				

[16 marks]

13.2 Here are the first four terms of a number sequence.

$$12, 17, 22, 27, \ldots$$

(a) Nick says that the number 3075 will not be in this sequence.
Is Nick correct?
Give a reason for your answer. **[1 mark]**

(b) Work out the 10th term in the sequence. **[2 marks]**

13.3 Here are the first three patterns in a sequence.

Each pattern is made of dots.

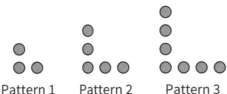

Pattern 1   Pattern 2   Pattern 3

> **EXAM TIP**
>
> The numbers in the sequence all have something in common.

(a) How many dots will there be in Pattern 5? **[1 mark]**

(b) Write the term-to-term rule for the number of dots in this sequence. **[1 mark]**

(c) Will one of the patterns in the sequence to contain 20 dots? **[1 mark]**

13.4 The first four terms of a linear sequence are a, 9, 15, b.
Work out the values of a and b. **[2 marks]**

13.5 Complete the table for each sequence, (a)-(d).
An example has been given.

	Position-to-term rule (nth term)	First four terms	Term-to-term rule	Seventh term	Hundredth term
	$2n + 6$	8, 10, 12, 14	Add 2	20	206
(a)	$3n - 1$				
(b)	$5n + 2$				
(c)	$6 - n$				
(d)	$10 - 3n$				

[16 marks]

13.6 Work out the first four terms of each of these sequences.

    (a) $n^2 + 5$ **[2 marks]**

    (b) $n^2 - 2n$ **[2 marks]**

    (c) $10 - n^2$ **[2 marks]**

13.7 The nth term of a sequence is $8n + 3$.

    (a)   Which term in the sequence is 51?   **[2 marks]**

    (b)   Show that number 64 is not a number in the sequence.   **[2 marks]**

    (c)   Work out the first number in the sequence that is greater than 100.   **[3 marks]**

> **EXAM TIP**
> Write and solve an inequality.

13.8 Complete the table for each sequence, (a)-(e).
An example has been given.

	Sequence	Term-to-term rule	Position-to-term rule (nth term)	Tenth term
	2, 6, 10, 14	Add 4	4n − 2	$(4 \times 10) - 2 = 38$
(a)	17, 23, 29, 35			
(b)	−1, 2, 5, 8			
(c)	4, 1, −2, −5			
(d)	20, 15, 10, 5			
(e)	3, 3.5, 4, 4.5			

[15 marks]

Exam-style questions

13.9 Here are the first three patterns in a sequence.

Each pattern is made of dots.

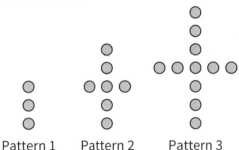

Pattern 1   Pattern 2   Pattern 3

EXAM TIP

Work out some terms in the sequence first.

(a) Work out an expression for the number of dots in the *n*th term of the sequence.   **[2 marks]**

(b) How many dots will there be in pattern 40?   **[2 marks]**

13.10 Here is a sequence.

$$3, 9, 27, 81, \ldots$$

Write down the next two terms in the sequence.   **[1 mark]**

13.11 An arithmetic progression has first term 5 and third term 11.

Work out an expression for the *n*th term of the sequence.   **[2 marks]**

13.12 Here are some special sequences.

Write the name of each one.

(a) 1, 4, 9, 16, 25, 36, …   **[1 mark]**

(b) 1, 1, 2, 3, 5, 8, …   **[1 mark]**

(a) 1, 8, 27, 64, 125, 216, …   **[1 mark]**

13.13 Here are the first three patterns in a sequence.

Each pattern is made of square tiles.

Pattern 1   Pattern 2   Pattern 3

(a) Write the number of tiles in the fourth pattern.   **[1 mark]**

(b) Work out an expression for the *n*th term of the sequence.   **[1 mark]**

13.14 (a)   A Fibonacci-type sequence starts:

2, 4, 6, 10, 16

Work out the 8th term.   **[2 marks]**

(b)   Another Fibonacci-type sequence starts: $x, 2x, 3x$

(i)   Work out the next two terms.

Write them in terms of x.   **[2 marks]**

(ii)   The 5th term of the sequence is 32. Work out the
first term in this sequence.   **[2 marks]**

13.15 A geometric sequence has nth term $\left(\dfrac{1}{2}\right)^{n}$

Write down the first three terms of the sequence.   **[2 marks]**

Questions referring to previous content

13.16 Work out the value of the fraction that is half way between $\dfrac{1}{4}$ and $\dfrac{7}{8}$.

[3 marks]

 13.17 The price of a coat is £53.76.

The price reduces by 20%.

Jo says the new price of the coat is £44.80.

Is Jo correct?

Give a reason for your answer.   **[3 marks]**

⚙ Knowledge

14 Units and measures

Length, mass and volume

You need to be able to choose an appropriate unit to measure length, mass and volume.

> **Worked example**
>
> Suggest a sensible **unit of measurement** for:
>
> 1. the height of an adult — metres or centimetres
> 2. the mass of a lorry — tonnes
> 3. the capacity of a kettle. — litres or millilitres

When suggesting units of measurement, check that your answers seem sensible: you should have an approximate idea of the size of **metric** measurements.

Scales

When reading off a scale, make sure that you know what each mark represents.

> **Worked example**
>
> Write down the values of A–F shown on the scales.
>
>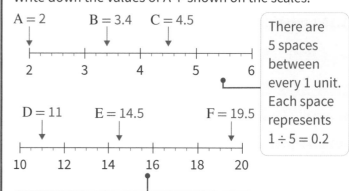
>
> A = 2   B = 3.4   C = 4.5
>
> There are 5 spaces between every 1 unit. Each space represents $1 \div 5 = 0.2$
>
> D = 11   E = 14.5   F = 19.5
>
> There are 4 spaces between every 2 units. Each space represents $2 \div 4 = 0.5$

Compound measures

A **compound measure** links two measurements. For example, a rate of pay could be £11 per hour and a rate of flow of water could be 3 litres per minute.

Speed, **density** and **pressure** are three compound measures you need to be familiar with. You can use their units to remember how to calculate them.

> **REVISION TIP**
>
> Speed is also measured in **miles** (distance) **per hour** (time). **Per** means divide, so speed = distance ÷ time.

$$\text{speed} = \frac{\text{distance}}{\text{time}}$$
= metres per second
$$= \frac{m}{s}$$

$$\text{density} = \frac{\text{mass}}{\text{volume}}$$
= grams per cubic centimetre
$$= \frac{g}{cm^3}$$

$$\text{pressure} = \frac{\text{force}}{\text{area}}$$
= newtons per square metre
$$= \frac{N}{m^2}$$

> **Worked example**
>
> 1. What is the size of force required to exert a pressure of $7\,N/cm^2$ on an area of $54\,cm^2$?
>
> $$\text{pressure} = \frac{\text{force}}{\text{area}}$$
>
>   — Select the equation and substitute in the values.
>
> $$7 = \frac{\text{force}}{54}$$
>
> $$7 \times 54 = \text{force}$$
> $$= 378\,N$$
>
>   > **WATCH OUT** ⚠
>   >
>   > Always check the units. You may need to convert one of the measures before you can complete the calculation.
>
> 2. The density of a piece of wood is $2.4\,g/cm^3$ and its mass is $1.8\,kg$. Work out the volume of the wood in cm^3.
>
> $$1.8\,kg = 1800\,g$$ — Convert kg to g.
>
> $$\text{density} = \frac{\text{mass}}{\text{volume}}$$
>
>   — Select the equation and substitute in the values.
>
> $$2.4 = \frac{1800}{\text{volume}}$$
>
> $$\text{volume} = \frac{1800}{2.4}$$
> $$= 750\,cm^3$$

Converting metric units

Convert between metric units by multiplying or dividing by powers of 10.

Length

$\times 10$ mm $\div 10$
cm
$\times 100$ $\div 100$
m
$\times 1000$ $\div 1000$
km

Mass

$\times 1000$ g $\div 1000$
kg
$\times 1000$ $\div 1000$
tonne

Volume

ml
$\times 1000$ $\div 1000$
l

milli- = one thousandth

centi- = one hundredth

kilo- = one thousand

Worked example

Sam's new wardrobe is 1950 mm high and has a mass of 13.5 kg.

1. What is the height of the wardrobe in cm?

   $1950 \div 10 = 195$ cm ●————(Convert mm to cm.)

2. What is the mass of the wardrobe in g?

   $13.5 \times 1000 = 13\,500$ g ●————(Convert kg to g.)

3. The wardrobe must be less than 75 in high to fit in Sam's room. Will the wardrobe fit? Explain your answer. Use the conversion 1 inch ≈ 2.54 cm.

   $75 \times 2.54 = 190.5$ cm ●————(Convert inches to cm.)

   The wardrobe won't fit, since 195 > 190.5

Converting units of area and volume

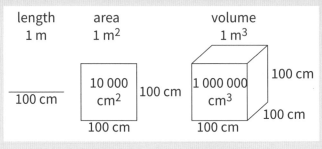

length
1 m

area
1 m^2

volume
1 m^3

100 cm

$10\,000 \text{ cm}^2$ 100 cm

$1\,000\,000 \text{ cm}^3$ 100 cm

100 cm 100 cm 100 cm

Area

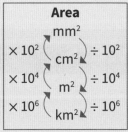

$\times 10^2$ mm² $\div 10^2$
cm²
$\times 10^4$ $\div 10^4$
m²
$\times 10^6$ $\div 10^6$
km²

Volume

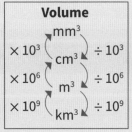

$\times 10^3$ mm³ $\div 10^3$
cm³
$\times 10^6$ $\div 10^6$
m³
$\times 10^9$ $\div 10^9$
km³

Worked example

A cube has a volume of 64 cm³ and a surface area of 96 cm².

1. Write the surface area in mm²

   (To convert cm to mm × 10, so to convert cm² to mm² × 10^2)

   surface area = $96 \times 10^2 = 9600$ mm²

2. Write the volume in mm³

   volume = $64 \times 10^3 = 64\,000$ mm³

   (To convert cm³ to mm³ × 10^3)

Key terms — Make sure you can write a definition for these key terms

compound measure   density   metric   pressure
speed   unit of measurement

14 Units and measures

Learn the answers to the questions below, then cover the answers column with a piece of paper and write as many as you can. Check and repeat.

	Questions		Answers
1	How do you convert from mm to m?		Divide by 1000 (divide by 10 to convert to cm and then by 100 to convert to m).
2	How do you convert from kg to g?		Multiply by 1000.
3	How do you convert from ml to l?		Divide by 1000.
4	What would be sensible units for the height of a house?		Metres.
5	What would be sensible units for the length of an ant?		Millimetres.
6	When reading values from a scale what should you check first?		The amount each division represents.
7	What is the formula for speed?	Put paper here	$\text{speed} = \dfrac{\text{distance}}{\text{time}}$
8	What is the formula for density?		$\text{density} = \dfrac{\text{mass}}{\text{volume}}$
9	What is the formula for pressure?		$\text{pressure} = \dfrac{\text{force}}{\text{area}}$
10	How can you calculate time if you know the distance and speed?		$\text{time} = \dfrac{\text{distance}}{\text{speed}}$
11	Name a metric unit that can be used for speed.		m/s, km/h
12	Rearrange $P = \dfrac{F}{A}$ to make A the subject.		$A = \dfrac{F}{P}$
13	How do you convert cm² into mm²?		Multiply by $10^2 = 100$.
14	How do you convert cm³ into m³?		Divide by $100^3 = 1\,000\,000$.

Previous questions

Now go back and use these questions to check your knowledge of previous topics.

	Questions		Answers
1	When you divide by a power of 10, what direction does the number move on a place value chart?		Right.
2	What place value column do you look at when rounding to the nearest million?	Put paper here	The hundred-thousands column.
3	What is a triangular number?		A number that can make a triangular dot pattern.
4	$a < b$. Which is the larger number?		b

Exam-style questions

14.1 Write down suitable metric units for measuring each item.

(a) The diameter of a 10p coin. **[1 mark]**

(b) The mass of a chocolate bar. **[1 mark]**

(c) The volume of shampoo in a bottle. **[1 mark]**

14.2 (a) Change 17 centimetres into millimetres. **[1 mark]**

(b) Change 2500 milligrams into grams. **[1 mark]**

(c) Change 0.35 litres into millilitres. **[1 mark]**

14.3 Work out 3.6 kg + 50 g.

Give your answer in kilograms. **[2 marks]**

14.4 Ringo is 1.68 m tall.

George is 8 cm taller than Ringo.

How tall is George?

Give your answer in metres. **[2 marks]**

14.5 Rodrigo puts some items in a box.

The table shows the mass of each item.

The box has a mass of 285 g.

Work out the total mass of the box and all of the items.

Give your answer in kilograms.

Item	Mass
Ornament	230 g
Six candles	159 g each
String	85 g
Tape	280 g
Five DVDs	78 g each

[3 marks]

14.6 Here are the lengths of three TV shows.

Show 1 is 45 minutes.

Show 2 is 23 minutes.

Show 3 is 68 minutes.

Work out the total time to watch all three shows.

Give your answer in hours and minutes. **[2 marks]**

Exam-style questions

 14.7 Write 0.25 hours in minutes. **[2 marks]**

 14.8 Write down the values of A and B.

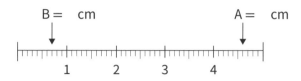

[2 marks]

 14.9 Car A drives 600 km in 7 hours and 30 minutes.

Car B drives 807 km in 9 hours.

Which car has the fastest average speed?

Answering A or B with no working to support it will get no marks. **[4 marks]**

 14.10 Water is poured into an empty tank at a rate of 20 cm³ per second.

After how long will the tank contain 2400 cm³ of water? State the units of your answer. **[2 marks]**

 14.11 The density of copper is 8.94 g/cm³.

A piece of copper has a volume of 0.6 cm³.

Work out the mass of the piece of copper. **[2 marks]**

 14.12 A baker uses:

36 ounces of sugar

2 pounds of flour

1 ounce = 28 g

1 pound = 0.45 kg

Work out the total mass of the sugar and flour.

Give your answer in kilograms. **[3 marks]**

> **EXAM TIP**
>
> You can convert between grams and kilograms to help you.

 14.13 The formula used to find pressure is

$$\text{pressure} = \frac{\text{force}}{\text{area}}.$$

A force of 36 N is applied to an area of 0.45 m².

Work out the pressure in N/m². **[2 marks]**

14.14 A sphere has a surface area of 40 cm².

Write the surface area to mm². **[2 marks]**

14.15 A cuboid has a volume of 120 cm³.

Write the volume to m³. **[2 marks]**

14.16 Cube A has a volume of 8 litres.

Cube B has a volume of 1500 cm³.

Write the ratio

volume of cube A : volume of cube B

in its simplest form. **[3 marks]**

Questions referring to previous content

 14.17 Work out the reciprocal of 1.5.

Write your answer as a fraction. **[1 mark]**

14.18 Tahira buys a car for £2500.

She then sells the car for £3200.

Work out her percentage profit. **[3 marks]**

⚙ Knowledge

15 Ratio

Ratios: an overview

A **ratio** describes how things are split into **parts**.

The ratio of black beads to red beads on this bracelet is 3:2.

Ratio problems can sometimes be solved by 'scaling up' a ratio. You do this by multiplying both sides by the same number.

Ratios compare parts to parts; **fractions** compare **parts** to the whole. For example, if the ratio of adults to children is 1:2 then $\frac{1}{3}$ of the total are adults and $\frac{2}{3}$ are children.

Ratios can also have three or more parts, for example $a:b:c$.

A ratio can be simplified fully by dividing both sides by their highest common factor (HCF).

> **Worked example**
>
> Simplify the ratio 49:28
>
> $\left(\frac{49}{7}\right):\left(\frac{28}{7}\right) = 7:4$
>
> > The HCF of 49 and 28 is 7, so divide both by 7.

> **LINK**
>
> To remind yourself about HCF, look back at Chapter 2.

Using ratio

> **Worked example**
>
> Kai has £90 which he wants to share in the ratio 1:5:3.
>
> How much is each **share** worth?
>
> ### Method 1
>
> > Draw a bar model split in the ratio 1:5:3
>
>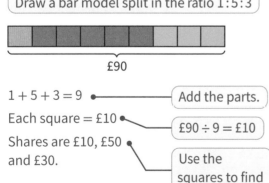
>
> £90
>
> $1 + 5 + 3 = 9$ •———— Add the parts.
>
> Each square = £10 •———— $£90 \div 9 = £10$
>
> Shares are £10, £50 and £30. •———— Use the squares to find each share.
>
> ### Method 2
>
> $1 + 5 + 3 = 9$ •———— Add up parts of the ratio.
>
> $£90 \div 9 = £10$ •———— Work out what one part is worth.
>
> $1 \times £10 = £10$
>
> $5 \times £10 = £50$
>
> $3 \times £10 = £30$ •———— Multiply to work out what each share is worth.
>
> > **REVISION TIP**
> >
> > Add your answers to check your total is the same as in the question.
> >
> > £10 + £50 + £30 = £90

Using ratio

WATCH OUT

These next two questions look very similar. Make sure you focus on the **information** and **instructions** given.

Worked example

Ben, Sima, and Lisa share some money in the ratio 3 : 4 : 5. Lisa gets £30. How much does Sarah get?

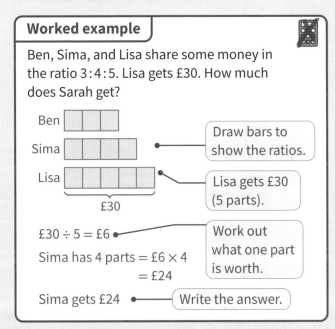

Draw bars to show the ratios.

Lisa gets £30 (5 parts).

Work out what one part is worth.

£30 ÷ 5 = £6

Sima has 4 parts = £6 × 4
= £24

Sima gets £24 — Write the answer.

Worked example

Ben, Sima, and Lisa share some money in the ratio 3 : 4 : 5. Lisa gets £30 more than Ben. How much does Sima get?

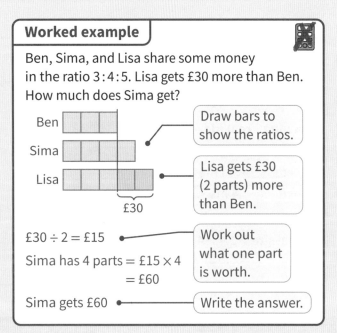

Draw bars to show the ratios.

Lisa gets £30 (2 parts) more than Ben.

Work out what one part is worth.

£30 ÷ 2 = £15

Sima has 4 parts = £15 × 4
= £60

Sima gets £60 — Write the answer.

Worked example

In a class of children, the ratio of 8-year-olds to 9-year-olds is 2:3.

25% of the 8-year-olds are left-handed.

$\frac{1}{3}$ of the 9-year-olds are left-handed.

What percentage of the class is right-handed?

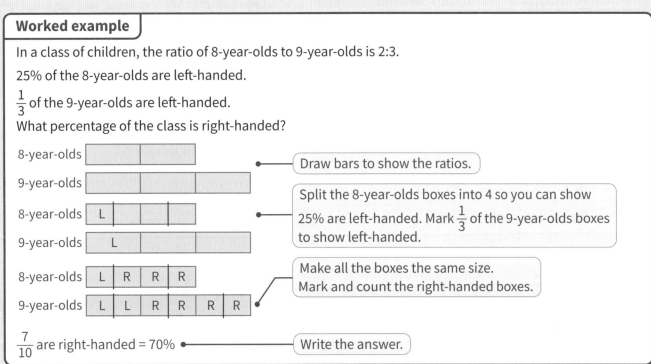

Draw bars to show the ratios.

Split the 8-year-olds boxes into 4 so you can show 25% are left-handed. Mark $\frac{1}{3}$ of the 9-year-olds boxes to show left-handed.

Make all the boxes the same size. Mark and count the right-handed boxes.

$\frac{7}{10}$ are right-handed = 70% — Write the answer.

15 Ratio

Ratios and scale

A **scale** can be written as a ratio, such as 1:400, or as a sentence.

You multiply the length on the drawing to get the real-life length.

You divide the real-life length to get the length on the drawing.

Worked example

A drawing of a tower is 1.4 cm tall. It is drawn to a scale of 1:400

How tall is the tower in real life?

drawing	real life
1	400
1 cm	400 cm
1 cm	4 m

— Make a table.

— Write the scale.

— Put in the units.

Size of drawing = 1.4 cm — Change to better units.

Actual size = 1.4 × 4

= 5.6 m — Scale up.

Worked example

On a map, 2 cm represents 3 km.

Write the scale of the map as a ratio in the form 1 : *n*

map	real
2 cm	3 km
2 cm	3000 m
2 cm	300 000 cm
1	150 000

— Simplify.

Problem solving with ratios

Worked example

Oskar mixes red and yellow paint in the ratio 2 : 3

1. Oskar needs 240 ml of red paint to paint a room.

   How much yellow paint does he need?

   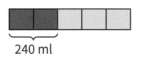

   240 ml

   Oskar needs 360 ml of yellow paint.

   — Draw a bar model in the ratio 2 : 3

   240 ml is 2 parts so 1 part
   = 240 ÷ 2 = 120
   Yellow paint is 3 parts, so 3 parts
   = 120 × 3 = 360

2. Oskar needs 15 litres of the mixed paint to paint his house.

   How much red paint does he need?

   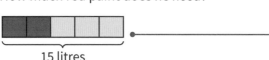

   15 litres

   1 part = 15 ÷ 5 = 3
   Red = 2 parts = 3 × 2 = 6

   Oskar needs 6 litres of red paint.

Key terms Make sure you can write a definition for these key terms

fraction   parts   ratio   scale   share

15 Ratio

Learn the answers to the questions below, then cover the answers column with a piece of paper and write as many as you can. Check and repeat.

	Questions		Answers
1	What is a ratio used for?		To compare two or more quantities in relation to each other.
2	To simplify a ratio fully you divide all the numbers in the ratio by what?		The highest common factor (HCF) of the numbers.
3	If a ratio of adults to children in a group is $4:7$, explain how to express the number of adults as a fraction of the whole group.		There are four parts representing adults, and $4 + 7 = 11$ in total. So, the fractions of adults is $\frac{4}{11}$.
4	To divide a quantity in a given ratio, what would the first step be?		Add up all the parts in the ratio.
5	What does a ratio of $1:100$ mean on a scale drawing?		1 unit in the drawing is equal to 100 units in real life.
6	On a scale drawing, the ratio is $1:n$. How do you find the real-life length?		Multiply the length on the drawing by n.
7	On a scale drawing, the ratio is $1:n$. How do you find a length on the drawing?		Divide the real-life length by n.
8	Is this statement true or false? A ratio can only have two parts.		False, you can have more than two parts; for example, $3:4:6$.
9	If the ratio of boys to girls is $2:3$, what fraction of the total are boys?		$\frac{2}{5}$
10	In a particular city, the ratio of red cars to blue cars is $r:b$. What is the ratio of blue cars to red cars?		$b:r$

Put paper here

Previous questions

Now go back and use these questions to check your knowledge of previous topics.

	Questions		Answers
1	How do you divide by a fraction?		Multiply by the reciprocal of the fraction.
2	What is the highest common factor of two or more numbers?		The largest number that is a factor of the numbers.
3	What is a multiple?		The result of multiplying a number by an integer.
4	How do you convert a proper fraction into a decimal?		Divide the numerator by the denominator.
5	What is an improper fraction?		A fraction where the numerator is bigger than the denominator.

Put paper here

Practice

15.1 Write the ratio 36 : 84 in its simplest form. **[1 mark]**

15.2 Write the ratio 1.2 : 0.4 in its simplest form. **[1 mark]**

15.3 Write the ratio 5 : 4 in the form 1 : n. **[1 mark]**

15.4 The ratio of red balls to yellow balls on a pool table is 4 : 3.

What fraction of the balls are red? **[1 mark]**

15.5 $\frac{2}{3}$ of the students in Lexi's class have a cat.

Write the ratio of students who have a cat to students
who do not have a cat. **[1 mark]**

15.6 The ratio of the cost of one metre of treated rope to the cost of one metre of
untreated rope is 4 : 3.

Complete the table of costs.

	2 metres	4 metres	11 metres
Treated		£6.00	
Untreated			

[3 marks]

15.7 The lengths of the sides of a triangle are in the ratio 5 : 12 : 13.

The shortest side has a length of 2 cm.

Work out the perimeter of the triangle. **[3 marks]**

> **EXAM TIP**
>
> This question combines
> ratio and geometry. Start
> by dividing each part of the
> ratio by 5.

15.8 Orange drink is made from orange cordial and water in the ratio 1 : 8.

Find the amount of water in 270 ml of this orange drink. **[2 marks]**

 15.9 In a card game, the ratio of losing cards to winning cards is 11 : 3.

There are 70 cards in the game.

How many of these cards are winning cards? **[2 marks]**

15.10 Nikisha mixes white paint with red paint in the ratio 2 : 3.

She uses 9 litres of red paint.

How much white paint does she use? **[2 marks]**

15.11 In a Geography exam, there is a shorter paper and a longer paper.

The marks are in the ratio 3 : 4.

The total for both papers is 98.

How many marks are there on the shorter paper? **[2 marks]**

 15.12 The angles in a triangle are in the ratio 3 : 2 : 3.

    (a)   Write down the name for this type of triangle. **[1 mark]**

    (b)   Work out the size of the smallest angle in the triangle. **[3 marks]**

15.13 The ratio of pencils to erasers is 7 : 2.

There are 90 more pencils than erasers.

How many pencils are there? **[2 marks]**

15.14 A camel and a giraffe are drawn to scale.

6 m

(a)   The actual height of the giraffe is 6 metres.

Estimate the actual height of the camel.

You **must** show your working.   [1 mark]

(b)   Saffi makes a scale drawing of the giraffe.

She uses a scale of 3 cm to represent 1 m.

What is the height of the giraffe in Saffi's scale drawing?

Give your answer in centimetres.   [1 mark]

> **EXAM TIP**
> Consider the sum of the angles in a triangle.

 15.15 The Seattle Space Needle is 184 metres tall.
Sam makes a model of the Space Needle, using a scale of 1 : 2000.

Work out the height of Sam's model.   [2 marks]

15.16 (a)   A map uses a scale of 2 cm to represent 5 km.
Write this scale in the form 1 : n.   [2 marks]

(b)   A different map has a scale of 1 : 400 000.

On this map, the distance between two villages is 5 cm.

What is the actual distance, in km, between these
two villages?   [2 marks]

15.17 In a cinema audience, the ratio of the number of people with a phone,
to the number of people without a phone, is 3 : 1.

90% of the people with a phone turned them off.

84 phones were not turned off.

Work out the total number of people in the cinema audience.   [4 marks]

Questions referring to previous content

15.18 Draw the graphs of:

(a) $y = 2$

(b) $x = -2$

(c) $y = x$

Label each line with its equation.

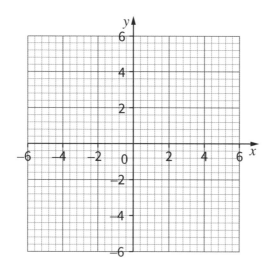

[3 marks]

⚙ Knowledge

16 Proportion

Direct proportion

When two values are in **direct proportion**, they will increase and decrease at the same rate.

For example, the number of apples and the cost of the apples are in direct proportion. If one apple costs 30p, then:

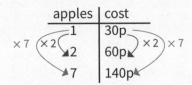

apples	cost
1	30p
2	60p
7	140p

×7 (×2) ×2 ×7

To solve direct proportion problems, you can use a common factor, or the **unitary method:**

- Divide to calculate the value of 1 unit.
- Multiply, if necessary, to find the value required.

The symbol for 'proportional to' is ∝.

Worked example: Common factors

1. A pack of 20 biscuits costs £1.50 and a pack of 35 of the same biscuits costs £2.80. Which is the better value?

   small pack

20	£1.50
5	£0.375

   ÷4 ... ÷4

   large pack

35	£2.80
5	£0.40

   ÷7 ... ÷7

   5 is a common factor.

   The smaller pack is better value.

2. A recipe for 12 portions of cheesecake requires 30 biscuits. How many biscuits are required for 32 portions of cheesecake?

portions	biscuits
12	30
4	10
32	80

   ÷3 ×8 ... ÷3 ×8

   80 biscuits are required for 32 portions.

Worked example: Unitary method

A pack of 240 teabags costs £2.25 and a pack of 150 of the same teabags costs £1.10.

Which is the better value?

240 pack

bags	price
240	£2.25
1	£0.009375

150 pack

bags	price
150	£1.10
1	£0.0073

Divide the price by the number of bags to get the price per unit.

The 150 pack is better value.

Compare the price per unit; lowest is best value.

Graphs showing direct proportion

A graph showing direct proportion is a straight line through the origin.
The equation is $y = kx$ where k is any number.

Worked example

This graph shows the exchange rate between pounds (£) and dollars ($) on a given day.

1. How much is $15 worth in pounds?

> Draw a straight line from $15 to the diagonal line. Then draw a straight line across to the £ axis and read the value.

$15 = £12

2. How many $ is in £32?

> From the graph, you know £16 = $20

£32 = $20 × 2 = $40 •——— Scale up

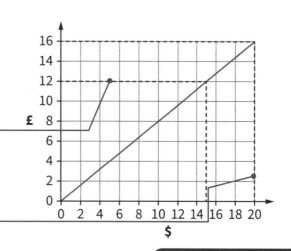

LINK
To remind yourself about straight line graphs, look back at Chapter 8.

Inverse proportion

Two values are in **inverse proportion** if, when one *increases*, the other *decreases* at the same rate.

For example, the number of taps and time taken to fill a sink are in inverse proportion.

time	taps
6 mins	1
3 mins	2
1.5 mins	4

÷2 on time, ×2 on taps

Notice that the product of the two values is constant.

Worked example

It takes 8 cleaners 3 hours to clean a block of offices.

1. How long does it take 6 cleaners to clean the offices?

cleaners	hours	cleaner-hours
8	3	8 × 3 = 24
6	$\frac{24}{6} = 4$	24

> Work out how many cleaner-hours the offices require.

> Work out how many hours are needed if there are 6 cleaners.

It takes 6 cleaners 4 hours to clean the offices.

2. How many cleaners are needed to clean the offices in 1.5 hours?

cleaners	hours	cleaner-hours
8	3	24
16	1.5	24

×2 on cleaners, ÷2 on hours

> Work out how many cleaners are needed if there are 1.5 hours. (16 × 1.5 = 24)

16 cleaners are needed to clean the offices in 1.5 hours.

 Key terms Make sure you can write a definition for these key terms

direct proportion   inverse proportion

16 Proportion

Learn the answers to the questions below, then cover the answers column with a piece of paper and write as many as you can. Check and repeat.

Questions | Answers

#	Question	Answer
1	What is the key feature of two quantities that are in direct proportion?	They increase and decrease at the same rate.
2	What is the key feature of two quantities that are in inverse proportion?	When one increases, the other decreases at the same rate.
3	What would a graph showing direct proportion look like?	A straight line through the origin.
4	What does $a \propto b$ mean?	a is proportional to b.
5	What is the equation for direct proportion?	$y = kx$
6	If x and y are in inverse proportion, what would happen to y if x is doubled?	y would halve.
7	If x and y are in direct proportion, what would happen to y if x is doubled?	y would double.
8	x is the number of identical hoses filling a swimming pool, y is the amount of time it takes. Are x and y in direct or inverse proportion?	Inverse proportion.
9	The graph of y is a straight line passing through the point (0, 1). Can x and y be in direct proportion?	No.
10	When $x = 5$, $y = 0$, can x and y be in proportion?	No.

Put paper here

Previous questions

Now go back and use these questions to check your knowledge of previous topics.

Questions | Answers

#	Question	Answer
1	How do you find 25% of a number?	Divide by 4 or multiply by 0.25.
2	What does $a \neq b$ mean?	a is not equal to b.
3	What type of graph is the curve $y = \frac{1}{x}$?	A reciprocal graph.
4	Solve $x^2 = 36$	$x = 6$ or $x = -6$
5	What are simultaneous equations?	Two (or more) equations that use the same variables that have the same solution.

Put paper here

Exam-style questions

16.1 Work out 32 grams as a proportion of 40 grams.

Give your answer as a percentage. **[2 marks]**

16.2 Alix has a ribbon 135 cm long.

Alix cuts a piece off the ribbon.

105 cm of ribbon is left.

What proportion of the original ribbon is left?

Give your answer as a fraction in its simplest form. **[2 marks]**

16.3 The conversion graph below can be used to convert between litres and pints.

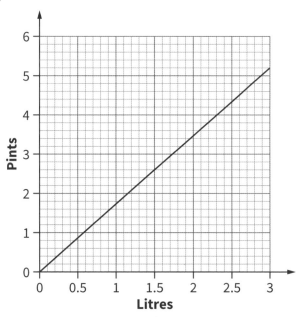

(a) Use the graph to convert 2 litres to pints. **[1 mark]**

(b) Use the graph to convert 4 litres to pints. **[1 mark]**

16.4 The variables x and y are in direct proportion.

Here is a table of values.

x	0	1	2	3	4
y			3	4.5	6

(a) Complete the table. **[2 marks]**

(b) Write the equation of the line through these points. **[1 mark]**

16.5 'Dogs love Bach' sells dog food in 3 kg bags.

Three of these bags cost £12.99.

'Woof and Ready' sells the same dog food in 2 kg bags.

Four of these bags cost £11.

Which is the best value for money: 'Dogs love Bach' or 'Woof and Ready'?

Show working to support your answer.   **[3 marks]**

> **EXAM TIP**
>
> Find the cost of 1 kg first.

16.6 Here are four graphs.

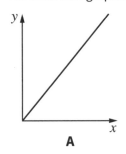 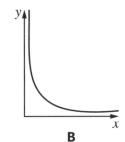 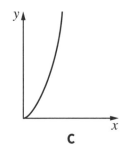 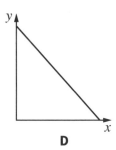

| A | B | C | D |

One of the graphs could show that y is inversely proportional to x.

Write down the letter of this graph.   **[1 mark]**

 16.7 12 builders complete a house in six days.

   (a) How many days would it take 18 builders to complete the same house?   **[2 marks]**

   (b) How many builders would be needed to complete the house in three days?   **[2 marks]**

 16.8 It would take 30 hours to fill a swimming pool using water from three taps.

   (a) How many minutes will it take to fill the pool using water from four taps?   **[2 marks]**

   (b) How many taps are needed to fill the pool with water in 10 hours?   **[2 marks]**

16.9 **(a)** Which one of these equations shows an inverse proportion relationship between x and y?

$$y = \frac{6}{x}$$

$$y = x^2$$

$$y = \sqrt{x}$$ **[1 mark]**

   (b) Use the equation you chose in part (a) to find the value of y when $x = 4$.   **[1 mark]**

   (c) Use the equation you chose in part (a) to find the value of x when $y = 1$.   **[1 mark]**

16.10 A T-shirt costs $30 in the US.

The same T-shirt costs £24 in the UK.

The exchange rate for pounds (£) to US dollars ($) is £1 = $1.31.

In which country is the T-shirt cheaper? **[2 marks]**

16.11 The table shows the prices of protractors, pencils and rulers.

Protractors	12p each or buy five and get the sixth free
Pencils	24p per roll or 10 rolls for £2
Rulers	18p each or buy one and get second half-price

Vicky buys exactly 25 of each item.

Work out the **total** cost. **[4 marks]**

Questions referring to previous content

 16.12 (a) Convert $\frac{5}{4}$ to a percentage. **[1 mark]**

(b) Convert 0.72 to a fraction in its simplest form. **[1 mark]**

(c) Convert 0.7% to a decimal. **[1 mark]**

16.13 (a) Part of a Fibonacci-type sequence is 3, 4, 7, ...

Write the next two terms. **[1 mark]**

(b) A linear sequence has first term 7 and third term 3.

Work out the 4th term of the sequence. **[2 marks]**

⚙ Knowledge

17 Angle facts

Angles and measurements

An **angle** is the amount of turn, usually from one line to another line connected at a point (**vertex**). A vertex is a corner of a shape or the point of an angle.

A **protractor** is used to measure angles. When using a protractor, make sure you place the cross of the protractor on the vertex and read round from 0°.

A **ruler** is used to measure straight lines.

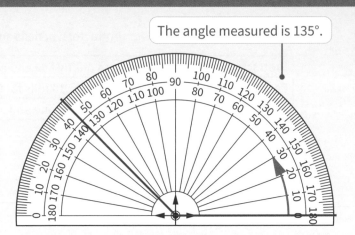

The angle measured is 135°.

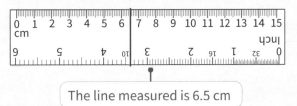

The line measured is 6.5 cm

Notation

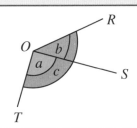

The line between O and R is called the line segment OR.

Angle a is called angle TOS.

Angle b is called SOR.

Angle c is called TOR.

The vertex is at O.

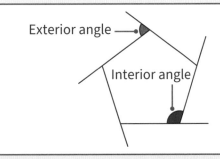

The angle inside the vertex of a shape is an **interior angle**.

The marked angle outside a shape is an **exterior angle**.

interior + exterior angles = 180°

Types of angle

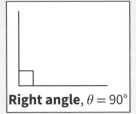

Right angle, $\theta = 90°$

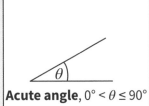

Acute angle, $0° < \theta \le 90°$

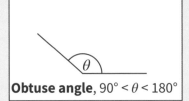

Obtuse angle, $90° < \theta < 180°$

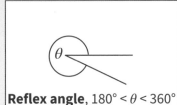

Reflex angle, $180° < \theta < 360°$

Two lines are **perpendicular** when the angle between them is exactly 90°.

Angles can be measured in a clockwise ↻ or anticlockwise ↺ direction.

Sums of angles

Vertically opposite angles are equal.

$a = b$

Angles on a straight line at the same vertex.
sum to 180°

$a + b = 180°$

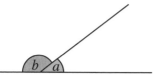

Angles around a point sum to 360°.

$a + b + c + d + e = 360°$

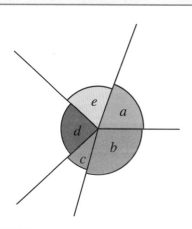

Angles in parallel lines

Parallel lines are the same distance from each other. Parallel lines never meet. They are shown on diagrams by arrows on the lines.

Transversal lines intersect (cross through) two or more lines.

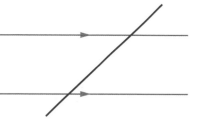

Angles a and b are **corresponding angles**.
Corresponding angles are always equal.
$a = b$

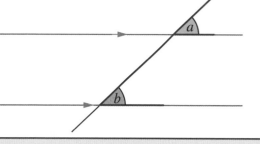

17 Angle facts

Angles in parallel lines

Angles c and d are **alternate angles.**
Alternate angles are always equal.
$c = d$

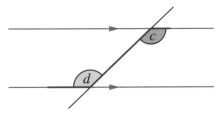

Angles e and f are **co-interior** angles.
Co-interior angles sum to 180°
$e + f = 180°$

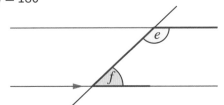

WATCH OUT ⚠

You must make sure you use the correct description (alternate, corresponding or co-interior).
If you do not state the correct reason using the correct word you will not get the marks in an exam!

Worked example

Find the values of x, y and z in the diagram.

Give reasons for your answers.

$x = 75°$ — Vertically opposite angles are equal.

$y = 180 - 75$
$\quad = 105°$ — Angles on a straight line add up to 180°.

$z = y = 105°$ — Corresponding angles are equal.

REVISION TIP 📝

There is more than one
way to do this.
For example, x and z are
co-interior angles.

Angles in triangles

Angles in a triangle sum to 180°.

$a + b + c = 180°$

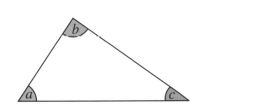

There are different types of triangles.

Equilateral

all sides equal
all angles equal

Isosceles

two sides equal
two angles equal

Scalene

no sides equal
no angles equal

Right-angled

has a 90° angle

Angles in triangles

Worked example

Find the missing angles.

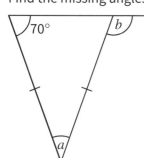

$70 + 70 + a = 180$

$a = 180 - 140$

$a = 40°$

The dashes tell us that those sides are equal, so this is an isosceles triangle. So, the unlabeled angle is 70°.

Angles in a triangle add up to 180°.

$70° + b = 180$

$b = 110°$

Angles on a straight line add up to 180°.

Angles in quadrilaterals

A **quadrilateral** is a 2D shape that has four straight sides.

Angles in a quadrilateral add up to 360°

REVISION TIP

Dashes on sides of a shape indicate that the two sides are equal. Match the number of dashes to find the pairs of equal sides.

Square

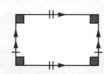

Rectangle

Kite

Rhombus

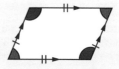

Parallelogram

Trapezium

Worked example

$ABCD$ is a parallelogram.

Calculate the size of $\angle BCD$

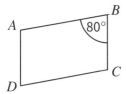

$\angle CDA = 80°$

$2 \times \angle BCD = 360 - 160 = 200$

$\angle BCD = 200 \div 2 = 100°$

Opposite angles in parallelogram are equal.

Angles in quadrilateral add up to 360°.

Key terms

Make sure you can write a definition for these key terms

acute angle   alternate angles   angle   co-interior angles
corresponding angles   intersect   obtuse angle
parallel lines   perpendicular   protractor   quadrilateral
reflex angle   right angle   ruler   transversal lines
triangle   vertex

Retrieval

17 Angle facts

Learn the answers to the questions below, then cover the answers column with a piece of paper and write as many as you can. Check and repeat.

Questions	Answers
1 What is an acute angle?	An angle that is less than 90°.
2 What is a reflex angle?	An angle that is greater than 180° and less than 360°.
3 What is an interior angle?	The angle at a vertex on the inside of a 2D-shape.
4 When are lines parallel?	When they are always an equal distance apart and they never meet.
5 What do angles at a point add up to?	360°
6 What do angles on a straight line add up to?	180°
7 Name the properties of an equilateral triangle.	All the sides are the same length and all the angles are equal.
8 Which type of triangle has sides that are all different lengths and angles that are all different sizes?	Scalene.
9 How many angles are equal in an isosceles triangle?	Two.
10 What do the angles in a triangle sum to?	180°
11 What is a transversal line?	A line that crosses two or more lines.
12 What instrument do you use to measure an angle?	A protractor.
13 What property do corresponding angles have?	They are equal.
14 What is the difference between a square and a rectangle?	A square has four sides of equal length, a rectangle has two pairs of sides of equal length.
15 What are the properties of a trapezium?	It is a quadrilateral with one pair of parallel sides.

Put paper here

Previous questions

Now go back and use these questions to check your knowledge of previous topics.

Questions	Answers
1 What is a mixed number?	A number and a fraction together.
2 What is the coefficient of the x term in the expression $ax^2 + bx$?	b
3 How do you convert a decimal into a percentage?	Multiply by 100.
4 How do you add two fractions with different denominators?	First write them both with a common denominator. Then add the numerators.
5 What does m represent in the equation $y = mx + c$?	The gradient.

Put paper here

124   **17** Angle facts

Exam-style questions

17.1 Find the size of **reflex** angle ABC.

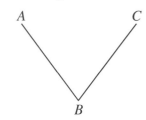

EXAM TIP

Measure the smaller angle first.

[1 mark]

17.2 Khabib says, "If you add together two acute angles, you always get an obtuse angle."

Is Khabib correct?

You must show how you get your answer.   [1 mark]

17.3 Work out the size of angle marked x.

Diagram NOT accurately drawn

[2 marks]

EXAM TIP

Use the sum of angles on a straight line.

17.4 The hour-hand of a clock is pointing directly at the number 1.

How many degrees does it have to turn
to point directly at the number 5?   [2 marks]

EXAM TIP

A clock has twelve hours, equally spaced around a point.

17.5

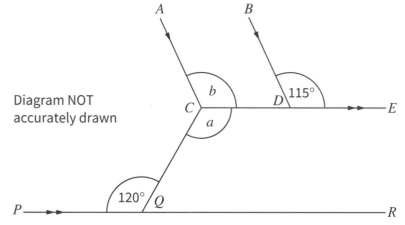

Diagram NOT accurately drawn

AC is parallel to BD.

CDE is parallel to PQR.

QC is a straight line.

(a) Work out the size of angle a. Give a reason for your answer.   [2 marks]

(b) Work out the size of angle b. Give a reason for your answer.   [2 marks]

Exam-style questions

17.6 *AB* and *CD* are straight lines.
Work out the value of *y*. **[1 mark]**

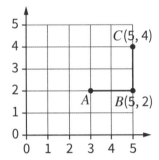

Diagram NOT
accurately drawn

EXAM TIP

Angle rules and solving
equation are combined
here. Remind yourself how
to solve equations.

17.7 Three points are shown on the coordinate grid.

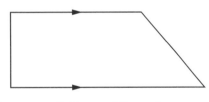

(a) Write down the coordinates of *A*. **[1 mark]**

(b) *ABCD* is a square. Plot point *D* on the grid. **[1 mark]**

(c) Write down the coordinates of *D*. **[1 mark]**

17.8 Here is a quadrilateral.

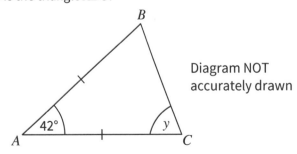

[1 mark]

Circle the name of this quadrilateral.

Rhombus   Kite   Parallelogram   Trapezium   **[1 mark]**

17.9 Here is the triangle *ABC*. **[2 marks]**

Diagram NOT
accurately drawn

Work out the size of angle *y*.

17.10 The quadrilateral $ABCD$ is a rhombus.

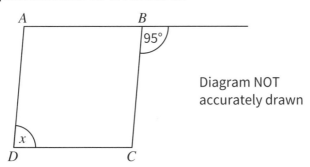

Diagram NOT accurately drawn

Work out the size of angle x.

Give a reason for each step of your working.　　　　　　　　**[3 marks]**

17.11 The four angles of a quadrilateral are x, $2x$, $3x$, and $20°$.

Work out the size of the smallest angle.　　　　　　　　**[3 marks]**

> **EXAM TIP**
>
> Find an equation in x and solve.

17.12 Angle $BFA = 44°$.

AE and BF are parallel.

Work out the size of angle FDE.　　　　　　　　**[3 marks]**

Questions referring to previous content

17.13 Given that
$$4.5 \times 192 = 864$$
find the value of:

(a) 4.5×19.2　　　　　　　　**[1 mark]**

(b) 450×0.0192　　　　　　　　**[1 mark]**

(c) $8.64 \div 0.45$　　　　　　　　**[1 mark]**

17.14 Seb says that $5x - 2 \equiv 3x$.

Is he correct?　　　　　　　　**[1 mark]**

Knowledge

18 Interior and exterior angles

Polygons

A **two-dimensional (2D) shape** is any flat shape or picture.

A **polygon** is a 2D shape with three or more straight sides, called **edges**.

A **regular polygon** is a polygon with equal sides and equal angles; an **irregular polygon** is a polygon that is not regular – in other words, at least one side or angle is different from the others.

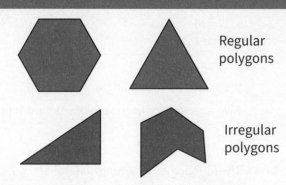

Regular polygons

Irregular polygons

These are examples of regular 2D polygons.

3 sides	4 sides	5 sides	6 sides	7 sides	8 sides	9 sides	10 sides
Triangle	Quadrilateral	Pentagon	Hexagon	Heptagon	Octagon	Nonagon	Decagon

A regular triangle is called an equilateral triangle.

A regular quadrilateral is a square.

Splitting into triangles

The number of triangles (drawn from the same vertex) that you can split a shape into is always two fewer than the number of sides.

For example, an octagon (eight sides) can be split into six triangles from the same vertex. This is two fewer than the number of sides $(8 - 6 = 2)$.

The angles in a triangle add up to 180°.

There are six triangles in an octagon, so:

sum of interior angles $= 6 \times 180° = 1080°$

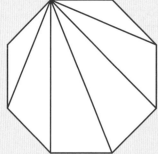

Formula box

Sum of interior angles =
(number of sides − 2) × 180°

Worked example

A heptagon has interior angles as shown.

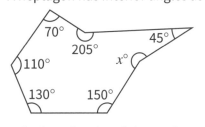

70°

205°

45°

110°

$x°$

130°   150°

Calculate the size of the angle marked x.

Sum of interior angles
$= (7 - 2) \times 180 = 5 \times 180 = 900°$

○— A heptagon has seven sides.

$70 + 205 + 45 + 150 +$
$130 + 110 = 710°$

○— Add the angles you already know.

$x = 900 - 710 = 190°$

○— Subtract this from the total of all the angles.

18

Corresponding angles

Worked example

The diagram shows a regular hexagon.

Find the angle x.

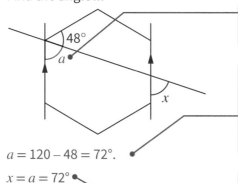

$a = 120 - 48 = 72°$.

$x = a = 72°$

Draw in angle a.

a and x are **corresponding angles**.

$a + 48° =$ interior angle of a hexagon.

Sum of interior angles of a hexagon $= (6 - 2) \times 180° = 720°$

So, one interior angle is

$720 \div 6 = 120°$

Corresponding angles are equal.

LINK

To remind yourself about angles on parallel lines, look back at Chapter 17.

Sum of exterior angles

Formula box

The sum of the exterior angles is the same for **all** polygons.

Sum of exterior angles $= 360°$

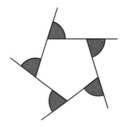

Worked example

The exterior angle of a regular polygon is 15°. How many sides does the polygon have?

$360 \div 15 = 24$

The shape has 24 exterior angles, so it has 24 sides.

REVISION TIP

The number of exterior angles in a polygon is the same as the number of sides.

The sum of exterior angles $= 360°$, so number of sides $\times$ exterior angle $= 360°$.

18 Interior and exterior angles

Using exterior angles to find interior angles

Worked example

Find the size of an interior angle of a regular heptagon.

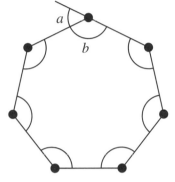

A heptagon has seven sides, so exterior angle

$a = 360 \div 7 = 51.4°$

a and b lie on a straight line.

$a + b = 180°$

$b = 180 - 51.4 = 128.6°$

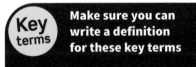

Key terms

Make sure you can write a definition for these key terms

congruent (congruence)   corresponding angles   edge
exterior angle   interior angle   irregular polygon
polygon   regular polygon   two-dimensional (2D) shape

18 Interior and exterior angles

Learn the answers to the questions below, then cover the answers column with a piece of paper and write as many as you can. Check and repeat.

	Questions	Answers
1	What is a polygon?	A 2D shape with three or more straight sides.
2	What is a regular polygon?	A polygon with sides of equal length and angles of equal size.
3	What is an irregular polygon?	A polygon that is not regular - in other words, at least one side is a different length or angle is a different size from the others.
4	What is another name for a straight side of a shape?	Edge.
5	What is a 6-sided polygon called?	A hexagon.
6	What is the formula for the sum of the interior angles in a polygon?	Sum of interior angles = (number of sides − 2) × 180.
7	What do the exterior angles of any polygon add up to?	360°.
8	If you are given one exterior angle of a regular polygon, how do you find how many sides it has?	Number of sides = 360 ÷ the exterior angle.
9	How many sides does a nonagon have?	Nine.
10	Why is a rhombus not a regular polygon?	Not all its angles are the same size.

Put paper here

Previous questions

Now go back and use these questions to check your knowledge of previous topics.

	Questions	Answers
1	What is a prime factor?	A factor that is also a prime number.
2	What is the formula used to find the gradient of a line given two points?	$\text{gradient} = \dfrac{\text{change in } y}{\text{change in } x}$
3	What does it mean to solve an equation?	To find a numerical value(s) for the variable(s).
4	How many parts are in the ratio $a:b:c$?	$a+b+c$.
5	What is the name given to the points where a quadratic curve crosses the x-axis?	The roots or solutions.

Put paper here

Exam-style questions

18.1 Write down the name of a 5-sided polygon. **[1 mark]**

 18.2 The diagram shows three sides of a regular polygon and one exterior angle.

Write down the name of this polygon. **[2 marks]**

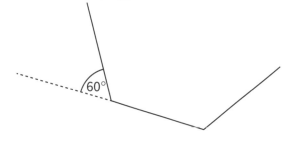

 18.3 Five of the interior angles in an irregular hexagon are 141°, 159°, 83°, 90° and 147°.

Find the size of the unknown interior angle. **[3 marks]**

18.4 The diagram shows a square, two equilateral triangles and two regular octagons.

EXAM TIP

Consider the rule for the sum of angles around a point.

Work out the size of the angle marked x.

You must show all your working.

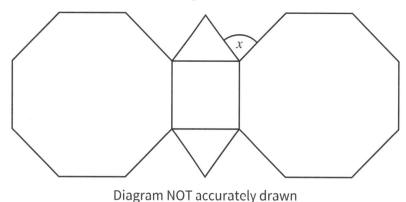

Diagram NOT accurately drawn **[4 marks]**

18.5 Jemima says she has drawn a regular polygon with an interior angle of 80°.

Sophia says that it is impossible.

Who is correct?

You must show how you get your answer. **[3 marks]**

EXAM TIP

Find the size of an exterior angle.

18.6 Here is a regular pentagon.

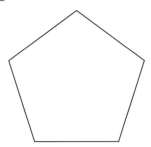

Work out the size of each interior angle. **[2 marks]**

18.7 Here is a regular 12-sided polygon.

O is the centre of the polygon.

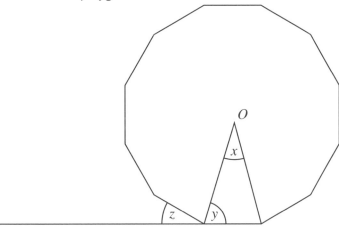

Work out the size of:

(a) The angle marked x **[2 marks]**

(b) The angle marked y **[2 marks]**

(c) The angle marked z **[2 marks]**

 18.8 The sum of the interior angles of an octagon is n.

The sum of the interior angles of a decagon is m.

Work out the value of $m - n$. **[2 marks]**

18.9 *PQRSTU* is a hexagon.

Angle *STU* = 2 × Angle *PQR*.

Work out the size of angle *STU*.

You must show our working. **[5 marks]**

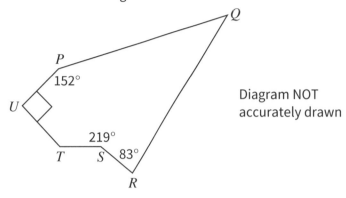

Diagram NOT
accurately drawn

Questions referring to previous content

18.10 *A* and *B* are two numbers.

They are written as a product of their prime factors.

$A = 2^3 \times 5 \times 11$

$B = 2 \times 3^2 \times 5$

(a) Find the highest common factor (HCF) of *A* and *B*. **[2 marks]**

(b) Find the lowest common factor (LCF) of *A* and *B*. **[1 mark]**

> **EXAM TIP**
>
> A Venn diagram might help in this question.

18.11 Chang makes some patterns out of matchsticks.

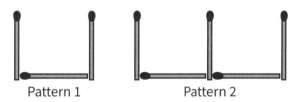

Pattern 1   Pattern 2

Pattern 3

(a) Draw Pattern 4. **[1 mark]**

(b) Work out how many matchsticks there will be in:

(i) the 7th pattern **[1 mark]**

(ii) the *n*th pattern **[2 marks]**

(c) Roham says 'Pattern 100 will contain 201 matchsticks.'

Roham is correct.

Show working to support Roham's answer. **[1 mark]**

19 3D shapes, plans, and elevations

Three-dimensional shapes

A **three-dimensional (3D) shape** is a solid shape.

3D shapes have **faces**, **edges** and **vertices** (singular: **vertex**).

Faces are the flat surfaces of a 3D shape.

Edges are the lines where two faces meet.

Vertices are the points where three or more edges meet (sometimes called a corner).

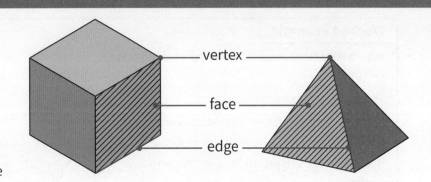

Prisms have a polygon as a base and a constant cross section joined by rectangles. A polygon is any 2D shape with straight sides.

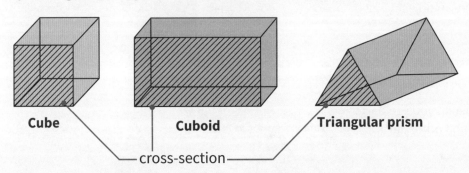

Cube

Cuboid

Triangular prism

cross-section

Note that a **constant** cross section means it is the same from one end to the other. Cubes and cuboids have more than one constant cross section.

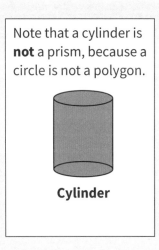

Note that a cylinder is **not** a prism, because a circle is not a polygon.

Cylinder

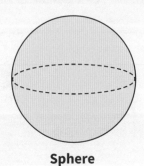

Sphere

A **sphere** is a 3D shape with one curved surface. It is the shape of a ball.

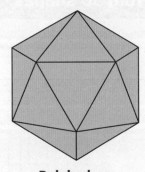

Polyhedron

A **polyhedron** is a solid shape with many faces. This one is called a dodecahedron; it has ten faces.

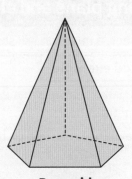

Pyramid

A **pyramid** is a 3D shape with flat faces. It has a polygon base and triangular faces which meet at a point.

Knowledge

19 3D shapes, plans and elevations

Three-dimensional shapes

> **Worked example**
>
> How many faces, edges and vertices does this prism have?
>
> This is a hexagonal-based prism.
>
> It has 8 faces (6 around the length and one at each end).
>
> It has 18 edges (6 around the length and 6 at each end).
>
> It has 12 vertices (6 at each end).

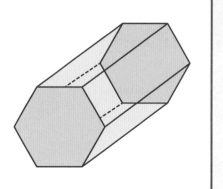

Plans and elevations

A **plan** is a view from directly above an object.

We can not see slopes in a plan.

An **elevation** is the view from the side or the front of an object.

Plans and elevations are useful to help you see parts of a 3D object that are hidden behind other parts.

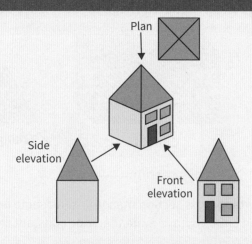

Drawing plans and elevations from 3D shapes

Sometimes, a question will show you a 3D shape and ask you to draw the plan or elevation.

> **Worked example**
>
> The 3D solid shown is made using eight centimetre cubes.
>
> Draw a plan of the solid on the grid.
>
>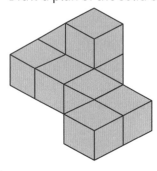
>
>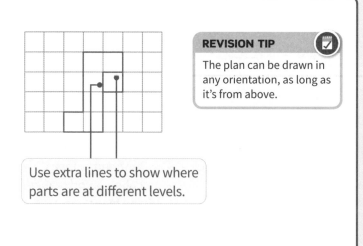
>
> Use extra lines to show where parts are at different levels.
>
> **REVISION TIP**
>
> The plan can be drawn in any orientation, as long as it's from above.

Drawing 3D shapes from plans and elevations

Sometimes, a question will show you a plan and elevation view and ask you to draw the 3D shape.

Worked example

The plan, front elevation and side elevation of a shape are shown. The shape is made up of identical cubes. Draw a 3D sketch of the shape.

Plan

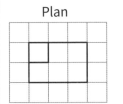

Front elevation

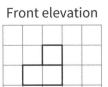

Side elevation

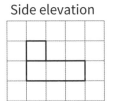

REVISION TIP

When you have drawn your 3D shape, think about what each of the plan and elevation views would look like. Are they the same as those given in the question?

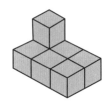

The plan shows that the base of the shape is 3 by 2 cubes. The front and side elevations both show that the top left part of the plan view is raised by a height of 1 cube.

Key terms Make sure you can write a definition for these key terms

elevation   edge   face   plan
three-dimensional (3D) shape   vertex (plural: vertices)

Retrieval

19 3D shapes, plans, and elevations

Learn the answers to the questions below, then cover the answers column with a piece of paper and write as many as you can. Check and repeat.

	Questions		Answers
1	What is a vertex?		The point where two or more edges meet.
2	What type of shape is the base of a prism?		A polygon.
3	What is a polygon?	Put paper here	Any 2D shape with three or more straight edges.
4	Why is a cylinder not a prism?		Because a circle is not a polygon.
5	What is a face of a 3D shape?	Put paper here	A flat surface.
6	What is an edge of a 3D shape?		Where two faces meet.
7	What is a plan view?		The view from directly above.
8	What is a side elevation?	Put paper here	The view from the side.
9	What is a polyhedron?		A solid shape with many faces.
10	What is another name for a triangular-based pyramid?		A tetrahedron.
11	What is a front elevation?	Put paper here	The view from the front.
12	How many vertices does a triangular prism have?	Put paper here	Six.
13	What type of shape is the base of a pyramid?		A polygon.

Previous questions

Now go back and use these questions to check your knowledge of previous topics.

	Questions		Answers
1	How is an inequality represented on a number line where the value is included?		A solid closed circle.
2	What is an acute angle?	Put paper here	An angle that measures less than 90°.
3	To simplify a ratio fully you divide all the numbers in the ratio by what?		The highest common factor of the numbers.
4	What is the sum of the exterior angles of any polygon?		360°

Exam-style questions

19.1 Write down the name of each of these 3D shapes. **[3 marks]**

(a) (b) (c) **[3 marks]**

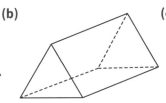

19.2 (a) Write down the name of this shape.

> **EXAM TIP**
>
> Vertices are points where three or more edges meet.

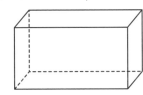

[1 mark]

(b) For the shape in part (a), write down the number of:

   (i) faces **[1 mark]**

   (ii) vertices **[1 mark]**

   (iii) edges. **[1 mark]**

19.3 For a pentagonal prism, write down the number of:

(a) faces

(b) edges

(c) vertices. **[3 marks]**

19.4 Use the diagram of a square-based pyramid for this question.

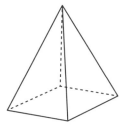

(a) Shade in exactly one face on the square-based pyramid. **[1 mark]**

(b) Draw a circle around any **one** of its vertices. **[1 mark]**

(c) Work out
'the number of faces + the number of vertices – the number of edges'
for this shape. **[2 marks]**

Exam-style questions

19.5 Here are the front and side elevations of a solid shape.

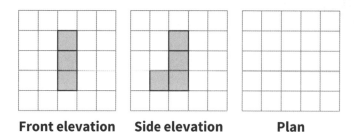

Front elevation   **Side elevation**   **Plan**

(a) Draw the plan of the solid shape.   **[1 mark]**

(b) Draw a 3D sketch of the solid shape.   **[2 marks]**

19.6 This solid shape is made from six identical cubes.

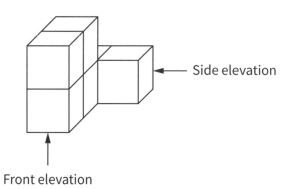

Side elevation

Front elevation

> **EXAM TIP**
>
> Plans can be drawn in any orientation, as long as it is from above.

On the grids below, draw the front elevation, side elevation, and plan.

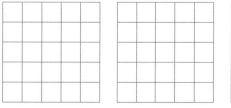

Front elevation   **Side elevation**   **Plan**   **[3 marks]**

19.7 Here are the plan, front elevation and side elevation of a solid shape.

They are drawn on a centimetre grid.

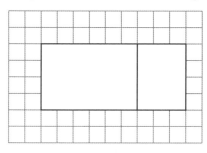 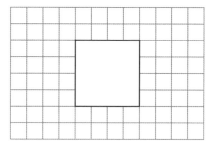 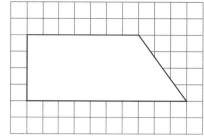

| **Plan** | **Front elevation** | **Side elevation** |

Draw a sketch of the solid shape.

Write the dimensions of the solid on your sketch. **[3 marks]**

Questions referring to previous content

19.8 The angles in a triangle are in the ratio $3:2:3$.

> **EXAM TIP**
> Consider the sum of angles in a triangle.

   (a)   Write down the name of this type of triangle. **[1 mark]**

   (b)   Work out the size of the smallest angle in the triangle. **[3 marks]**

19.9 **(a)**   *AB* and *CD* are parallel lines.

        Work out the size of angle *x*.

        Give a reason for your answer.

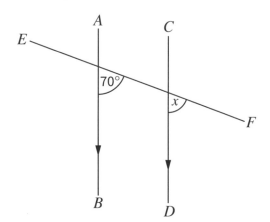

[2 marks]

   (b)   Work out the size of angle *y*.

        Give a reason for each stage of your working.

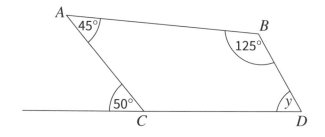

20 Perimeter, area, and volume

Perimeter and compound shapes

The **perimeter** is the total distance around the outside of a 2D shape.

A **compound shape** is two or more shapes joined together to create a single shape.

This is a compound shape.

To calculate its perimeter, add all the side lengths together.

But be careful – you have to work out all the missing lengths first!

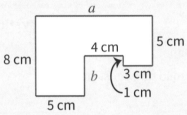

$$a = 5 + 4 + 3$$
$$= 12 \text{ cm}$$
$$b = 8 - 5 + 1$$
$$= 4 \text{ cm}$$
$$p = 8 + 12 + 5 + 3 + 1 + 4 + 4 + 5$$
$$= 42 \text{ cm}$$

Area

Area is the flat space inside a 2D shape .

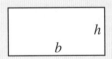

area of rectangle = base × perpendicular height
$$= bh$$

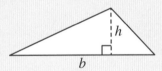

area of triangle $= \dfrac{(\text{base} \times \text{height})}{2}$
$$= \frac{1}{2} bh$$

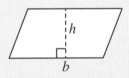

area of parallelogram = base × perpendicular height
$$= bh$$

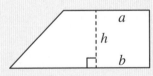

area of trapezium $= \dfrac{1}{2}(a + b)h$

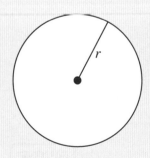

area of circle = π × radius squared
$$= \pi r^2$$

To find the area of a compound shape:

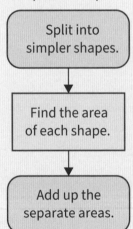

Split into simpler shapes.

Find the area of each shape.

Add up the separate areas.

Area

Worked example

Calculate the area of this shape.

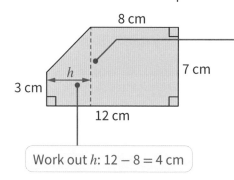

8 cm

7 cm

3 cm

h

12 cm

Split the shape into a rectangle and a trapezium.

REVISION TIP

There will often be more than one way to split the shape up. Can you think of another way to divide this shape to find its area?

Work out h: $12 - 8 = 4$ cm

total area = area of trapezium + area of rectangle

$$= \frac{1}{2} \times 4(3 + 7) + (8 \times 7)$$

$$= 2(3 + 7) + (8 \times 7)$$

$$= 2(10) + 56$$

$$= 76 \text{ cm}^2$$

For area, we use units squared because we are multiplying two lengths together.

Nets and surface area

A **net** is a 2D shape that folds up to make a 3D shape.

On a dice, the opposite faces have dots that add up to 7. Try to visualise how this net will fold into a dice.

The **surface area** of a shape is the sum of the areas of each face.

Think about what shape each face is. Find the area of each face and then add together.

Drawing a net can help you with this.

Worked example

Draw a net of this triangular prism, then calculate its surface area.

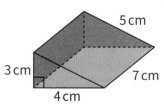

5 cm

3 cm

7 cm

4 cm

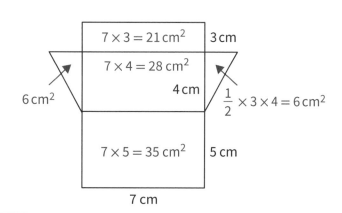

$7 \times 3 = 21 \text{ cm}^2$ 3 cm

$7 \times 4 = 28 \text{ cm}^2$

4 cm

6 cm^2

$\frac{1}{2} \times 3 \times 4 = 6 \text{ cm}^2$

$7 \times 5 = 35 \text{ cm}^2$ 5 cm

7 cm

The net has two triangles and three rectangles. Work out the area of each and write it on the net to make sure you don't miss any out.

surface area $= 21 + 28 + 35 + 6 + 6 = 96 \text{ cm}^2$

Knowledge

20 Perimeter, area, and volume

Volume

The **volume** is a measure of the space inside a 3D shape.

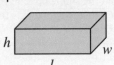

volume of a cuboid
= length × width
× height
= *lwh*

volume of a prism
= area of cross-
section × height

volume of a cylinder
= area of cross-
section × height

Worked example

Calculate the volume of this prism.

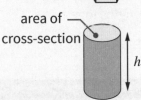

area of triangular cross-section = $\frac{1}{2} \times 3 \times 6$

volume = $9 \times 12 = 108\,\text{cm}^3$

For volume, we use cubic units because we are multiplying three lengths together.

Composite solids

A **composite solid** is a 3D shape that is made by 'sticking together' other 3D shapes.

You can calculate the volume of a composite solid by dividing it into 3D shapes.

Worked example

Calculate the volume of this composite solid.

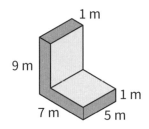

Method 1

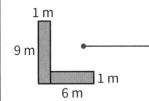

Find the area of the cross section by splitting the L-shape into two rectangles.

area of cross section = $(9 \times 1) + (6 \times 1) = 15\,\text{m}^2$

volume = area of cross section × length
= $15 \times 5 = 75\,\text{m}^3$

Method 2

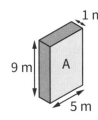 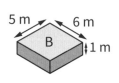

Split into two cuboids.

volume of cuboid A = $9 \times 5 \times 1 = 45\,\text{m}^3$

volume of cuboid B = $6 \times 5 \times 1 = 30\,\text{m}^3$

volume of solid = $45 + 30 = 75\,\text{m}^3$

 Key terms **Make sure you can write a definition for these key terms**

area   composite solid   compound shape   net
perimeter   volume   surface area

20 Perimeter, area, and volume

Learn the answers to the questions below, then cover the answers column with a piece of paper and write as many as you can. Check and repeat.

Questions | Answers

#	Question	Answer
1	What is the perimeter of a shape?	The distance around the outside of a shape.
2	What is the area of a shape?	The space inside a 2D shape.
3	What is the formula used to find the area of a triangle?	Area $= \frac{1}{2} \times$ base $\times$ perpendicular height.
4	What is the formula used to find the area of a trapezium?	Area $= \frac{1}{2}(a+b)h$
5	What is formula used to find the area of a parallelogram?	Area = length of base $\times$ perpendicular height.
6	What is formula used to find the area of a rectangle?	Area = length $\times$ width or base $\times$ height.
7	What is a compound shape?	A shape made up of two or more simpler shapes.
8	How can you find the area of a compound shape?	Split it into simpler shapes, find the area of each shape and then add the areas together.
9	What is the surface area of a 3D shape?	The sum of the areas of the faces of a 3D shape.
10	What is the net of a 3D shape?	A 2D shape that folds up to make the 3D shape.
11	What can you do to help calculate the surface area of a 3D shape?	Draw the net.
12	What is the volume of a 3D shape?	The space inside a 3D shape.
13	How do you find the volume of a cuboid?	Multiply the length by width by height.
14	How do you find the volume of a prism?	Multiply the area of the cross-section by the length.
15	What units do you use for volume?	Cubic units, such as cm³ (pronounced cubic centimetres).

Put paper here

Previous questions

Now go back and use these questions to check your knowledge of previous topics.

Questions | Answers

#	Question	Answer
1	What is the formula for percentage decrease?	Percentage (%) decrease $= \left(\dfrac{\text{actual decrease}}{\text{original amount}}\right) \times 100$.
2	What are like terms?	Terms whose variables are the same.
3	What does $5a$ mean?	5 multiplied by a.
4	What is a polygon?	A shape with three or more straight sides.
5	What is a twelve-sided 2D-shape called?	A dodecagon.

Put paper here

Practice

Exam-style questions

20.1 (a) Draw a straight line of length 5.4 cm. **[1 mark]**

(b) Measure the total perimeter of the triangle in mm.

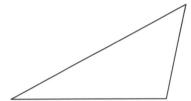

[2 marks]

20.2 Work out the area of each shape.

(a)

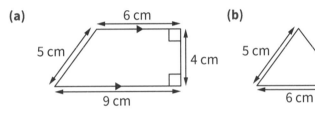

(b)

(c)

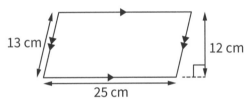

[6 marks]

> **EXAM TIP**
>
> For area we use units squared because we are multiplying two lengths together.

20.3 Work out the area of this rhombus.

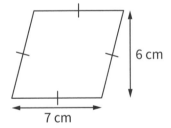

[2 marks]

20.4 Here is a prism.

The volume of the prism is 180 cm³.

Work out the area of its cross-section.

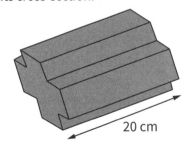

[1 mark]

20.5 This cuboid is 5 cm long and 2 cm wide.

Its volume is 40 cm³.

Work out the surface area of the cuboid.

State the units of your answer.

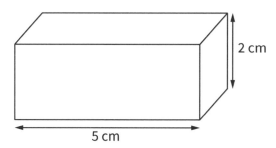

2 cm

5 cm

[4 marks]

20.6 The length of the rectangle is twice the length of the square.

Work out the perimeter of the rectangle.

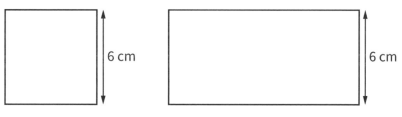

6 cm

6 cm

Diagrams NOT accurately drawn

[2 marks]

20.7 Find the area of this shape.

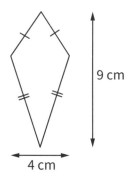

9 cm

4 cm

[2 marks]

Exam-style questions

20.8

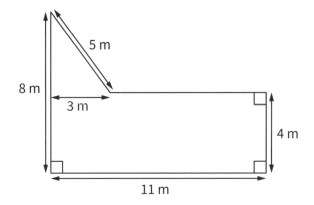

(a) Work out the perimeter of this shape.
State the units of your answer. **[2 marks]**

(b) Work out the area of this shape.
State the units of your answer. **[3 marks]**

EXAM TIP

For area we use units squared because we are multiplying two lengths together.

20.9 Here is a regular hexagon.

Work out the area of this hexagon.

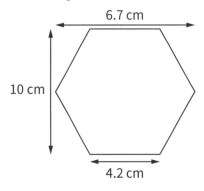

[2 marks]

EXAM TIP

Treat the hexagon like a compound shape and split it into two shapes.

20.10 Here is a cuboid.

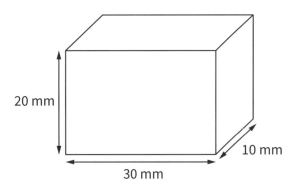

(a) Work out the volume of the cuboid in mm³. **[1 mark]**

(b) Work out the surface area of the cuboid in mm³. **[2 marks]**

20.11 Here is a hexagonal prism.

The prism has a height of 8 m.

The area of its cross section is 25 m².

Work out the volume of the prism in cubic metres (m³).

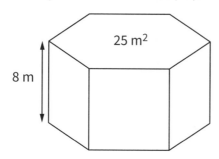

[2 marks]

20.12 Write an expression for the area of this L-shape.

Give your answer in its simplest form.

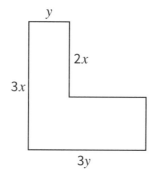

[2 marks]

Questions referring to previous content

 20.13 Each exterior angle of a regular polygon is 24°.

Work out the number of sides the polygon has. [2 marks]

20.14 Here is a list of numbers:

2 6 9 15 24 27

From the list, write down all the numbers that are

(a) cube numbers [1 mark]

(b) factors of 12 [1 mark]

(c) triangular numbers. [1 mark]

⚙ Knowledge

21 Circles, cylinders, cones, and spheres

Parts of a circle

Here are the parts of a circle:

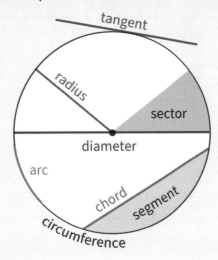

Radius: The distance of a point on the circle to the centre.

Diameter: The distance across the circle through the centre.
diameter = 2 × radius

Circumference: The perimeter of a circle.

Chord: A line that joins two points on a circle.

Segment: The region formed by a chord and the part of the circumference between the two points.

Tangent: A line that touches the circumference of a circle in exactly one point, and is perpendicular to the radius at the point of contact.

Arc: Part of the circumference of the circle.

Sector: Part of the circle formed by two radii and an arc. It is shaped like a slice of cake!

The importance of Pi (π)

Pi (π) is an important number when calculating measurements of circles. It is approximately 3.14159265 and is written using the symbol π.

Use the Pi button on your calculator when calculating with Pi.

> **Formula box**
>
> For a circle with radius, r and diameter, d:
>
> circumference, $C = \pi d$ or $2\pi r$
>
> $$\text{area, } A = \pi r^2$$
>
> For a semicircle:
>
> $$\text{area} = \frac{\text{area of circle}}{2}$$

> **Worked example**
>
> A circle has a diameter of 15 cm.
>
>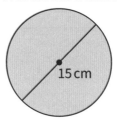
>
> 15 cm
>
> 1. Work out the circumference of the circle.
>
> $C = \pi d$
>
> $= \pi \times 15$
>
> $= 47.1 \text{ cm (to 1 decimal place)}$
>
> 2. Work out the area of the circle.
>
> $A = \pi r^2$
>
> $= \pi \times 7.5^2$ ← The radius is half the diameter.
>
> $r = \dfrac{15}{2} = 7.5 \text{ cm}$
>
> $= 167.7 \text{ cm}^2$
>
>   (to 1 decimal place)

Arcs and sectors

For a sector with a radius of r and an angle of θ:

$$\text{area} = \frac{\theta}{360} \times \text{area of full circle}$$

$$= \frac{\theta}{360} \times \pi r^2$$

$$\text{arc length} = \frac{\theta}{360} \times \text{circumference of full circle}$$

$$= \frac{\theta}{360} \times \pi r$$

Worked example

A sector of a circle is shown.

Work out the following. Give your answers to 1 decimal place.

1. The arc length of the sector.

$$\text{arc length} = \frac{\theta}{360} \times \pi r$$

$$= \frac{230}{360} \times 2 \times \pi \times 7$$

$$= 28.1 \text{ cm}^2$$

2. The area of the sector.

$$\text{area} = \frac{\theta}{360} \times \pi r^2$$

$$= \frac{230}{360} \times 2 \times \pi \times 7^2$$

$$= 98.3 \text{ cm}^2$$

Cylinders

A **cylinder** is a 3D shape like a prism but with a circular cross-section.

Formula box

$$\text{volume of a cylinder} = \text{area of circular face} \times \text{height}$$

$$= \pi r^2 h$$

$$\text{curved surface area of a cylinder} = \text{circumference circle} \times \text{height}$$

$$= 2\pi r h$$

$$\text{total surface area of a closed cylinder} = \text{curved surface area} + (2 \times \text{area of base})$$

$$= 2\pi r h + 2\pi r^2$$

LINK

To remind yourself about volume, surface area, and nets, look back at Chapter 20.

Worked example

Calculate the surface area of this closed cylinder.

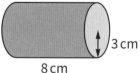

3 cm

8 cm

$$= 2\pi r h + 2\pi r^2$$

$$= (2\pi \times 3 \times 8) + (2 \times \pi \times 3^2)$$

$$= 48\pi + 18\pi$$

$$= 56\pi$$

$$= 207.3 \text{ cm}^2 \text{ (to 1 d.p.)}$$

total surface area of a closed cylinder = curved surface area + (2 × area of base)

Knowledge

Spheres

A **sphere** is a 3D shape where every point of its surface is the same distance from its centre.

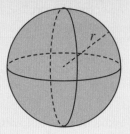

Formula box

For a sphere with radius r:

volume of a sphere $= \frac{4}{3}\pi r^3$

surface area of a sphere $= 4\pi r^2$

REVISION TIP

The phrase 'Give your answer in terms of π' means your answer should be an exact multiple of π. You shouldn't multiply by 3.141... at the end.

REVISION TIP

These formulae will be given to you in the exam. You don't need to learn them.

Worked example

A sphere has a surface area of $36\pi r^2$.

Calculate the volume of the sphere in terms of π.

$4\pi r^2 = 36\pi$ ⟵ surface area of a sphere $= 4\pi r^2$

$\dfrac{4\pi r^2}{4\pi} = \dfrac{36\pi}{4\pi}$ ⟵ divide both sides by 4π

$r^2 = 9$

$r = \sqrt{9}$

$r = 3\,\text{cm}$

volume of a sphere $= \frac{4}{3}\pi r^3$

$= \frac{4}{3} \times \pi \times 3^3$

$= \frac{4}{3} \times \pi \times 27$

$= 36\pi\,\text{cm}^3$

 Key terms — Make sure you can write a definition for these key terms

arc	chord	circumference	cone
diameter	Pi (π)	pyramid	radius
	sector	segment	tangent

Cones and pyramids

A **cone** is a 3D shape with a circular base and one vertex.

A **pyramid** is a 3D shape with a polygon base, and triangular sides that meet at one vertex.

Formula box

volume of pyramid
$= \frac{1}{3} \times$ area of base $\times$ height

volume of cone
$= \frac{1}{3} \times$ area of base $\times$ height
$= \frac{1}{3}\pi r^2 h$

curved surface area of cone $= \pi r l$

area of base of cone $= \pi r^2$

total surface area of cone $= \pi r l + \pi r^2$

where,

r is the radius is the base

h is the height

l is the slant length.

REVISION TIP

These formulae will be given to you in the exam. You don't need to learn them.

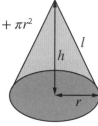

Worked example

The dimensions of a cone are shown.

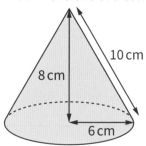

Work out, in terms of π:

1. the volume of the cone

   volume of cone $= \frac{1}{3}\pi r^2 h$

   $= \frac{1}{3} \times \pi \times 6^2 \times 8$

   $= 98\pi\,\text{cm}^3$

2. the total surface area of the cone.

   curved surface area $= \pi r l = \pi \times 6 \times 10$
   $= 60\pi\,\text{cm}^2$

   area of base $= \pi r^2 = \pi \times 6^2 \times 10 = 36\pi\,\text{cm}^2$

   total surface area $= 60\pi + 36\pi = 96\pi\,\text{cm}^2$

21 Circles, cylinders, cones, and spheres

Learn the answers to the questions below, then cover the answers column with a piece of paper and write as many as you can. Check and repeat.

Questions	Answers
1 What is the perimeter of a circle called?	The circumference.
2 What is the radius?	The distance from the centre of a circle to the edge.
3 What is a sector?	A 'slice' of a circle between two radii and an arc.
4 How do you find the diameter when you know the radius?	Multiply the radius by 2.
5 What is the formula used to find the area of a circle?	$A = \pi r^2$
6 What is the formula used to find the circumference of a circle?	$C = \pi d$ or $C = 2\pi r$
7 Describe how you find the area of a semicircle.	Find the area of the circle using $A = \pi r^2$ and then divide the answer by 2.
8 What is the formula used to find the length of an arc?	Arc length $= \dfrac{\theta}{360} \times$ circumference of full circle.
9 Describe how to find the volume of a cylinder.	Find the area of the circular face and then multiply it by the height/length.
10 What is the formula used to find the volume of a pyramid?	Volume of pyramid $= \dfrac{1}{3} \times$ area of base $\times$ height.
11 What is the formula used to find the volume of a sphere?	$\dfrac{4}{3}\pi r^3$

Put paper here

Previous questions

Now go back and use these questions to check your knowledge of previous topics.

Questions	Answers
1 What is the formula used to find the area of a triangle?	Area $= \dfrac{1}{2} \times$ base $\times$ height.
2 What is the equation of a straight line?	$y = mx + c$
3 What two algebraic methods can you use to solve simultaneous equations?	Elimination, substitution.
4 What is a turning point of a quadratic graph?	A maximum or minimum point of the graph.

Put paper here

Practice

Exam-style questions

 21.1 Here is a circle with a radius of 3 mm.

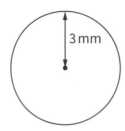

3 mm

(a) Find the area of the circle.

Give your answer to correct to 3 significant figures. **[3 marks]**

(b) Find the circumference of the circle.

Give your answer correct to 3 significant figures. **[3 marks]**

21.2 The centre of this circle is marked with a cross.

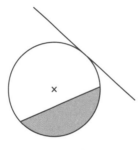

×

(a) Write down the mathematical name of the straight line that is touching the circle. **[1 mark]**

(b) Write down the mathematical name of the shaded part of the circle. **[1 mark]**

 21.3 Here is a circle with diameter 8 cm.

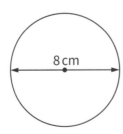

8 cm

(a) Find the area of the circle in terms of π. **[1 mark]**

(b) Find the circumference of the circle in terms of π. **[2 marks]**

 21.4 A circle has an area of 25π cm². Work out the circumference of the circle. Give your answer in terms of π. **[3 marks]**

> **EXAM TIP**
> Find the radius of the circle.

21.5 Here is a semicircle with a diameter of 9 cm.

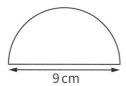

9 cm

(a) Work out the area of the semicircle.

Give your answer correct to 1 decimal place. **[2 marks]**

(b) Work out the perimeter of the semicircle.

Give your answer correct to 1 decimal place. **[2 marks]**

 21.6

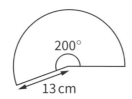

200°

13 cm

(a) Work out the area of this sector.

Give your answer correct to 1 decimal place. **[3 marks]**

(b) Work out the arc length of this sector.

Give your answer correct to 1 decimal place. **[3 marks]**

 21.7 A circle of radius 18 cm is divided into six equal sectors.

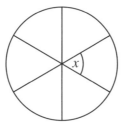

x

(a) Work out the size of angle *x*. **[1 mark]**

(b) Work out the area of one sector. **[2 marks]**

21.8 A baked bean can has a height of 11 cm and a radius of 4 cm.

(a) Work out the volume of the can.

Give your answer correct to 1 decimal place. **[2 marks]**

(b) There is a label around the curved surface of the can.

Work out the area of the label.

Give your answer correct to 1 decimal place. **[4 marks]**

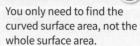

EXAM TIP

You only need to find the curved surface area, not the whole surface area.

Exam-style questions

21.9 The diagram shows a shape made from three semicircles.

Work out the perimeter of this shape.

Give your answer correct to 3 significant figures.

EXAM TIP

You will need to know the diameters of all three semi-circles.

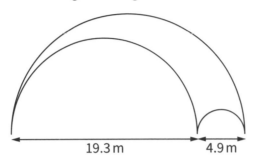

19.3 m   4.9 m   **[3 marks]**

21.10 A sphere has a radius of 18.2 cm.

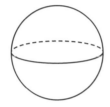

EXAM TIP

For a sphere with radius r,

volume $= \frac{4}{3}\pi r^3$

surface area $= 4\pi r^2$

(a) Find the volume of the sphere.

Give your answer correct to 1 decimal place. **[2 marks]**

(b) Find the surface area of the sphere.

Give your answer correct to 1 decimal place. **[2 marks]**

21.11 A sphere has a surface area of 400π cm².

Work out the radius of the sphere. **[2 marks]**

EXAM TIP

Form and solve an equation for r.

21.12 Here is a cone.

The base of the cone has a radius of 10 cm.

The vertical height of the cone is 24 cm.

The slant height of the cone is 26 cm.

For a cone with base radius r, height h and slant height l,

volume $= \frac{1}{3}\pi r^2 h$

surface area $= \pi r^2 + \pi r l$

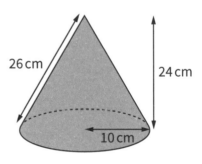

26 cm   24 cm

10 cm

(a) Work out the volume of the cone.

Give your answer in terms of π. **[2 marks]**

(b) Work out the surface area of the cone.

Give your answer in terms of π. **[3 marks]**

21.13 The Great Pyramid of Giza has a square base.

The length of one side of the base is 230 m.

The vertical height of the pyramid is 147 m.

Work out the volume of the pyramid.

Give your answer correct to 2 significant figures.

EXAM TIP

Find the area of the base first.

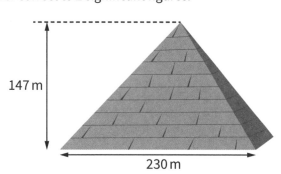

147 m

230 m **[3 marks]**

21.14 Here is a cone.

The area of the cone's curved surface is $21\pi \, \text{cm}^2$.

Work out the area of the base of the cone.

Give your answer correct to 1 decimal place.

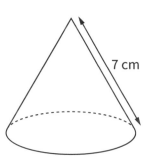

7 cm

[5 marks]

21.15 This solid shape is made from a hemisphere and a cylinder.

Work out the volume of the solid.

Give your final answer in terms of π.

EXAM TIP

volume of a hemisphere $= \frac{2}{3}\pi r^3$

volume of a cylinder $= \pi r^2 h$

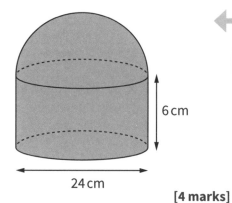

6 cm

24 cm

[4 marks]

Questions referring to previous content

21.16 Solve these simultaneous equations.

$2x - 3y = 18$

$3x + 4y = -7$ **[4 marks]**

21.17 A square has an area of $x^2 + 6x + 9$

(a) Factorise the expression for the area.

(b) Write an expression for the side length of the square in terms of x.

(c) Write an expression for the perimeter of the square in terms of x. **[2 marks]**

Knowledge

22 Similarity and congruence

Congruent shapes

Congruent shapes are exactly the same size and shape.

- Each pair of corresponding angles are equal.

- Each pair of corresponding sides are equal.

The shapes may be reflected, rotated or translated, but still be congruent.

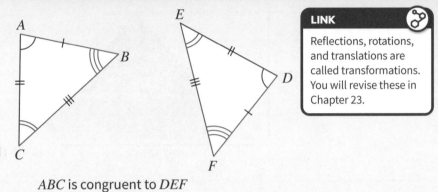

ABC is congruent to *DEF*

LINK

Reflections, rotations, and translations are called transformations. You will revise these in Chapter 23.

Congruent conditions

There are different conditions that you can use to show two triangles are congruent.

Corresponding sides are sides connecting the same angles on both shapes.

SSS	Side-Side-Side	All three corresponding sides are the same.	
SAS	Side-Angle-Side	Two corresponding sides and the angle between them are the same.	
ASA	Angle-Side-Angle	Two angles and any side are the same.	
RHS	Right angle-Hypotenuse-Side	Both are right-angled triangles; the hypotenuse and one other side are the same.	

Be careful: If only the three angles are equal (AAA), it doesn't mean that the two triangles are congruent. This means the triangles are **similar**.

Congruent conditions

Worked example

Give a reason why these two triangles are congruent.

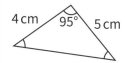
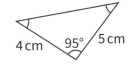

They are congruent because they satisfy the condition SAS.

Side 1 = 4 cm

Angle between the two sides = 95°

Side 2 = 5 cm

Worked example

These two triangles are congruent.

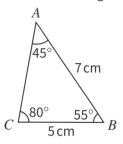
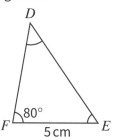

1. State the length of DE.

   $DE = 7$ cm

   DE corresponds to AB since it is opposite the 80° angle.

2. State the size of $\angle DEF$.

   $\angle DEF = \angle ABC = 55°$

Similar shapes

Similar shapes have exactly the same shape but different sizes.

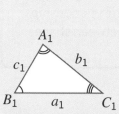
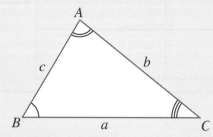

Each pair of corresponding angles are equal
Corresponding sides are in the same position

$A = A_1$, $B = B_1$, $C = C_1$
Multiply every side in first triangle by 2 to get the lengths in the second triangle:

$a = 2 \times a_1$

$b = 2 \times b_1$

$c = 2 \times c_1$

The number you multiply sides in one shape by to get sides in the other shape is called the **scale factor** (SF).

Here, the scale factor is 2.

One shape is an enlargement of the other.

Formula box

$$\text{scale factor (SF)} = \frac{\text{new length}}{\text{original length}}$$

Knowledge

Similar shapes

Worked example

Triangles ABC and DEF are similar.

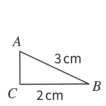

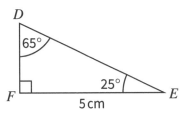

1. Work out the length of DE

   length of $DE = 3 \times \dfrac{5}{2} = 7.5 \, \text{cm}$ • ⟶ scale factor $= \dfrac{\text{new length}}{\text{original length}} = \dfrac{5}{2}$

2. State the size of $\angle CAB$

   $\angle CAB = \angle FDE = 65°$ • ⟶ Similar shapes have equal corresponding angles.

	triangle ABC	scale factor	triangle DEF
base	2 cm	$\times \dfrac{5}{2}$	5 cm
	$\times 1.5 \downarrow$		$\times 1.5 \downarrow$
side	3 cm	$\times \dfrac{5}{2}$	7.5 cm

You could use a table like this one to help you spot the relationships between shapes.

Key terms — Make sure you can write a definition for these key terms

congruent shapes   corresponding sides
scale factor   similar

22 Similarity and congruence

Learn the answers to the questions below, then cover the answers column with a piece of paper and write as many as you can. Check and repeat.

	Questions	Answers
1	What does congruent mean?	Exactly the same size and shape.
2	What does SSS mean?	Side-Side-Side: All three corresponding sides are of equal length on both triangles.
3	What does ASA mean?	Angle-Side-Angle: Two angles and any side are equal.
4	What does RHS mean?	Right angle-Hypotenuse-Side: Both are right-angled triangles, the hypotenuse and one other side are equal.
5	What are the four different ways that two triangles can be congruent?	SSS (Side-Side-Side). SAS (Side-Angle-Side). ASA (Angle-Side-Angle). RHS (Right angle-Hypotenuse-Side).
6	How do you calculate the scale factor?	$\text{scale factor} = \dfrac{\text{new length}}{\text{original length}}$
7	Are an object and its enlargement congruent or similar shapes?	They are similar shapes.
8	When using the SAS condition for congruence, which angles need to be equal?	The angle between the two pairs of corresponding sides.
9	Are all equilateral triangles similar?	Yes, as all pairs of corresponding angles are 60°.
10	True or False? All right-angled triangles are similar.	False: The other two angles also have to be equal for a pair of right-angled triangles to be similar.

Put paper here

Previous questions

Now go back and use these questions to check your knowledge of previous topics.

	Questions	Answers
1	How do you convert from cm² to mm²?	Multiply by 100.
2	How do you multiply fractions?	Multiply the numerators and multiply the denominators.
3	What is simple interest?	A fixed amount of interest calculated as a percentage of the original amount invested.
4	What is an algebraic expression?	A collection of letters and numbers with no equals sign.
5	What is a quadratic equation?	An equation where the highest power of the variable is 2.

Put paper here

Exam-style questions

22.1 In each pair, the two triangles are congruent.

Write down the reason for congruence for each pair.

Choose from SSS, SAS, ASA or RHS.

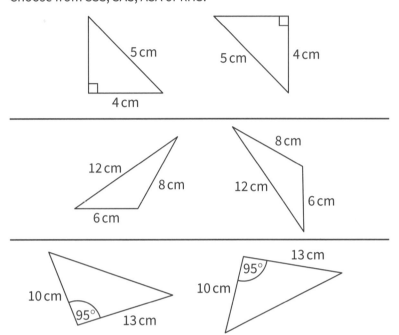

[3 marks]

22.2 Write the letters of the two shapes that are congruent.

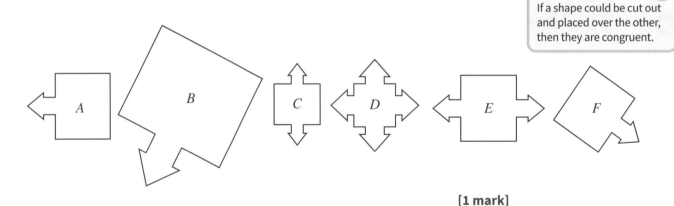

[1 mark]

22.3 On the grid, shade three more squares so that shape N is congruent to shape M.

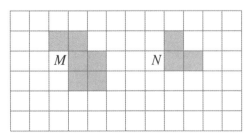

[1 mark]

22.4 Triangles *ABC* and *FED* are congruent.

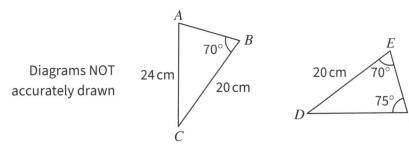

Diagrams NOT accurately drawn

(a) Write down the length of *DF*. **[1 mark]**

(b) Write down the size of angle *CAB*. **[1 mark]**

22.5 Two of these rectangles are similar.
Write down the letters of these two rectangles.

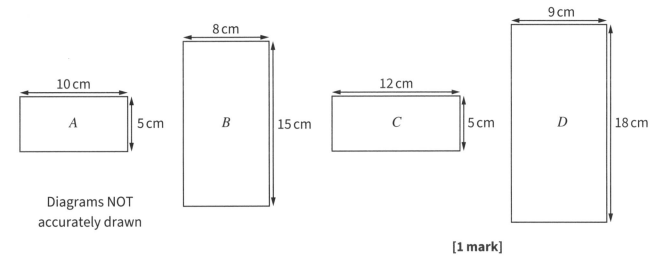

Diagrams NOT accurately drawn

[1 mark]

 22.6 These two triangles are similar.
Work out the length *y*.

Diagrams NOT accurately drawn

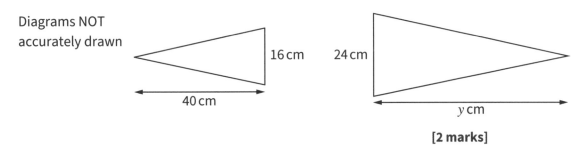

[2 marks]

Exam-style questions

22.7 Triangles *ABC* and *DEF* are similar.

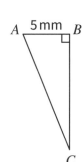

Diagrams NOT accurately drawn

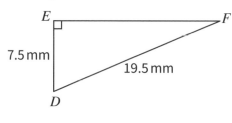

Find the length of *AC*. **[2 marks]**

22.8 In the diagram, *EB* is parallel to *DC*. *ABE* and *ACD* are similar triangles.

Diagrams NOT accurately drawn

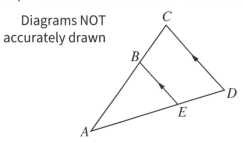

AC = 11.5 cm, *AB* = 9.2 cm and *AE* = 8.4 cm.

Work out the length of *ED*. **[2 marks]**

22.9 Sonny and Blair each draw a triangle.

Sonny's triangle has angles of sizes 45°, 60° and *x*°.

Blair's triangle has angles of sizes 60°, 75° and *y*°.

Sonny says that the two triangles must be congruent. Blair says that they are similar.

Who is correct?
You must show how you get your answer. **[3 marks]**

22.10

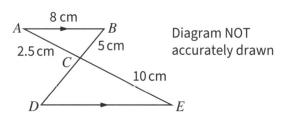

Diagram NOT accurately drawn

Triangles *ABC* and *EDC* are similar.

AB is parallel to *DE*.

ACE and *BCD* are straight lines.

AB = 8 cm	*AC* = 2.5 cm
BC = 5 cm	*CE* = 10 cm

(a) Work out the length of *CD*. **[2 marks]**

(b) Work out the length of *DE*. **[2 marks]**

22.11

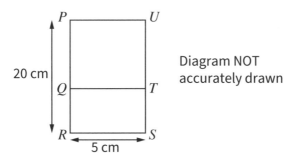

Diagram NOT accurately drawn

Rectangle *PUSR* is mathematically similar to rectangle *RQTS*.

PR = 20 cm and *RS* = 5 cm.

Work out the area of rectangle *RQTS*. **[4 marks]**

Questions referring to previous content

22.12 This flag has a white cross on a red background.

Work out the area of the white cross.

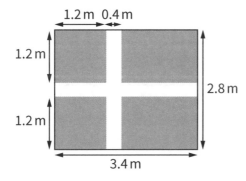

[3 marks]

22.13 Draw the graph of $y = 4x - 3$ for values of x from 0 to 3.

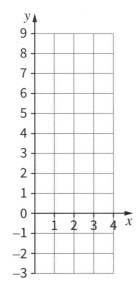

[2 marks]

Knowledge

23 Transformations

Types of transformation

A **transformation** is something that alters a shape's position and/or its size.

There are four types of transformation:

Reflection: The shape is reflected in a line of reflection (also called a mirror line or line of symmetry).

Rotation: The shape is pivoted around a fixed point (the centre of rotation).

Translation: The shape is moved to a different position.

Enlargement: The shape changes its size.

REVISION TIP

The **image** of a reflection, rotation or translation is always **congruent** to the **object**.

REVISION TIP

The image of an enlargement is always similar to the object.

WATCH OUT !

The **object** is the original shape.

The **image** is the result after the transformation.

Remember: you look at your image in a mirror.

object — image

LINK

To remind yourself about similarity and congruence, look back at Chapter 22.

Reflection

Describe a reflection by giving the line of symmetry.

Worked example

1. Describe the single transformation that maps $ABCD$ to $A'B'C'D'$.

$A'B'C'D'$ $A'B'C'D'$ is the reflection of $ABCD$ in the mirror line $x = -1$

LINK

To remind yourself about equations and straight lines, look back at Chapter 8.

2. Draw the reflection of the trapeziuim $ABCD$ in the mirror line $y = x$.

Draw the line $y = x$

Draw a line from each vertex which passes through $y = x$ at right angles.

Mark the point which is the same distance on the other side of $y = x$. This is a vertex of the reflection.

Join the reflected vertices up.

Rotation

Describe a rotation by giving:

1 The angle through which the shape is rotated, such as 90°.

2 The direction of rotation, clockwise or anticlockwise.

3 The centre of rotation, such as the origin or another point.

Rotation

Worked example

Describe the transformation that maps *ABC* to *DEF*.

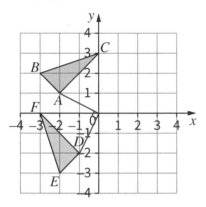

The transformation is a rotation of 90° anticlockwise about the origin (the point (0, 0)).

REVISION TIP

Use tracing paper to help you (you can ask for tracing paper in an exam).

Enlargement

Describe an enlargement by giving the **scale factor** and **centre of enlargement**.

To find the centre of enlargement, draw lines through the corresponding vertices of the object and see where they meet.

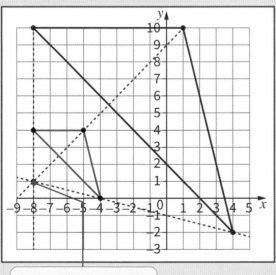

centre of enlargement

Translation

Describe a translation by giving the **column vector**.

$\begin{pmatrix} 2 \\ 3 \end{pmatrix}$ tells you to move 2 right and 3 up.

Negative values tell you to move left or down.

$\begin{pmatrix} -2 \\ -3 \end{pmatrix}$ tells you to move 2 left and 3 down.

When you translate a shape, the object and image are congruent and have the same **orientation** (unlike rotations and reflections).

LINK

You will learn more about vectors in Chapter 26.

Worked example

1. Describe the transformation that maps shape *A* on to shape *B*.

   Shape *A* has been moved down 6, but has not moved left or right.

   Translation by the vector $\begin{pmatrix} 0 \\ -6 \end{pmatrix}$

2. Translate shape *A* by vector $\begin{pmatrix} -4 \\ -5 \end{pmatrix}$ and label the image *C*.

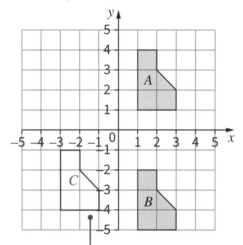

The vector $\begin{pmatrix} -4 \\ -5 \end{pmatrix}$ tells you to move shape *A* left 4 and down 5.

23 Transformations

Enlargement

Worked example

Enlarge triangle ABC by scale factor 2 with centre of enlargement $(0, 0)$.

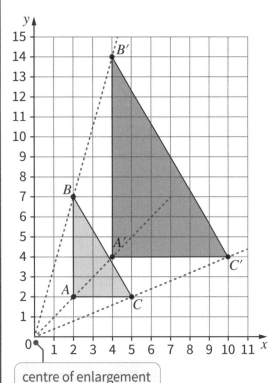

centre of enlargement

2 right; **2** up. ●——— Measure the distance of vertex A from the centre of enlargement.

$2 \times 2 = \mathbf{4}; 2 \times 2 = \mathbf{4}$ ●———

$(0, 0) \Rightarrow (\mathbf{4}, \mathbf{4})$ ●——— Multiply these numbers by the scale factor.

$A' = (4, 4)$

$B' = (4, 7)$

$C' = (10, 4)$ ●——— Add these numbers to the centre of enlargement to find vertex A'.

Repeat the process for B and C to plot vertices B' and C'.

Worked example

Enlarge the shape by scale factor 0.5 from centre of enlargement $(1, 1)$.

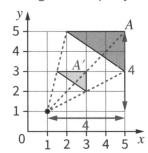

4 right, 4 up ●——— Measure the distance of vertex A from the centre of enlargement.

$4 \times 0.5 = 2$

$4 \times 0.5 = 2$ ●——— Multiply by the scale factor.

$(1, 1) \rightarrow (3, 3) = A'$ ●——— Add to centre of enlargement to find A'.

 Key terms — Make sure you can write a definition for these key terms

centre of enlargement   column vector   congruent   enlargement   image   object   orientation   reflection   rotation   scale factor   similar   transformation   translation

23 Transformations

Learn the answers to the questions below, then cover the answers column with a piece of paper and write as many as you can. Check and repeat.

Questions	Answers
1 What are the four types of transformation?	Reflection, rotation, translation, enlargement.
2 What do you need to know in order to draw the reflection of a shape on a graph?	The equation of the line of symmetry.
3 What is a shape called before and after a transformation?	Before the transformation it is called the object and after it is called the image.
4 What three pieces of information do you need to know in order to describe the rotation of a shape?	The angle, the direction and the centre of rotation.
5 When you rotate a shape, are the object and image congruent or similar?	Congruent.
6 What can you ask for in an exam to help with drawing rotations?	Tracing paper.
7 How do you write a translation mathematically?	Using a column vector.
8 To enlarge a shape, what two pieces of information do you need?	The scale factor and the centre of enlargement.
9 When you enlarge a shape, are the object and image congruent or similar?	Similar.
10 What happens when you enlarge a shape by a scale factor between 0 and 1?	The image is smaller than the object.
11 If you are given the object and the image, how do you find the centre of enlargement?	Draw lines through the corresponding vertices and see where they meet. This point is the centre of enlargement.

Put paper here

Previous questions

Now go back and use these questions to check your knowledge of previous topics.

Questions	Answers
1 What is a regular shape?	A shape that has all sides the same length and all angles the same size.
2 What is the formula that is used to calculate the sum of the interior angles in a polygon?	Sum of interior angles = (number of sides − 2) × 180°.
3 What can you say about the size of two corresponding angles on parallel lines?	They are equal.
4 What is the area of a 2D shape?	A measure of the space inside a 2D shape.
5 How do you find the area of a compound shape?	Split it into simpler shapes, find the area of each shape and then add the areas up.

Put paper here

Practice

Exam-style questions

23.1 **(a)** Reflect shape *A* in the mirror line shown.

Label the image *A'*.

> **EXAM TIP**
>
> Reflect one vertex at a time.

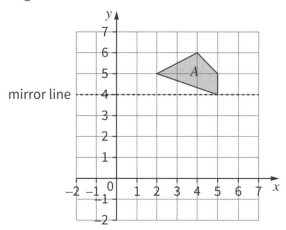

[2 marks]

(b) Write down the equation of the mirror line. [1 mark]

23.2 Describe fully the single transformation that maps triangle *A* onto triangle *B*.

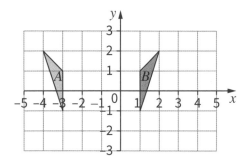

[2 marks]

23.3 **(a)** Reflect shape *P* in the mirror line.

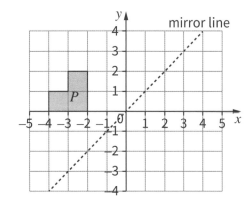

[2 marks]

(b) Write down the equation of the mirror line. [1 mark]

23.4 Rotate point P 180° about the origin.

Label the new point P'.

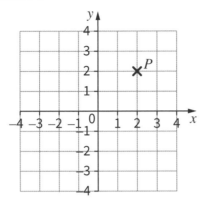

[1 mark]

23.5 (a) Rotate rectangle A 90° clockwise about (2, 3).

Label the new rectangle B.

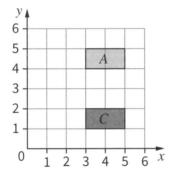

[2 marks]

(b) Describe fully the translation that maps rectangle A to rectangle C.

[2 marks]

> **EXAM TIP** 🎯
> Your description will be similar to that in part (a).

23.6 (a) Rotate triangle P 180° about the origin.

Label the new triangle Q.

> **EXAM TIP** 🎯
> Remember you can use tracing paper to help you.

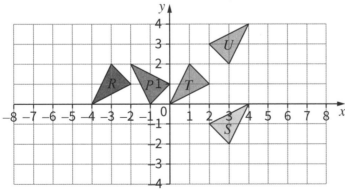

[1 mark]

(b) Triangle P rotates 90° anticlockwise about (0, 2) onto one of the other triangles in the grid.

Write down the letter of the triangle P maps onto.

[1 mark]

23.7 Translate the T-shape by vector $\begin{pmatrix} 4 \\ 0 \end{pmatrix}$.

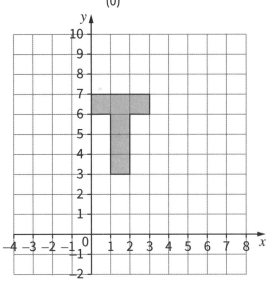

[1 mark]

23.8 Write down the letter of the shape that is an enlargement of shape A.

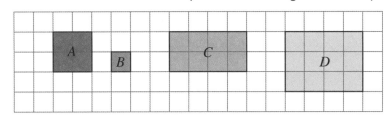

[1 mark]

23.9 Describe fully the transformation that maps rectangle $ABCD$ to rectangle $A'B'C'D'$.

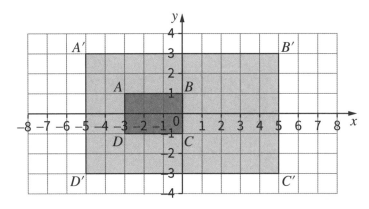

[3 marks]

EXAM TIP

Draw lines through corresponding vertices and see where they meet.

23.10

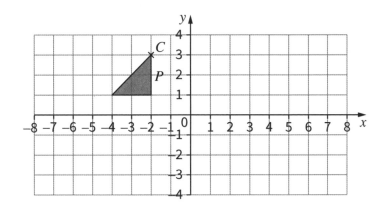

(a) Enlarge triangle P by scale factor 2, centre C.

Label your image Q. **[2 marks]**

(b) Enlarge triangle P by scale factor $\frac{1}{2}$, centre $(2, -1)$.

Label your image R. **[2 marks]**

Questions referring to previous content

23.11 Rani deposited some money in this savings account.

At the end of one year, she has £711.22 in her account.

This includes her interest for the first year.

How much money did she deposit in the account? **[2 marks]**

23.12 Which graph could be the graph of $y = \frac{1}{x}$.

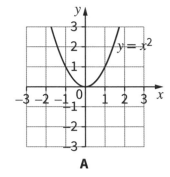
A

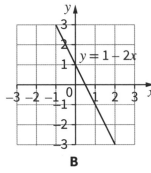
B

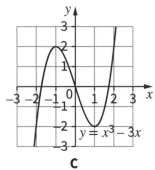
C

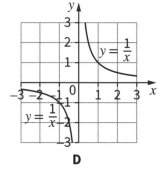
D

[2 marks]

⚙ Knowledge

24 Pythagoras and trigonometry

Pythagoras' theorem

Use **Pythagoras' theorem** to find missing side lengths in right-angled triangles.

Pythagoras' theorem: $c^2 = a^2 + b^2$

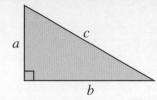

Worked example

Work out the missing side lengths in these triangles.

7 cm

x

15 cm

$$x^2 = 7^2 + 15^2$$
$$x = \sqrt{7^2 + 15^2}$$
$$= 16.6\,\text{cm (to 1 d.p.)}$$

3.5 cm

y 9.8 cm

$$9.8^2 = 3.5^2 + y^2$$
$$y^2 = 9.8^2 - 3.5^2$$
$$y = \sqrt{9.8^2 - 3.5^2}$$
$$= 9.2\,\text{cm (to 1 d.p)}$$

LINK

To remind yourself about rearranging equations, look back at Chapter 7.

Worked example

The points A and B have coordinates $(1, 2)$ and $(4, -2)$. Calculate the length of AB.

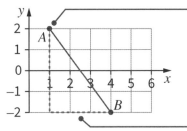

Plot the points A and B on a coordinate grid.

Make a right-angled triangle by drawing a vertical line from A and a horizontal line from B.

$$(AB)^2 = 3^2 + 4^2 = 25$$
$$AB = \sqrt{25} = 5$$

The triangle has a base of 3 and a height of 4.

Trigonometry

Use **trigonometry** to find missing side lengths or angles in right-angled triangles.

Hypotenuse: The longest side of a right-angled triangle.

Opposite: Opposite the angle θ.

Adjacent: Next to the angle θ.

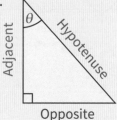

Formula box

There are three trigonometric ratios that we can use to find missing sides or angles.

$$\sin \theta = \frac{\text{opposite}}{\text{hypotenuse}}$$
$$\cos \theta = \frac{\text{adjacent}}{\text{hypotenuse}}$$
$$\tan \theta = \frac{\text{opposite}}{\text{adjacent}}$$

REVISION TIP

Use this mnemonic to remember the trigonometric ratios.

SOH-CAH-TOA

Solving trigonometry problems

Worked example

Work out the value of x in this triangle.

angle = 32°

13 cm side is **adjacent** 32°.

x cm side is **opposite** 32°.

S<u>O</u>H C<u>A</u>H ⃝T<u>O</u>A⃝

$\tan \theta = \dfrac{\text{opposite}}{\text{adjacent}}$

$\tan 32 = \dfrac{x}{13} \Rightarrow x = 13 \tan 32$

$x = 8.1 \text{ cm (1 d.p.)}$

> Write down the information you know.

> Underline the side you know and the side you need to find. Use the one that has two underlined letters.

> Substitute in the values.

> Use a calculator.

WATCH OUT ⊙

A lot of students lose marks because they don't know how to use their calculator properly.

Find these buttons:

| sin | cos | tan |

To work out the inverse of cos, sin or tan, you will probably have to press **shift** or **inv** first.

Sometimes you will be given two side lengths and asked to work out an angle.

The method is the same, even though you don't know what the angle is yet.

Worked example

A plank of wood is propped up against a wall. The plank rests 0.5 m from the base of the wall and makes an angle of 70° with the floor.

Work out the length of the plank to the nearest centimetre.

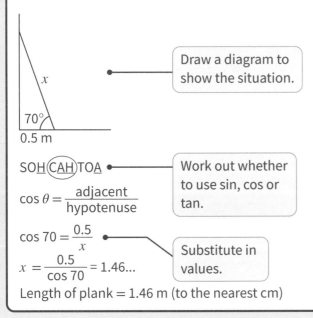

> Draw a diagram to show the situation.

S<u>O</u>H ⃝C<u>A</u>H⃝ T<u>O</u>A

$\cos \theta = \dfrac{\text{adjacent}}{\text{hypotenuse}}$

$\cos 70 = \dfrac{0.5}{x}$

$x = \dfrac{0.5}{\cos 70} = 1.46...$

Length of plank = 1.46 m (to the nearest cm)

> Work out whether to use sin, cos or tan.

> Substitute in values.

Worked example

Work out the size of the angle marked x in this triangle.

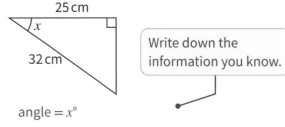

angle = $x°$

The 25 cm side is **adjacent** to angle $x°$.

The 32 cm side is the **hypotenuse**.

$\cos \theta = \dfrac{\text{adjacent}}{\text{hypotenuse}}$

$\cos x = \dfrac{25}{32}$

$x = \cos^{-1}\left(\dfrac{25}{32}\right)$

$x = 38.6°$

> Write down the information you know.

> You have the adjacent and the hypotenuse.

> Substitute in values.

> Use a calculator.

Trigonometric values

Here are the exact values you need to know (or be able to calculate quickly) in an exam.
You can use the triangles or memorise the table.

First, draw a right-angled isosceles triangle with base and height of 1.

Now draw an equilateral triangle with side lengths 2 and split it into two right-angled triangles.

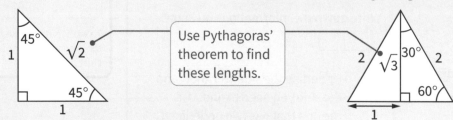

Use Pythagoras' theorem to find these lengths.

angle, θ	sin, θ	cos, θ	tan, θ
0°	0	1	0
30°	$\frac{1}{2}$	$\frac{\sqrt{3}}{2}$	$\frac{\sqrt{3}}{3}$
45°	$\frac{1}{\sqrt{2}} = \frac{\sqrt{2}}{2}$	$\frac{1}{\sqrt{2}} = \frac{\sqrt{2}}{2}$	1
60°	$\frac{\sqrt{3}}{2}$	$\frac{1}{2}$	$\sqrt{3}$
90°	1	0	n/a

Key terms — Make sure you can write a definition for these key terms

adjacent   angle of depression   angle of elevation
hypotenuse   opposite   Pythagoras' theorem   trigonometry

24 Pythagoras and trigonometry

Learn the answers to the questions below, then cover the answers column with a piece of paper and write as many as you can. Check and repeat.

Questions | Answers

	Questions		Answers
1	What kind of triangles can Pythagoras' theorem be used with?	Put paper here	Right-angled triangles.
2	What is Pythagoras theorem?		$c^2 = a^2 + b^2$
3	What is the value of sin 30?		0.5
4	What is the value of tan 45?	Put paper here	1
5	How do you know whether to use sin, cos or tan?		Label the triangle with the angle and the sides you know or want to find out. Write SOH CAH TOA. Underline the sides you know or want to find out. Use the part that has two underlined letters.
6	Is $\dfrac{\text{opposite}}{\text{adjacent}}$ the formula for sin θ, cos θ or tan θ?	Put paper here	tan θ
7	What is the value of cos 60?		0.5
8	If tan $\theta = 5$, how do you find θ using your calculator?		Use $\tan^{-1}(5)$.
9	What is the value of cos 90?	Put paper here	0
10	When finding the distance between two points on a grid, what theorem can you use?		Pythagoras' theorem.

Previous questions

Now go back and use these questions to check your knowledge of previous topics.

Questions | Answers

	Questions		Answers
1	What is a net?	Put paper here	A 2D shape that can be folded up to form a 3D shape.
2	What is a formula?		An equation which links different variables in a real-life relationship.
3	In algebra, what do we mean by $\dfrac{7}{x}$?		7 divided by x.
4	What does the A in BIDMAS stand for?		Addition.
5	How do you find the next term in a Fibonacci sequence?		Add the previous two terms to get the next one.

Practice

24.1 Only one of these triangles in right-angled.

Write down the letter of the right-angled triangle.

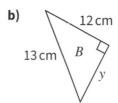

8 cm | 12 cm
A
10 cm

16 cm | 19 cm
B
14 cm

20 cm | 21 cm
C
13 cm

24 cm | 25 cm
D
7 cm

[2 marks]

> **EXAM TIP**
>
> Pythagoras' theorem is only true for right-angled triangles.

24.2 Work out the length of the unknown side in each of these right-angled triangles.

a)

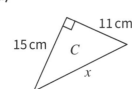

6 cm
A
8 cm
x

b)

12 cm
13 cm B
y

[6 marks]

24.3 Work out the length of the unknown side in each of these right-angled triangles.

Give your answers correct to 1 decimal place.

a)

11 cm
15 cm C
x

b)

y
D 34 cm
29 cm

[6 marks]

24.4 Point A has coordinates $(-1, 3)$. Point B has coordinates $(2, 8)$.

Work out the length of the line AB.

Give your answer correct to 3 significant figures. **[4 marks]**

24.5 The diagram shows a biscuit in the shape of an isosceles triangle.

Work out the height of this biscuit.

Give your answer to the nearest millimetre.

20 cm

10 cm

[3 marks]

 24.6 Work out the length of the unknown side in each of these right-angled triangles.

Give your answers correct to 2 decimal places.

a)

x

35°

16 cm

b)

27°

42 cm

y

c)

67°

14 cm

z

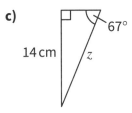

d)

p

32°

6 cm

e)

47°

10 cm

q

f)

8 cm

62°

r

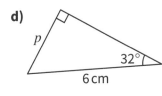
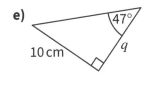
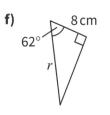

[12 marks]

 24.7 Here is a trapezium.

Work out the height of this trapezium.

Give your answer correct to 3 significant figures.

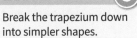

EXAM TIP

Break the trapezium down into simpler shapes.

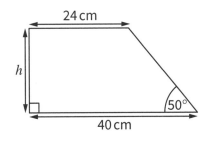

24 cm

h

50°

40 cm

[3 marks]

24.8 The helicopter is 1000 m above the ground.

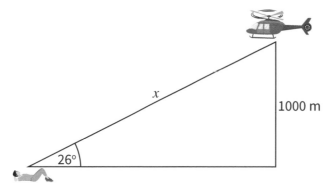

Work out x, the distance from Taylor to the helicopter.

Give your answer correct to 2 significant figures. **[2 marks]**

24.9 Write down the value of $\sin x$.

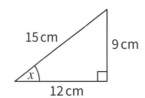

[1 mark]

24.10 Work out the size of angle x in each of these triangles.

Give your answers correct to 1 decimal place.

a) 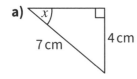 **b)**  **c)**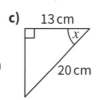

[6 marks]

24.11 Triangle PQR is an isosceles triangle.

Work out the size of angle PQR.

Give your answer correct to 1 decimal place.

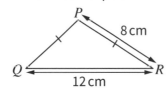

[4 marks]

EXAM TIP

Split the isosceles triangles into two right-angled triangles. Be careful – angle QPR is **not** a right angle.

24.12 Write down the value of $\cos 0°$. **[1 mark]**

24.13 Work out the length of the side labelled x in each of these triangles.

a)

b)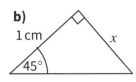

c)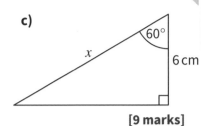

[9 marks]

24.14 Write down the value of

    (a)   cos 45°   **[1 mark]**

    (b)   tan 45° + sin 30°   **[2 marks]**

    (c)   sin 60°   **[1 mark]**

    (d)   tan 60° − cos 90°   **[2 marks]**

Questions referring to previous content

 24.15 These two triangular prisms both have the same volume.
Work out the height h.

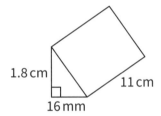 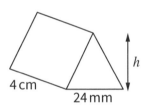

[4 marks]

24.16 AB and CD are parallel.

By forming and solving an equation, find the value of x.

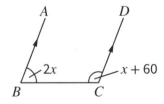

[3 marks]

⚙ Knowledge

25 Constructions, loci, and bearings

Drawing triangles

You can use a ruler and a protractor to accurately draw
a triangle when you know:

- angle-side-angle (ASA), or
- side-angle-side (SAS), or
- hypotenuse and one other side of a right-angled triangle (RHS).

LINK

In Chapter 22 you learned that ASA, SAS,
and RHS are tests for congruent triangles.
This means that there is only one possible
way that you can draw the triangle if you are
given these things.

Worked example

In the triangle ABC, $AB = 6\,\text{cm}$, $BC = 8\,\text{cm}$ and
$ABC = 62°$.
Draw the triangle ABC.

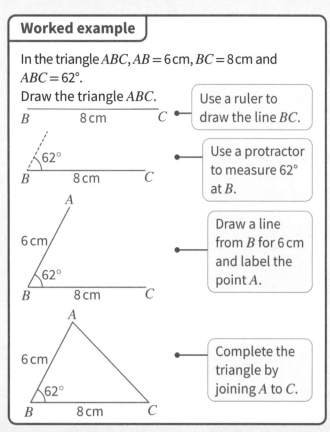

Use a ruler to
draw the line BC.

Use a protractor
to measure 62°
at B.

Draw a line
from B for 6 cm
and label the
point A.

Complete the
triangle by
joining A to C.

Worked example

In the triangle PQR, $RPQ = 43°$, $RQP = 57°$
and $PQ = 7\,\text{cm}$.
Draw triangle PQR.

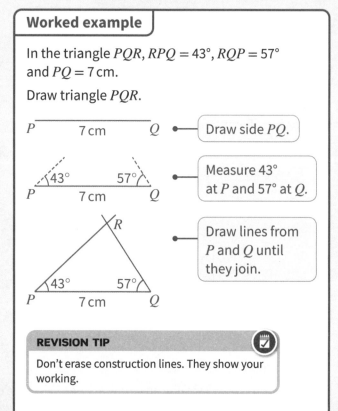

Draw side PQ.

Measure 43°
at P and 57° at Q.

Draw lines from
P and Q until
they join.

REVISION TIP

Don't erase construction lines. They show your
working.

Constructing triangles

To **construct** a shape means to draw it accurately with a ruler and
a pair of compasses.

If you know the lengths of all three sides of a triangle, but no angles,
you can use a ruler and a pair of compasses to construct the triangle.

REVISION TIP

To make a triangle, any two
sides of the triangle must have a
sum greater than the third side.

Worked example

Construct a triangle with side lengths 7 cm, 4 cm and 5 cm.

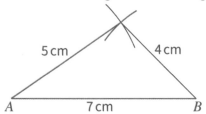

Use a ruler to draw a horizontal 7 cm line, AB.

Set compasses to 5 cm. Put compasses point at A and draw an arc.

Set compasses to 4 cm. Put compasses point at B and draw an arc.

Draw lines from A and B to where the arcs cross.

Drawing bisectors

Perpendicular lines are lines at 90° to each other (at right angles).

A **bisector** cuts a line or an angle exactly in half.

So, a **perpendicular bisector** cuts a line exactly in half at right angles.

The shortest distance from a point to a line is the **perpendicular distance**.

The perpendicular bisector can be used to find the midpoint of a line.

Worked example

Draw the perpendicular bisector of AB.

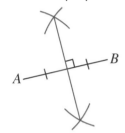

Put compasses at A. Draw arcs above and below the line.

Put compasses at B. Draw arcs above and below the line.

Join up the points where the arcs meet.

REVISION TIP

If your arcs don't cross then your compasses aren't wide enough – ensure they are open wider than half way.

Your compasses must be set to the same width when repeating at B.

Worked example

Draw the perpendicular from the dot though the line.

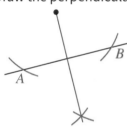

Put compasses on the dot. Draw two arcs on the line. Label the intersects A and B.

Put compasses at A. Draw an arc below the line.

Put compasses at B. Draw an arc below the line.

Draw the line from the dot through where the arcs meet.

Worked example

Use compasses to bisect the angle.

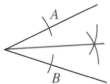

Put compasses on the vertex. Draw an arc on each line. Label the intersects A and B.

Put compasses at A. Draw an arc to the right of the angle.

Put compasses at B. Draw an arc to the right of the angle.

Draw the line from the angle through where the arcs meet.

⚙ Knowledge

25 Constructions, loci, and bearings

Loci

Loci are the sets of points that satisfy one or more given condtions.

The **locus of points** a fixed distance from a point is a circle.

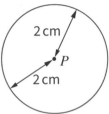

All the points that are 2 cm from P lie on the red circle.

The locus of points a fixed distance from a line.

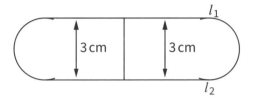

All the points that are 3 cm from l_1 lie on the red line, l_2.

The locus of points **equidistant** from two points is a perpendicular bisector of those two points.

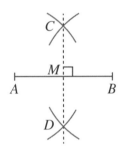

All the points that are equidistant from both A and B lie on the line CD.

The locus of points equidistant from two points is a perpendicular bisector of those two points.

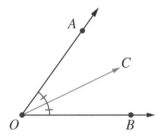

All the points that are **equidistant** from both OA and OB lie on the line OC.

Remember: **Equi**distance means 'the same distance'.

Worked example

Draw the locus of points that are 5 cm from the line AB.

Shade the region where the points are:

- less than 5 cm from the line AB, and
- closer to point B than point A.

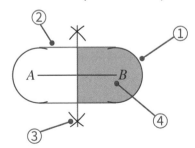

① Draw **semicircles** of radius 5 cm from each end of the line AB.

② Extend the arcs beyond the top and bottom points.

Draw parallel lines 5 cm either side of the line.

③ Draw the perpendicular bisector of the line AB.

④ Shade the part that is closer to B.

Bearings

A **compass** (not a pair of compasses!) shows the direction of magnetic north, east, south and west.

A **bearing** is a way to give a direction of travel.

Bearings are measured **clockwise** from north.

Bearings always have **three** figures; for example, a bearing of 3° is written as 003°.

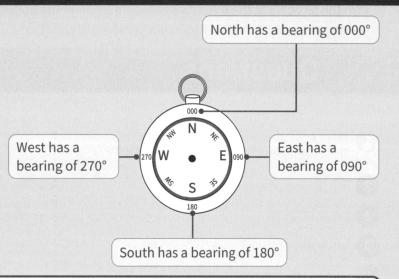

North has a bearing of 000°

West has a bearing of 270°

East has a bearing of 090°

South has a bearing of 180°

LINK

To remind yourself about measuring angles in degrees, look back at Chapter 18.

Worked example

A boat sails south-east from a rock.

1. What is the bearing of the boat from the rock?

   It helps to draw a diagram, like these.

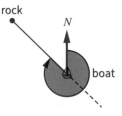

   rock ● - - - - - E

   boat
   SE

   $90 + 45 = 135°$ — You measure the bearing of the boat from the rock.

2. What is the bearing of the rock from the boat?

   rock

   N

   boat

   215° — You measure the bearing of the rock from the boat.

Retrieval

25 Constructions, loci and bearings

Learn the answers to the questions below, then cover the answers column with a piece of paper and write as many as you can. Check and repeat.

	Questions		Answers
1	What is the first step for drawing a perpendicular bisector of a line segment?	Put paper here	Put the point of the compasses at one end of the line. Open the compasses to more than half the length of the line. Draw arcs above and below it.
2	What are perpendicular lines?		Lines that cross at 90°.
3	What is the perpendicular distance?		The shortest distance from a point to a line.
4	What does bisect mean?	Put paper here	To cut in half.
5	What is the perpendicular bisector of an angle?		A line that cuts an angle in half.
6	What shape is the locus of points that are a fixed distance from a point?		A circle.
7	What direction are bearings measured in?	Put paper here	Clockwise from north.
8	What does the locus of points equidistant from two points look like?		The perpendicular bisector of the two points.
9	What are the four points of a compass?		North, east, south, west.
10	What is a compass used for?	Put paper here	To measure direction.
11	How many figures do bearings have?		Three.
12	What is the bearing of North?		000°
13	What is the bearing of West?		270°

Previous questions

Now go back and use these questions to check your knowledge of previous topics.

	Questions		Answers
1	What is a plan view of a 3D shape?		The view from directly above.
2	To simplify a ratio fully you divide all the numbers in the ratio by what?	Put paper here	The highest common factor (HCF) of the numbers.
3	What is a prism?		A 3D shape with a polygon base (it has straight sides) and a constant cross-sectional area.
4	What is the perimeter of a 2D shape?		The distance around the edges of a 2D shape.
5	What is a vertex?		Where sides or edges meet on a 2D or 3D shape.

Exam-style questions

25.1 Draw the locus of points that are exactly 2 cm from a point P.   **[2 marks]**

25.2 (a) Only one of these triangles can be constructed. Which one?

     A: A triangle with sides 7 cm, 8 cm and 16 cm

     B: A triangle with sides 3 cm, 4 cm and 6 cm

     C: A triangle with sides 9 cm, 12 cm and 22 cm

     D: A triangle with sides 15 cm, 30 cm and 60 cm   **[1 mark]**

(b) Using a ruler and a pair of compasses, construct the triangle you have chosen in part **a**.   **[2 marks]**

25.3 (a) Construct the perpendicular bisector of the line AB.

> **EXAM TIP**
> You must show your construction lines.

    [2 marks]

(b) Construct the bisector of angle CDE.

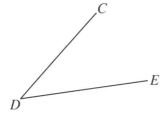

    [2 marks]

25.4 Draw this triangle accurately.

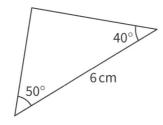

> **EXAM TIP**
> Start with the 6 cm side.

    [2 marks]

25.5 Construct a line perpendicular to FH, at the point G.

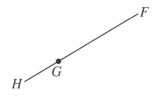

> **EXAM TIP**
> Start by drawing arcs either side of G.

    [3 marks]

Exam-style questions

25.6 Draw, accurately, triangle ABC with side lengths
$AB = 6.4\,$cm, $AC = 4.8\,$cm and angle $BAC = 120°$ **[3 marks]**

25.7 Here is a plan of a triangular field.

Rani uses the land that is:
closer to CD than CE and
less than 500 m from C.

> **EXAM TIP**
> You will need to draw a bisector and a circle. Remember to show your construction lines.

Show, by shading on the diagram, the region of land that Rani uses.

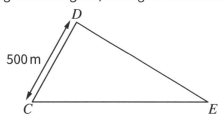

[4 marks]

25.8 The diagram shows two points, A and B, on a map.

(a) Find the bearing of B from A.

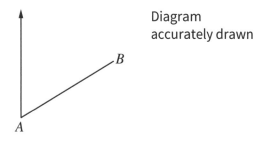

Diagram accurately drawn

[1 mark]

(b) Draw a line on a bearing of 110° from B. **[1 mark]**

25.9 The diagram shows two points, P and Q, on a map.

Work out the bearing of Q from P.

> **EXAM TIP**
> Remember that you want the **clockwise** angle.

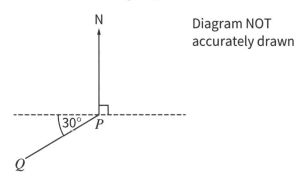

Diagram NOT accurately drawn

[2 marks]

25.10 The scale drawing shows the positions of two lifeboats, *A* and *B*.

A swimmer is
on a bearing of 040° from lifeboat *A*
and
on a bearing of 300° from lifeboat *B*.

Mark the position of the swimmer with a cross.

•
B

•
A

[3 marks]

Questions referring to previous content

25.11 Describe fully the **single** transformation that maps shape *A* onto shape *B*.

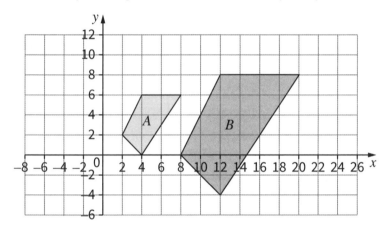

[3 marks]

25.12 *x*, *y* and *z* form a Pythagorean triple.

If *z* = 5 and *x* = 4 what is the value of *x*?

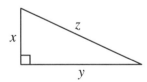

[1 mark]

⚙ Knowledge

26 Vectors

Vector notation

A **vector** is a way of describing movement.
Vectors have both direction and magnitude (size).

One way to write a vector is as a **column vector**. ●────────────●

Other notations for representing vectors include:

An arrow	**A bold letter**	**An underlined letter**
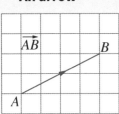	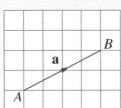	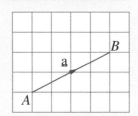

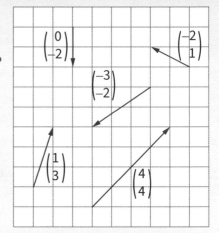

In the example above, the vector $\overrightarrow{BA}$ could be written as $-\mathbf{a}$ or $-\underline{a}$.
It is a parallel vector of the same length but opposite direction.

LINK 🔗

You revised translations of shapes
using column vectors in Chapter 23.
The top number tells you how far
right or left the shape moves, and the
bottom number tells you how far up
or down it moves.

Multiplying a vector by a scalar

A **scalar** is a quantity with just size. A number is a scalar.

Scalars can be used as scale factors or multipliers.

To multiply column vectors by a scalar, multiply the top and bottom values by the number.

For example:

$$3\begin{pmatrix} -1 \\ 8 \end{pmatrix} = \begin{pmatrix} 3 \times -1 \\ 3 \times 8 \end{pmatrix} = \begin{pmatrix} -3 \\ 24 \end{pmatrix}$$

Worked example

$\mathbf{a} = \begin{pmatrix} 2 \\ 3 \end{pmatrix}$. Using this information, draw $\mathbf{a}$ and $2\mathbf{a}$ on a grid.

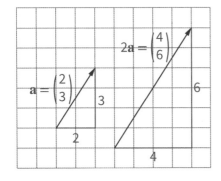

2 is a scalar. It only has magnitude
(size).

$$2\mathbf{a} = 2\begin{pmatrix} 2 \\ 3 \end{pmatrix} = \begin{pmatrix} 2 \times 2 \\ 2 \times 3 \end{pmatrix} = \begin{pmatrix} 4 \\ 6 \end{pmatrix}$$

$\mathbf{a}$ is a vector. It has both direction
and magnitude.

Notice how $\mathbf{a}$ and $2\mathbf{a}$ are parallel.

Adding and subtracting vectors

To add column vectors, add the top values and then add the bottom values.
For example:

$$\begin{pmatrix} 4 \\ -3 \end{pmatrix} + \begin{pmatrix} 2 \\ 7 \end{pmatrix} = \begin{pmatrix} 4+2 \\ -3+7 \end{pmatrix} = \begin{pmatrix} 6 \\ 4 \end{pmatrix}$$

You can show this on a grid.

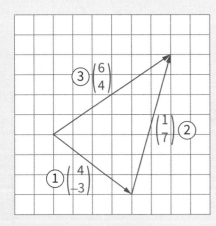

①   Draw $\begin{pmatrix} 4 \\ -3 \end{pmatrix}$.

②   The end of $\begin{pmatrix} 4 \\ -3 \end{pmatrix}$ becomes the start point for $\begin{pmatrix} 2 \\ 7 \end{pmatrix}$.

③   The vector sum $\begin{pmatrix} 6 \\ 4 \end{pmatrix}$ is the single vector which takes you directly from the starting point to the finishing point.

Worked example

$\mathbf{a} = \begin{pmatrix} 4 \\ -2 \end{pmatrix}$ and $\mathbf{b} = \begin{pmatrix} -5 \\ 0 \end{pmatrix}$.

Use this information to

1. work out the column vectors

    $\mathbf{a} + \mathbf{b}$ and $2\mathbf{b} - \mathbf{a}$

$$\mathbf{a} + \mathbf{b} = \begin{pmatrix} 4 \\ -2 \end{pmatrix} + \begin{pmatrix} -5 \\ 0 \end{pmatrix}$$

$$= \begin{pmatrix} 4-5 \\ -2+0 \end{pmatrix}$$

$$= \begin{pmatrix} -1 \\ -2 \end{pmatrix}$$

$$2\mathbf{b} - \mathbf{a} = 2\begin{pmatrix} -5 \\ 0 \end{pmatrix} - \begin{pmatrix} 4 \\ -2 \end{pmatrix}$$

$$= \begin{pmatrix} -10 \\ 0 \end{pmatrix} - \begin{pmatrix} 4 \\ -2 \end{pmatrix}$$

$$= \begin{pmatrix} -10-4 \\ 0-(-2) \end{pmatrix}$$

$$= \begin{pmatrix} -14 \\ 2 \end{pmatrix}$$

2. show the vectors $\mathbf{a}$, $\mathbf{b}$ and $\mathbf{a} + \mathbf{b}$ on a square grid.

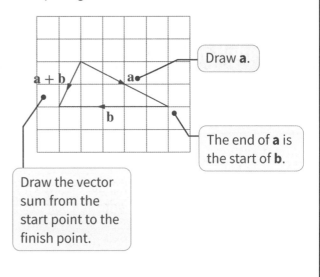

Draw $\mathbf{a}$.

The end of $\mathbf{a}$ is the start of $\mathbf{b}$.

Draw the vector sum from the start point to the finish point.

Knowledge

26 Vectors

Parallel vectors

On this diagram, vector $\overrightarrow{CD}$ is also **a** as it has the same size and direction as the vector $\overrightarrow{AB}$.

Two vectors are **parallel** if one is a multiple of another.

The vector $-\mathbf{a}$ is the same size as **a** and parallel to **a** because it is $-1 \times \mathbf{a}$, but it is in the opposite direction to **a**.

A vector that is parallel to **a** but a different length will be a multiple of **a**, such as $2\mathbf{a}$.

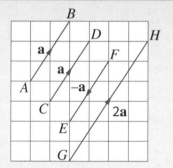

Worked example

$OABC$ is a parallelogram.

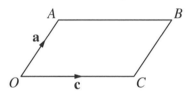

> **REVISION TIP**
>
> If two vectors are parallel, one is a multiple of the other.

> **REVISION TIP**
>
> Remember to underline the letter if you write vectors by hand.

$\overrightarrow{OA} = \mathbf{a}$ and $\overrightarrow{OC} = \mathbf{c}$

Write down these vectors in terms of **a** and **c**

$\overrightarrow{CO} \quad = -\underline{c}$ •————— it is parallel to $\overrightarrow{OC}$ but in the opposite direction.

$\overrightarrow{OB} \quad = \overrightarrow{OA} + \overrightarrow{AB} = \underline{a} + \underline{c}$

$\overrightarrow{AC} \quad = \overrightarrow{AO} + \overrightarrow{OC} = -\underline{a} + \underline{c}$ •————— you could write $\underline{c} - \underline{a}$, the order doesn't matter.

Using simultaneous equations

You can form a pair of simultaneous equations to solve for x and y.

Worked example

$4\begin{pmatrix} x \\ 1 \end{pmatrix} = \begin{pmatrix} -y \\ 2x \end{pmatrix}$ Work out the values of x and y.

$4x = -y \; ① \;$ •————— Equate the top components and bottom components, and write as a pair of simultaneous equations.

$4 = 2x \; ②$

$\dfrac{4}{2} = \dfrac{2x}{2} \Rightarrow x = 2 \;$ •————— From ②

$4 \times 2 = -y \Rightarrow y = -8 \;$ •————— Substitute $x = 2$ in ①

$x = 2, y = -8$

> **Key terms** Make sure you can write a definition for these key terms
>
> column vector   parallel   scalar   vector

26 Vectors

Learn the answers to the questions below, then cover the answers column with a piece of paper and write as many as you can. Check and repeat.

Questions	Answers
1 What is a vector used for?	To describe movement from one point to another.
2 What other way can the vector **a** be written?	a̲.
3 How do you know when vectors are parallel?	They are multiples of each other.
4 What do you know about the relationship between **a** and −**a**?	−**a** is the same size as **a** and is parallel to **a**, but is in the opposite direction.
5 What do you know about the relationship between **a** and 2**a**?	2**a** is parallel and in the same direction as **a**, but it is twice as long.
6 What does the top value in a column vector tell you?	How far to move right (+ve) or left (−ve).
7 What does the bottom value in a column vector tell you?	How far to move up (+ve) or down (−ve).
8 How do you add column vectors?	Add the top values together and add the bottom values together.
9 How do you multiply a column vector by a number?	Multiply both the top and bottom values by the number.
10 How can you represent 3**a** on a grid?	3**a** is three lots of the vector **a** drawn end to end.

Put paper here

Previous questions

Now go back and use these questions to check your knowledge of previous topics.

Questions	Answers
1 What are the four types of transformation?	Reflection, rotation, translation, enlargement.
2 What does $a \propto b$ mean?	a is proportional to b.
3 What is the value of tan 45?	1
4 When you translate a shape, are the object and the image similar or congruent?	Congruent.
5 What is the formula used to find the circumference of a circle?	$2\pi r$ or πd

Put paper here

Practice

26.1 Write the column vectors representing **f**, **g** and **h**.

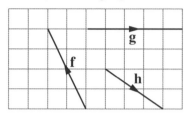

[3 marks]

26.2 (a) On the grid below, draw the vector $\begin{pmatrix} 3 \\ -4 \end{pmatrix}$.

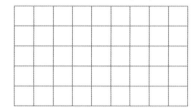

[1 mark]

(b) Write down the column vector in the
opposite direction to $\begin{pmatrix} 3 \\ -4 \end{pmatrix}$.

[1 mark]

26.3 Here is vector **a** drawn on a grid.

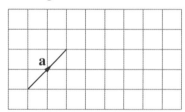

On the same grid, draw and label the vector −2**a**.

[1 mark]

26.4 Here is vector **b** drawn on a grid.

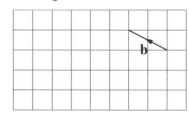

> **EXAM TIP**
>
> Write down a column vector
> for **b** first.

Write a column vector that is parallel to **b** and three times its length. **[2 marks]**

26.5 $\mathbf{p} = \begin{pmatrix} 4 \\ 3 \end{pmatrix}$ $\mathbf{q} = \begin{pmatrix} 2 \\ -5 \end{pmatrix}$

Draw a triangle of vectors representing:

$\mathbf{p}, \mathbf{q}$ and $\mathbf{p} + \mathbf{q}$

EXAM TIP

Remember to draw an arrow on each vector to indicate its direction.

[4 marks]

26.6 *ABCD* is a rectangle.

Write the column vector that represents $\overrightarrow{OC}$.

EXAM TIP

Draw point *C* on the grid and use this to help you.

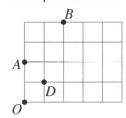

[2 marks]

26.7 **(a)** The vector $\overrightarrow{OA} = \mathbf{a}$

Write down a vector that is parallel to $\overrightarrow{OA}$ and three times as long as $\overrightarrow{OA}$. **[1 mark]**

(b) The vector $\overrightarrow{OB} = \mathbf{b}$

Write down a vector that is parallel to $\overrightarrow{OB}$, the same length as OB, and in the opposite direction to $\overrightarrow{OB}$. **[1 mark]**

26.8 *OPQR* is a rhombus.

$\overrightarrow{OP} = \mathbf{p}$
$\overrightarrow{OR} = \mathbf{r}$

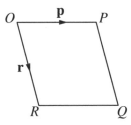

Write these vectors in terms of $\mathbf{p}$ and $\mathbf{r}$.

(a) $\overrightarrow{PO}$ **[1 mark]**

(b) $\overrightarrow{OP} + \overrightarrow{PQ}$ **[1 mark]**

(c) $\overrightarrow{QO}$ **[2 marks]**

Exam-style questions

26.9 $n = \begin{pmatrix} -2 \\ 3 \end{pmatrix}$ $m = \begin{pmatrix} -1 \\ 4 \end{pmatrix}$

Find as a column vector

(a)   4n   [1 mark]

(b)   n + m   [1 mark]

(c)   2m − 3n   [2 marks]

EXAM TIP

Write the top and bottom of the vectors as separate equations.

26.10 $2 \begin{pmatrix} -x \\ 3 \end{pmatrix} = \begin{pmatrix} y \\ x \end{pmatrix}$

Work out the value of x and the value of y.   [4 marks]

26.11 *PQRSTU* is a regular hexagon.

$\overrightarrow{OP} = 2a$

$\overrightarrow{OQ} = 3b$

EXAM TIP

A regular hexagon is made from six equilateral triangles.

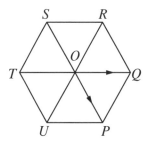

Write these vectors in terms of **a** and **b**.

(a) $\overrightarrow{OT}$ [1 mark]

(b) $\overrightarrow{PQ}$ [2 marks]

(c) $\overrightarrow{OU}$ [2 marks]

(d) $\overrightarrow{UQ}$ [3 marks]

Questions referring to previous content

26.12 Write down the value of

(a)   sin 0°.   [1 mark]

(b)   sin 60°.   [1 mark]

(c)   cos 45°.   [1 mark]

(d)   tan 30°.   [1 mark]

26.13 Describe the single transformation that maps
shape A onto to shape B.

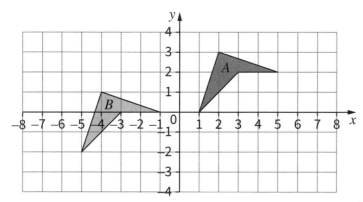

[2 marks]

⚙ Knowledge

27 Theoretical probability, mutually exclusive events, possibility spaces, and probability experiments

Theoretical probability

Probability is the likelihood that something will happen. It is always a value between 0 and 1.

Probabilities can be written as fractions, decimals or percentages.

A **theoretical probability**, written as P(event), is the probability that an event will happen.

If all possible outcomes are equally likely, then the theoretical probability is defined as:

$$\text{probability of an event happening} = \frac{\text{number of ways the event can happen}}{\text{total number of possible outcomes}}$$

The probability scale

LINK

To remind yourself about fractions, decimals and percentages, look back at Chapter 4.

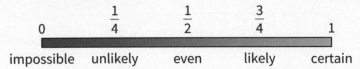

0	$\frac{1}{4}$	$\frac{1}{2}$	$\frac{3}{4}$	1
impossible	unlikely	even	likely	certain

Worked example

Saeed has a pack of 10 cards showing the numbers 1 to 10.
He selects one at random. Write down the probability it is:

1. a 5

   $P(5) = \frac{1}{10}$ •————— There are 10 cards and one of them is a 5.

2. an odd number

   $P(\text{odd}) = \frac{5}{10} = \frac{1}{2}$ •————— Five of the cards have an odd number.

   WATCH OUT ⊘

   If a question uses the terms 'less than' or 'more than', do **not** include the number itself.

3. less than 8.

   $P(\text{less than 8}) = \frac{7}{10}$ •————— Seven of the numbers are less than 8.

Mutually exclusive events

Mutually exclusive events are events that can't happen at the same time.

For example, a number cannot be both odd and even.

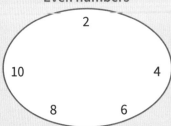

Odd numbers   Even numbers

The probabilities of all possible mutually exclusive outcomes must add up to 1.

P(event happening) = 1 − P(event not happening)

Mutually exclusive events

Each card in a pack shows a shape that may be a triangle, a square, a pentagon or a hexagon.

The probability of selecting a pentagon is the same as the probability of selecting a hexagon.

Complete the table.

Shape	triangle	square	pentagon	hexagon
Probability	0.38	0.26	0.18	0.18

The four probabilities must add up to 1.

$1 - (0.38 + 0.26) = 0.36$

$P(\text{pentagon}) = P(\text{hexagon}) = \dfrac{0.36}{2} = 0.18$

Possibility spaces

A **sample space** (sometimes called a possibility space) is a list of all the possible outcomes of two events.

Suppose a coin is flipped and a card is drawn from a pack.

- The coin can be heads (**H**) or tails (**T**).
- The card can be red (**R**) or black (**B**).

You can write this

- as a systematic list (**HR, HB, TR, TB**)
- in a two-way table:

Card

Coin		B	R
	H	HB	HR
	T	TB	TR

Worked example

At a sandwich shop, you can choose white or brown bread, cheese or ham, and salad or no salad. Write your choices as a systematic list.

W, C, S
W, C, NS
W, H, S
W, H, NS
B, C, S
B, C, NS
B, H, S
B, H, NS

Abbreviate each outcome: W, B, C, S, NS
Write a list, changing one option at a time.

Worked example

A four-sided dice and a six-sided dice are rolled and results added together.

Draw a two-way table to show the outcomes.

six-sided dice

four-sided dice	1	2	3	4	5	6
1	2	3	4	5	6	7
2	3	4	5	6	7	8
3	4	5	6	7	8	9
4	5	6	7	8	9	10

result of the four-sided dice = 2
result of the six-sided dice = 3
2 + 3 = 5

⚙ Knowledge

27 Theoretical probability, mutually exclusive events, possibility spaces, and probability experiments

Frequency trees

Frequency trees show the outcomes of two or more events, and the frequencies with which they occur.

Worked example

This frequency tree shows the numbers of dogs and cats in a sample that have been microchipped.

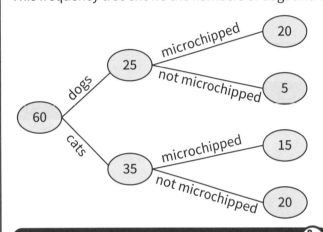

1. A cat or dog is chosen at random. What is the probability it has been microchipped?

   $\frac{35}{60} = \frac{7}{12}$

   Total of microchipped cats and dogs = 20 + 15 = 35.

2. A dog is chosen at random. What is the probability it has not been microchipped?

   $\frac{5}{25} = \frac{1}{5}$

   You only need to consider the 25 dogs. 5 of them have not been microchipped.

LINK 🔗

In Chapter 28 you will meet tree diagrams, which show the probability on the branches rather than the frequencies.

Probability experiments

If you do not know the probability of an event you can estimate probability from a **probability experiment** by finding the **relative frequency**.

$$\text{relative frequency} = \frac{\text{number of times the event happened}}{\text{total number of trials}}$$

The more trials in the experiment, the more accurate the estimate of the probability.

REVISION TIP 📝

By increasing the number of times you repeat an experiment you can get a better estimate for the real probability. This is because, with more repeats, the relative frequency gets closer and closer to the real probability.

Worked example

Jamie has an unfair dice.

He rolls the dice 60 times and scores a 5 on 20 rolls. Estimate the probability of rolling 5 on Jamie's dice.

$$\text{estimate for P(5)} = \frac{\text{number of 5s Jamie rolled}}{\text{total number of rolls}}$$
$$= \frac{20}{60}$$
$$= \frac{1}{3}$$

Key terms Make sure you can write a definition for these key terms

frequency tree   mutually exclusive events   possibility space
probability   probability experiment   relative frequency
theoretical probability

27 Theoretical probability, mutually exclusive events, possibility spaces, and probability experiments

Learn the answers to the questions below, then cover the answers column with a piece of paper and write as many as you can. Check and repeat.

Questions | Answers

	Questions	Answers
1	What does probability tell us?	How likely an event is to happen.
2	What range of values can probability take?	Any value between 0 and 1.
3	If two possible outcomes are equally likely, what is the probability of each event happening?	$\frac{1}{2}$
4	What do probabilities that are mutually exclusive add up to?	1
5	What is significant about mutually exclusive events?	They cannot both happen at the same time.
6	Name two ways a possibility space can be represented.	A systematic list or a two-way table.
7	What is the estimated probability of an event, calculated from an experiment, called?	Relative frequency.
8	How can you improve the accuracy of an estimate of the probability?	Increase the number of trials.
9	What check should you do with a frequency tree?	Check the numbers on the final branches add up to the total at the start.
10	What is an unfair dice?	A dice on which the probability of obtaining each outcome is not equal.

Put paper here

Previous questions

Now go back and use these questions to check your knowledge of previous topics.

Questions | Answers

	Questions	Answers
1	What would a graph showing direct proportion look like?	A straight line through the origin.
2	What is inverse proportion?	If two values are in inverse proportion, then one will increase while the other decreases at the same rate. For example, if one doubles, the other halves.
3	What is a reflex angle?	An angle that is greater than 180° but less than 360°.
4	What is a 9-sided polygon called?	A nonagon.
5	Why is a cylinder not a prism?	Because a circle is not a polygon.

Put paper here

⬤ Practice

Exam-style questions

 27.1 In a bag of sweets, 20 are purple, 16 are green, 24 are red, and 20 are black.

   (a)   A sweet is picked at random.

   Work out the probability that the sweet is red.   **[1 mark]**

   (b)   A sample of 20 sweets are picked at random.

   Work out the expected number of red sweets in this sample.   **[1 mark]**

 27.2 The probability of a report being submitted on time is 0.85.

   (a)   Out of 60 reports, how many would you expect to be submitted on time?   **[1 mark]**

   (b)   Out of 170 reports, 160 are submitted on time.

   Is this more or fewer than you would have expected?
   Explain your answer.   **[2 marks]**

 27.3 An fair 8-sided dice has the numbers 1, 2, 2, 3, 3, 4, 4 and 4 on its faces.

   (a)   The dice is thrown once.

   Write down the probability that it lands on 4.   **[1 mark]**

   (b)   Seren is going to throw the dice 40 times.

   Work out an estimate for the number of times it will land on 3.   **[2 marks]**

27.4 An ordinary fair dice is thrown.
Write down the probability of

   (a)   throwing a 1   **[1 mark]**

   (b)   throwing an odd number   **[1 mark]**

   (c)   throwing a 3 or a 5.   **[1 mark]**

27.5 This spinner has eight equal sections.

This probability scale shows the probability of three events, A, B and C.

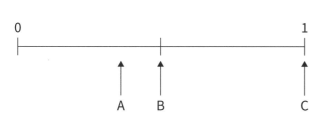

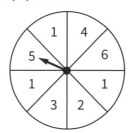

Write the letter of each event next to its description.

(a) The spinner lands on a multiple of 2. [1 mark]

(b) The spinner lands on an integer. [1 mark]

(c) The spinner lands on a number greater than 2. [1 mark]

27.6 A bag contains only blue balls and red balls.

The ratio of blue balls to red balls is $1:2$.

Dayo takes a ball at random from the bag.

Find the probability that Dayo takes a red ball. [1 mark]

27.7 Here are five letter cards.

One of the cards is chosen at random.

$P(S) = 0.2$

$P(S \text{ or } A) = 0.6$

(a) Write the missing letter on the blank card. [1 mark]

(b) One of the five cards is chosen at random.
What is the probability that the letter on this
card is in the word PASTA? [1 mark]

27.8 Two people play a game.

The probability of winning the game is x.

The probability of losing the game is $x + \dfrac{1}{2}$.

The game cannot end in a draw.

Work out the value of x. [2 marks]

27.9 The probability that it will snow today is 0.1.

What is the probability that it will **not** snow today? [1 mark]

27.10 In a prize draw, raffle tickets are numbered 1 to 50.

Write down the probability that the winning ticket number

(a)   is 39   **[1 mark]**

(b)   is **not** a multiple of 8.   **[2 marks]**

27.11 There are only white, yellow, pink and orange counters in a bag.

The table shows the probabilities of taking at random a white, yellow or pink counter from the bag.   **[2 marks]**

Colour	White	Yellow	Pink	Orange
Probability	0.3	0.15	0.26	

(a)   Complete the table.

(b)   A counter is taken at random from the bag.

What is the probability that the counter is not white or pink?   **[2 marks]**

(c)   There are 200 counters in the bag.

Work out how many of the counters are yellow.   **[2 marks]**

27.12 Here are two 4-sided spinners.

Each spinner is spun once and their scores are added together.

(a)   Complete the possibility space grid.

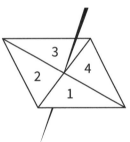

                                                                               [2 marks]

(b)   Work out the probability that the total is less than 4.   **[1 mark]**

27.13 40 people took a driving test.

16 of these people wore glasses.

15 people without glasses failed.

16 people passed.

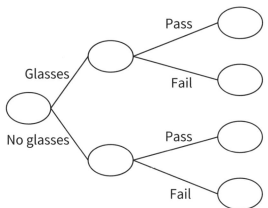

(a) Use this information to complete the frequency tree. **[2 marks]**

(b) One of the people is chosen at random.
Find the probability that this person wore glasses and
passed the test. **[1 mark]**

(c) One of the people who failed is chosen at random.
Find the probability that this person wore glasses.

 27.14 When a drawing pin is dropped it can land point down or point up.

(a) Sheena drops a drawing pin 50 times and records some of the results.

Complete the table.

	Point up	Point down
Frequency	35	
Relative frequency		0.3

[2 marks]

(b) Sheena drops the drawing pin 100 more times.

It lands point up 60 times.

Mark is going to drop the drawing pin once.

Use all Sheena's results to work out an estimate for
the probability that the drawing pin will land point down. **[1 mark]**

Questions referring to previous content

 27.15 Solve

    (a) $2x + 4 = 9$ **[2 marks]**

    (b) $19 = 3y - 2$ **[2 marks]**

    (c) $-4 = 5q + 6n$ **[2 marks]**

 27.16 Work out the sum of the interior angles of an octagon. **[2 marks]**

Knowledge

Expected results

The **expected frequency** of an event is the number of times you expect it to happen.

expected frequency = probability × number of trials

Worked example

The probability that a person is left-handed is estimated to be 9%.

There are 780 students in a school.

Estimate how many are left-handed.

expected frequency = probability × number of trials

$$= 0.09 \times 780$$
$$= 70.2$$

About 70 students are left-handed.

> Round the final answer, as the number of students must be a whole number.

Worked example

Miles rolls a dice 200 times and gets a 6 on 30 rolls. He claims this means the dice is biased. Explain whether or not you think Miles is correct.

expected frequency = probability × number of trials

$$= \frac{1}{6} \times 200 = 33.333...$$

This is close to the actual result of 30, so Miles is wrong; the dice appears to be fair.

> With a fair dice, the probability of a 6 is $\frac{1}{6}$.

> **REVISION TIP**
>
> An unfair coin or spinner or dice is said to be **biased**.

Tree diagrams

A **tree diagram** helps you to calculate the probability of two or more events.
For example, if you toss a coin two times:

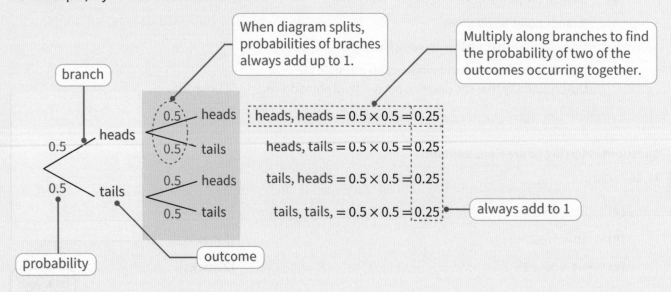

When diagram splits, probabilities of braches always add up to 1.

Multiply along branches to find the probability of two of the outcomes occurring together.

branch

0.5 heads
0.5 — heads   heads, heads = 0.5 × 0.5 = 0.25
0.5 — tails   heads, tails = 0.5 × 0.5 = 0.25
0.5 tails
0.5 — heads   tails, heads = 0.5 × 0.5 = 0.25
0.5 — tails   tails, tails, = 0.5 × 0.5 = 0.25   always add to 1

probability

outcome

Tree diagrams

Worked example

A bag contains two black, four-sided dice, and four red, six-sided dice. Tam picks a dice randomly and rolls it. The tree diagram shows the probabilities.

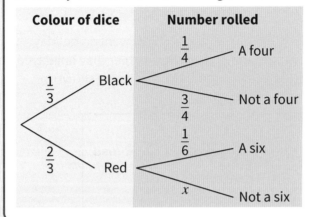

1. Work out the value of x.

$$x = 1 - \frac{1}{6} = \frac{5}{6}$$

> Probabilities on each set of branches must add up to 1.

2. Work out the probability of picking a black dice and rolling a 4.

$$P(\text{black dice and 4}) = \frac{1}{3} \times \frac{1}{4} = \frac{1}{12}$$

> Multiply along the branches.

Set notation and Venn diagrams

A set is a collection of numbers, letters or objects. You need to know some notation to describe sets.

- The symbol ξ means the **universal set**.

- You can describe a set using curly brackets; for example, {1, 2, 3, 4} or {odd numbers}.

- $x \in A$ means x is a **member** of the set A.

- $A \cap B$ means the **intersection** of sets A and B (numbers in **both** sets).

- $A \cup B$ means the **union** of sets A and B (numbers in **either** set).

- A' means the **complement** of set A (numbers **not** in set A).

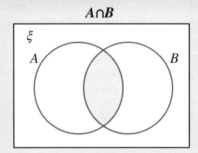

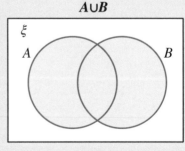

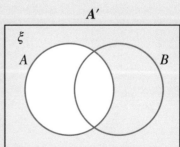

Knowledge

28 Expected results, tree diagrams, set notation, and probability from tables and diagrams

Set notation and Venn diagrams

Worked example

$\xi = \{1,2,3,4,5,6,7,8,9,10\}$

$A = \{\text{odd numbers}\}$

$B = \{\text{prime numbers}\}$

1. Draw a **Venn diagram** to show this information.

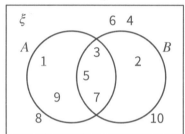

2. Write down the numbers that are in set $A \cap B$

   $A \cap B$ means the intersection of sets A and B.

   3, 5 and 7

Worked example

60 families were asked if they went on holiday last year and, if they did, whether they holidayed in the UK or abroad. The results are shown in the Venn diagram.

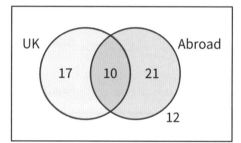

Work out the probability that a randomly chosen family

1. went abroad on holiday

   $P(\text{abroad}) = \dfrac{10 + 21}{60} = \dfrac{31}{60}$

2. didn't go on holiday

   $P(\text{no holiday}) = \dfrac{12}{60} = \dfrac{1}{5}$

3. went on holiday in both the UK and abroad.

   $P(\text{UK and abroad}) = \dfrac{10}{60} = \dfrac{1}{6}$

 Key terms — Make sure you can write a definition for these key terms

biased   complement   expected frequency   intersection
member   tree diagram   union   universal set   Venn diagram

28 Expected results, tree diagrams, set notation, and probability from tables and diagrams

Learn the answers to the questions below, then cover the answers column with a piece of paper and write as many as you can. Check and repeat.

Questions		Answers
1	What is the expected frequency of an event?	The number of times you expect the event to happen.
2	What is the formula used to find the expected frequency of the event?	Expected frequency = probability of the event occurring × number of trials.
3	In probability, what does biased mean?	Unfair.
4	Why might we use a probability tree diagram?	To calculate the probability of two or more events.
5	What calculation is made along the branches of a probability tree diagram?	Multiplication.
6	What do the probabilities on each set of branches add up to?	1
7	What is the symbol for the universal set?	ξ
8	What does $A \cap B$ mean?	A and B; the intersection of the Venn diagram.

Put paper here

Previous questions

Now go back and use these questions to check your knowledge of previous topics.

Questions		Answers
1	What do the exterior angles of any polygon add up to?	360°
2	How many vertices does a cuboid have?	8
3	What is a compound shape?	A shape made up of two or more simpler shapes.
4	What is a line that touches the circumference of a circle in exactly one point called?	A tangent.
5	What does it mean for two shapes to be similar?	They are the same shape but not the same size.

Put paper here

Practice

Exam-style questions

28.1 A baseball player has two attempts to hit each ball.
The tree diagram shows the probabilities.

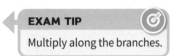

EXAM TIP

Multiply along the branches.

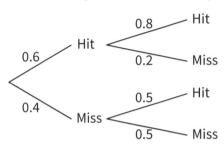

Work out the probability that the player misses on both attempts. **[2 marks]**

28.2 Maryam plays one game of tennis and one game of chess.

The probability that Maryam will win at tennis is $\frac{2}{3}$.

The probability that Maryam will win at chess is $\frac{5}{8}$.

(a) Complete the probability tree diagram.

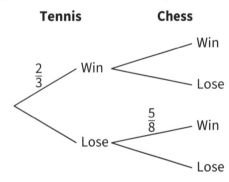

[2 marks]

(b) Work out the probability that Maryam wins both games. **[2 marks]**

28.3 60 people were asked if they read fiction or non-fiction books.

20 people read only non-fiction.

5 people do not read fiction or non-fiction.

28 people read only fiction.

Complete the Venn diagram.

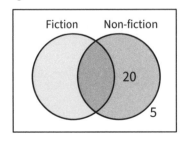

[2 marks]

28.4 There are 79 students in a college.

44 study art.

12 study both art and music.

11 don't study either.

Complete the Venn diagram.

EXAM TIP
Fill in the intersection first.

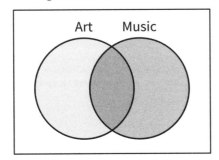

[4 marks]

28.5 In the Venn diagram, $A \cap B = \{7, 9\}$

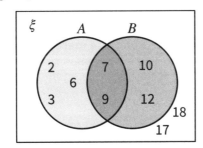

Write the numbers that are in the set

(a) $A \cup B$ [1 mark]

(b) A' [1 mark]

28.6 Here are some squares and circles.

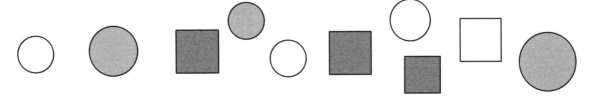

(a) Complete the two-way table.

	Grey	White	Total
Circle			6
Square	3		
Total		4	

[3 marks]

(b) One of the shapes is chosen at random.
Work out the probability that it is white. [1 mark]

28.7 $\xi = \{1, 2, 4, 8, 16, 25, 27, 64\}$, $A = \{$square numbers$\}$, $B = \{$cube numbers$\}$

    (a)   Draw a Venn diagram to show this information.   **[4 marks]**

    (b)   Write the numbers that are in the set $A \cap B$.   **[1 mark]**

28.8 A total of 35 snooker and darts players are rated in ability as either good or average.

    10 of the 14 snooker players are rated as average, whereas 12 players are rated good in either snooker or darts.

    (a)   Construct a two-way table to show this information.   **[4 marks]**

    (b)   One of the players is chosen at random.

        Write the probability that they are a snooker player who is rated as good.   **[1 mark]**

> **EXAM TIP**
>
> Check all row and column totals.

28.9 $\xi = \{1, 2, 3, 5, 6, 9, 10, 11, 17, 21, 25\}$, $P = \{$prime numbers$\}$, $G = \{$numbers greater than 10$\}$

    (a)   Draw a Venn diagram for this information.   **[4 marks]**

    (b)   One of the numbers in the diagram is chosen at random.

        Find the probability that the number is in:

        (i)   set $P \cap G$ **[1 mark]**

        (ii)   set G' **[1 mark]**

        (iii)   set P only.   **[1 mark]**

Questions referring to previous content

28.10 Jason can either win or lose a game.

    (a)   Jason plays the game three times.

           Complete this list of possible outcomes.   **[2 marks]**

    (b)   For each game P(win) = P(lose).

           Work out the probability that he wins at least one
           of the games.   **[2 marks]**

 28.11 Work out $\dfrac{1.6 + (-0.35)}{3.27 - (-1.3)}$.

    Give your answer correct to 2 decimal places.   **[2 marks]**

29 Tables, charts, and graphs

Types of data

	Definition	Example
Data	Any information you can collect.	The heights of people who live in London.
Quantitative data	Numerical data; a quantity or amount.	The number of students in a class.
Qualitative (or categorical) data	Non-numerical data; a quality or characteristic.	The colour of a person's hair.
Discrete data	Data that can only take specific values or numbers	The number of pets people own.
Continuous data	Data that can take any value.	The heights of trees in an orchard.
Primary data	Data that you collect yourself.	Favourite ice cream flavours of students in your class.
Secondary data	Data that someone else collected.	The number of castles in England in 1600.

Frequency tables

The total number of times something happened is called the **frequency**.

Frequency tables are used to collect **data**.

Ungrouped frequency tables are suitable for **discrete data**, such as the number of days it rained each week over a period of 11 weeks.

Days it rained	Frequency
0	2
1	③
2	5
3	1

> This means that there were three weeks where it only rained on one day.

Grouped frequency tables are used for **continuous data**, such as height.

> Notice the groups do not need to be the same width.
>
> $127 \leq h < 135$ is 8 cm wide, but $135 \leq h < 150$ is 15 cm wide.

Height (cm)	Frequency
$120 \leq h < 127$	④
$127 \leq h < 135$	7
$135 \leq h < 150$	12

> This means there were four people whose heights were between 120 cm and 127 cm.

Two-way tables

You can use a **two-way table** to organise data into two categories. For example, the number of students in different year groups and their favourite sport.

	Year 10	Year 11	TOTAL
Football	50	41	**90**
Hockey	46	⑤52	**98**
Tennis	37	49	**86**
TOTAL	**133**	**142**	**275**

> This shows that hockey is the favourite sport for 52 students in Year 11.

Bar charts

Bar charts are used for qualitative (categorical) data.

In a **bar chart**, the height of each bar shows the frequency. A **vertical line chart** uses lines instead of bars.

When drawing a bar chart

- label both axes

- make sure bars are the same width

- leave an equal gap between the bars.

Dual bar charts show two sets of data on the same bar chart.

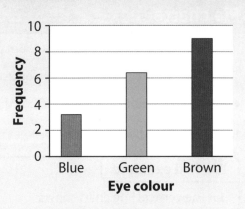

Worked example

The dual bar chart shows the average number of different drinks sold per day at a café. What is the most popular drink on weekdays?

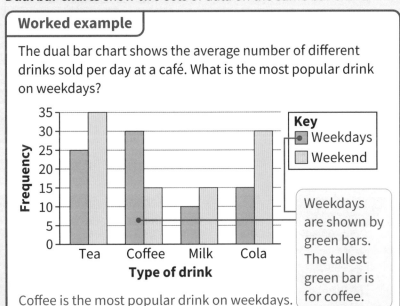

Key
- Weekdays
- Weekend

Weekdays are shown by green bars. The tallest green bar is for coffee.

Coffee is the most popular drink on weekdays.

The same data can be shown on a **composite bar chart**.

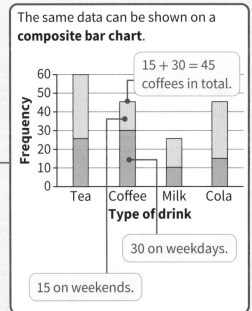

15 + 30 = 45 coffees in total.

30 on weekdays.

15 on weekends.

Pictograms

Pictograms are used for **qualitative data**. They use images to represent the data. For example, you could represent eye colour with a pictogram that uses pictures of eyes.

Eye colour	Number of children
Brown	◉ ◉ ◉ ◉
Hazel	◉ ◉ ◉
Blue	◉ ◉ ◉
Green	◉ ◉ ◉ ◉

Key
◉ = 4 Children

Remember to add a key and use pictures that are simple to draw.

Line graphs

Line graphs (or time-series graphs) show how data change over time. Time is always on the horizontal axis. For example, the average temperature for each month for a year.

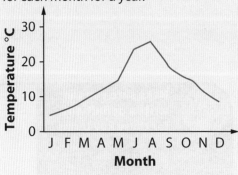

Pie charts

In a **pie chart**, the frequency or amount of something is shown as a sector of a circle.

There are two main things you can be asked with a pie chart.

- Draw a pie chart (this may be using data from different type of chart).

- Work out values from a pie chart.

Worked example

1. The vertical line chart shows the reasons for staff absence at a school.

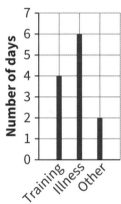

Reason for absence

Draw a pie chart to show this data.

$\text{Total} = 4 + 6 + 2 = 12$ ●————— Find the total number of days of absence.

$\text{Proportion} = \dfrac{4}{12} = \dfrac{1}{3}$ ●————— Find the proportion of absence days caused by training.

$\text{Angle of sector } \dfrac{1}{3} \times 360$
$= 120°$

The angles of all sectors in a circle always add up to 360°.

Repeat to find the angles for 'Illness' and 'Other', and draw the pie chart.

Key
- ■ Training
- ■ Illness
- ■ Other

Remember to add a key.

2. A greengrocer has 81 pieces of fruit. He records the number of apples, bananas and pears.

   He draws a pie chart to show the results. Calculate how many apples there were.

   $\dfrac{a}{81} = \dfrac{160}{360} = \dfrac{4}{9}$ ●—————

   Use equivalent fractions.

   $\dfrac{\text{number of apples, } a}{\text{total pieces of fruit}} = \dfrac{\text{angle for apples}}{\text{total angle in circle}}$

   $a = \dfrac{4 \times 81}{9} = 36$ apples

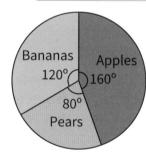

Key terms

Make sure you can write a definition for these key terms

bar chart   continuous data   data   discrete data
dual bar chart   frequency   frequency table   grouped
line graph   pictogram   pie chart   primary data
qualitative data   quantitative data   secondary data
two-way table   ungroupedvertical line chart

29 Tables, charts, and graphs

Learn the answers to the questions below, then cover the answers column with a piece of paper and write as many as you can. Check and repeat.

Questions	Answers
1 What is quantitative data?	Numerical data.
2 What is qualitative data?	Non-numerical; a quality that describes something.
3 Is hair colour quantitative or qualitative?	Qualitative.
4 Is shoe size an example of discrete or continuous data?	Discrete.
5 What type of data can you represent using a pictogram?	Qualitative.
6 When can data be arranged in a two-way table?	When data falls into two different sets of categories; for example, the number of students in different year groups and their favourite sport.
7 What is the formula used to calculate the number of items in a pie chart sector?	Number of items $= \left(\dfrac{\text{angle of sector}}{360}\right) \times$ total number.
8 What is the formula used to find the size of an angle of a pie chart sector, if you know the number of items in the sector?	Angle $= \left(\dfrac{\text{number of items in sector} \times \text{total number of items}}{360}\right)$.

Put paper here

Previous questions

Now go back and use these questions to check your knowledge of previous topics.

Questions	Answers
1 What is the hypotenuse?	The longest side of a right-angled triangle.
2 What is the value of sin 30?	0.5
3 How are bearings measured?	Clockwise from north.
4 How do you add two column vectors?	Add the top numbers together, and then add the bottom numbers together.
5 How do you factorise the difference of two squares, $x^2 - a^2$?	$(x + a)(x - a)$

Put paper here

Practice

Exam-style questions

29.1 Jon asks 20 pupils how many minutes it takes them to get to school each day.

Here are the results.

5	25	15	6	3	5	20	16	20	9
7	3	18	21	11	10	10	17	4	8

Complete the grouped frequency table for this data.

Time (minutes)	Frequency
0–5	
6–10	
11–15	
16–20	
21–25	

[2 marks]

29.2 Children were asked how many pets they have.
The bar chart shows the results.

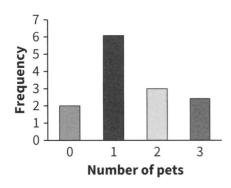

How many children were surveyed? **[1 mark]**

29.3 The pictogram shows information about children's favourite ice cream.

30 children chose strawberry.

Vanilla	
Strawberry	🍦🍦🍦🍦🍦🍦🍦
Chocolate	🍦🍦🍦🍦🍦🍦🍦🍦🍦🍦🍦

Key

🍦 = _____ children

(a) Complete the key. **[1 mark]**

(b) How many children chose chocolate? **[1 mark]**

(c) 20 children chose vanilla.

Use this information to complete the pictogram. **[1 mark]**

29.4 The table shows how 30 people travel to work.

Car	Walk	Bus	Train
15	7	3	5

Show this information on a bar chart.

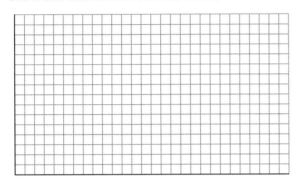

[3 marks]

29.5 The composite bar chart shows the sale of socks and shoes over three months.

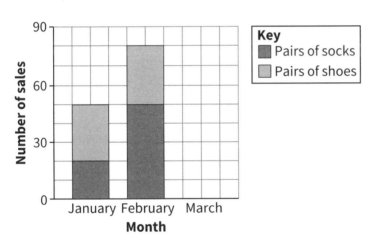

Key
- Pairs of socks
- Pairs of shoes

(a) Write down the number of pairs of socks sold in January. **[1 mark]**

(b) In February, more pairs of shoes were sold than pairs of socks.
How many more? **[1 mark]**

(c) In March, 50 pairs of shoes and 30 pairs of socks were sold.
Use this information to complete the bar chart. **[2 marks]**

29.6 The table shows a shop's profit each month from January to July.

Month	Jan	Feb	Mar	Apr	May	Jun	Jul
Profit (£)	3000	3500	4200	4500	4000	5000	6000

(a) Draw a time series graph for this data.

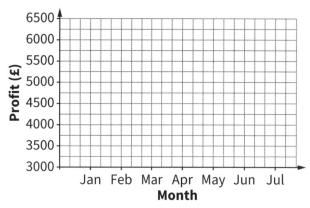

[2 marks]

(b) Describe the general trend of the data. [1 mark]

29.7 The time series graph shows the number of people at football matches over 8 weeks.

> **EXAM TIP**
> You might find it helpful to draw on the graph to help you make your prediction.

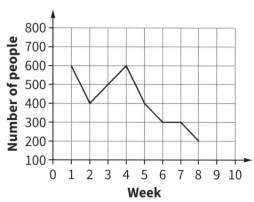

(a) Describe the general trend of the data. [1 mark]

(b) Which two weeks had the greatest number of people? [1 mark]

(c) Use the general trend to predict the attendance in Week 9. [1 mark]

29.8 200 people took part in a survey.

The pie chart shows their ages.

Work out how many people aged 16–24 took the survey.

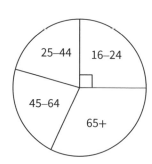

[1 mark]

29.9 Sam asked students to name their favourite type of book.

Here are her results.

Draw an accurate pie chart for her results.

Favourite type	Science fiction	Fantasy	Romance	Other	Total
Frequency	34	20	6	12	

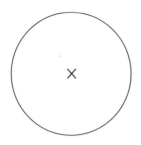

[3 marks]

29.10 The pie charts show some information about GCSE grades at two secondary schools.

Winterton High

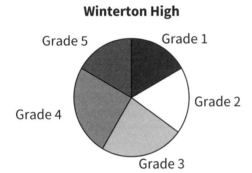

Summerton High

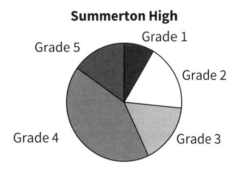

Jusuf says "More students got Grade 4 at Winterton High."

Give a reason why Jusuf could be wrong. [2 marks]

Questions referring to previous content

29.11 A square has a perimeter of 20 cm.

Work out the area of the square. [2 marks]

29.12 A bird spots a worm on the ground.

The worm is 50 m away from the bird at an angle of 40°.

Work out the vertical height, x, of the bird above the ground.

Give your answer correct to 2 significant figures.

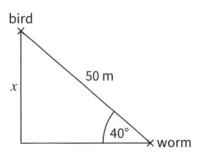

[3 marks]

Knowledge

30 Sampling and averages

Types of data

	Definition	Examples		
Data	Any information you can collect.	The heights of people who live in London.	The number of children in different classes of a school.	The number of eggs that chickens on a farm lay.
Population	The entire group of things that you can choose from.	All the people who live in London.	All the classes in the school.	All the chickens that live on the farm.
Sample	A smaller set within the population that you can collect data from.	One person from every street in London.	One class from each year group in the school.	Five chickens from the farm.
Biased sample	A sample that doesn't represent the population well.	A group of men from a basketball team.	Classes only in the junior school.	The five healthiest chickens on the farm.

In a **random sample**, each member of the **population** is equally likely to be chosen.

Data from a sample can be used to estimate properties of the whole population.

The larger the sample, the more accurate the estimates.

> ### Worked example
>
> Jessica wants to know how many books the students in her school read each month.
>
> There are 1000 students in her school, so she wants to use a sample.
>
> She decides to go to the library and ask students how many books they have read that month.
>
> 1. What type of data will Jessica have?
>
>   Quantitative, primary data •————————— It is numerical and Jessica has collected it herself.
>
> 2. Jessica asks 10 students in total, and finds that two of them have read more than five books that month.
>
>   Use this data to estimate how many students in the entire school have read more than five books that month.
>
> $\frac{2}{10} = \frac{1}{5}$ •————————— Find the proportion in the sample who have read more than five books.
>
> $\frac{1}{5} \times 1000 = 200$ students •————————— Multiply the proportion in the sample by the total number of students.
>
> 3. Explain why the sample might be biased and your previous estimate may not be accurate.
>
>   Not all students in the school have an equal chance of being in the sample, and students in the library are likely to have read more books than average.

Averages

Average	Description	Example
Mean	The sum of all values divided by the total number of values.	The mean of 3, 4, 8, 5 is $\frac{3+4+8+5}{4}=\frac{20}{4}=5$
Median	The middle value when the data is put in order. If there are two middle values, find the mean of the two middle values.	The median of 3, 4, 5, 7 is $\frac{4+5}{2}=\frac{9}{2}=4.5$
Mode	The most commonly occurring value. There can be no mode, one mode or multiple modes.	The mode of 3, **4**, 7, 5, 3, **4**, 8, **4**, 6 is 4
Range	The difference between the largest and smallest values.	The range of 3, 4, 7, 5 is $7-3=4$

Ungrouped frequency tables

You can find the **mean**, **median**, **mode**, and **range** when data is in an ungrouped frequency table.

Worked example

The table shows the number of sunny days per week over a period of three weeks.

Number of sunny days	0	1	2	3	4	5	6	7
Frequency	3	8	4	2	1	1	0	2

Work out the

1. median

   $\frac{(1+1)}{2}=1$ — Write out the data in a list, and find the middle value(s).

   0, 0, 0, 1, 1, 1, 1, 1, 1, ①, ①, 2, 2, 2, 2, 3, 3, 4, 5, 7, 7

2. mode

   1 — Mode is the number with the highest frequency.

3. mean

   $\frac{45}{21}$
   $= 2.1$ (1 d.p.)

   Add a row to the frequency table for number of days × frequency

No. days × frequency	0	8	8	6	4	5	0	14	= 45 total

   REVISION TIP

   When finding the mean, remember that you always divide by the sum of all the frequencies.

4. range.

   $7-0=7$ — The difference between the largest and smallest values.

Knowledge

30 Sampling and averages

Grouped frequency tables

You can find an estimate for the mean, as well as the **modal class** (the group with the highest frequency) and the **median class** (the group that the middle value lies in) for data given in a grouped frequency table.

> **Worked example**
>
> The lengths of 25 pieces of string are recorded in the table.
>
> | Length of string (s cm) | Number of pieces of string |
> |---|---|
> | $0 < s \leq 8$ | 12 |
> | $8 < s \leq 12$ | 6 |
> | $12 < s \leq 20$ | 7 |
>
> **1.** Write down the modal class
>
> $0 < s \leq 8$ —— The modal class it has the highest frequency, 12.
>
> **2.** Work out which class the median lies in.
>
> 13 lies between 12 and 18, so the 13th value lies in the $8 < s \leq 12$ class.
>
> There are 25 pieces of string, so the median will be the 13th. Add a running total column to the table.
>
> | Length of string (s cm) | Frequency | Running total |
> |---|---|---|
> | $0 < s \leq 8$ | 12 | 12 |
> | $8 < s \leq 12$ | 6 | 18 |
> | $12 < s \leq 20$ | 7 | 25 |
>
> **3.** Calculate an estimate for the mean.
>
> Estimate for mean $= \dfrac{220}{25} = 8.8$ cm
>
> Add columns for the midpoint and midpoint × frequency
>
> | Length of string (s cm) | Midpoint | Frequency | Midpoint × frequency |
> |---|---|---|---|
> | $0 < s \leq 8$ | 4 | 12 | 48 |
> | $8 < s \leq 12$ | 10 | 6 | 60 |
> | $12 < s \leq 20$ | 16 | 7 | 112 |
> | **Totals** | | **25** | **220** |
>
> **REVISION TIP**
>
> It is not possible to find the exact mean because we do not know all the exact values. So, we estimate by assuming that, for each group, every string had length equal to the midpoint of the group.

 Key terms — Make sure you can write a definition for these key terms

biased sample   mean   median   median class   modal class
mode   population   random sample   range   sample

30 Sampling and averages

Learn the answers to the questions below, then cover the answers column with a piece of paper and write as many as you can. Check and repeat.

	Questions	Answers
1	What is quantitative data?	Numerical data.
2	What is a random sample?	A sample in which each member of the population is equally likely to be chosen.
3	How do you calculate the mean of a list of data values?	Add up all the values and divide by the total number of values.
4	How do you calculate the median of a list of data values?	List the data in ascending order and select the middle value.
5	What do you do if there are two middle values when finding the median?	Find the mean of the two middle values.
6	What is the mode?	The most frequently occurring value.
7	What is the range?	The difference between the highest and lowest value.
8	How do you calculate the mean of ungrouped data in a frequency table?	Multiply each value by its frequency, add up these values, and divide by the total of the frequencies.
9	For grouped data, what is the median class?	The class that the middle value lies in.
10	For grouped data, what is the modal class?	The group with the highest frequency.
11	Why is the mean from a grouped frequency table just an estimate?	Because we do not know the exact values in each group, we estimate that all the values in each group take the middle value in that group.
12	How do you find the middle value between two numbers?	Add them together and divide by 2.
13	What is meant by the term biased?	Unfair.
14	What is primary data?	Data you collect yourself.

Put paper here (repeated in central margin)

Previous questions

Now go back and use these questions to check your knowledge of previous topics.

	Questions	Answers
1	What is Pythagoras' theorem?	$c^2 = a^2 + b^2$
2	What is the formula used to find the volume of a cylinder?	volume $= \pi r^2 h$
3	When you are rounding to the nearest whole number, which number do you need to consider first?	The first decimal.
4	What is the value of cos 90?	0
5	What is the tan ratio?	$\tan \theta = \dfrac{\text{opposite}}{\text{adjacent}}$

Put paper here (repeated in central margin)

Practice

30.1 Brita carries out a survey of 20 people to see what type of music they like best.

The table gies information about her results.

Type of music	Number of people
classical	8
rock and roll	7
country	5

Which type of music is the mode? **[1 mark]**

30.2 Maria is planning an event for 180 students.

She asks a sample of 40 students what type of event they would like.

Each student chooses one event.

The table shows information about her results.

> **EXAM TIP**
>
> First find the fraction of the sample who want a day at the funfair.

Type of celebration	Frequency
Cinema trip	11
Party	10
Meal out	11
Day at funfair	8

(a) Work out how many of the 180 students you think would like a day at the funfair. **[2 marks]**

(b) State **any** assumption you have made **and** explain how this may affect your answer. **[1 mark]**

 30.3 Here are the heights in cm of 7 boys in a class.

154   151   152   157   150   148   159

(a) Find the median.

(b) Find the range. **[1 mark]**

 30.4 Bertrand rolled an 8-sided dice 16 times. His scores were:

2	4	3	2	8	6	2	2
7	1	1	2	4	6	8	6

(a) Write down the mode. **[1 mark]**

(b) Find the median. **[2 marks]**

(c) Work out the mean. **[2 marks]**

(d) Work out the range. **[1 mark]**

30.5 The mean of 10 numbers is 63.

The mean of four of the numbers is 51.

Work out the mean of the remaining 6 numbers. **[3 marks]**

 30.6 Ellie rolled a dice 20 times. Her results are shown below.

5	3	4	6	3	1	3	3	5	3
6	6	2	3	1	1	1	5	4	2

(a) Complete the frequency table to show Ellie's results.

Score on dice	Tally	Frequency
1		
2		
3		
4		
5		
6		

[2 marks]

(b) Write

(i) the mode **[1 mark]**

(ii) the range **[1 mark]**

(iii) the median. **[1 mark]**

 30.7 Rob measures 100 worms.

The table shows his results.

Length (x cm)	Frequency, f	Midpoint	$f \times$ midpoint
$0 < x \leq 8$	50	4	200
$8 < x \leq 16$	30	12	
$16 < x \leq 24$	20		400
Total	**100**		

(a) Complete the table. **[2 marks]**

(b) Write down the modal class. **[1 mark]**

(c) Work out an estimate for the mean length. **[2 marks]**

Exam-style questions

30.8 71 people take part in a 5 km race.

The table shows their finishing times in minutes.

Time (*t* minutes)	Frequency
$20 < t \leq 25$	10
$25 < t \leq 30$	17
$30 < t \leq 35$	24
$35 < t \leq 40$	11
$40 < t \leq 45$	9

    (a) Find the class interval that contains the median. **[2 marks]**

    (b) Work out your estimate for the mean finishing time.

           Give your answer to the nearest minute. **[3 marks]**

> **EXAM TIP**
> Add extra columns to the table to help you.

    (c) Explain why your answer to part **b** is only an estimate. **[1 mark]**

30.9 Nana says, 'I can't estimate the mean score because I don't know the value of *y*.'

Score (*x*)	Frequency
$0 < t \leq 4$	$3y$
$4 < t \leq 8$	$7y$

> **EXAM TIP**
> Follow the usual method using the expressions given for the frequency instead.

Nana is wrong. Work out an estimate of the mean score. **[3 marks]**

30.10 This sign was displayed in a dentist surgery.

> 88 appointments were missed last month.
>
> These missed appointments were a total of 36 hours.

Work out the mean length of time for each appointment.

Give your answer in minutes. **[3 marks]**

Question referring to previous content

30.11 The lines AB and DC are parallel.

ABC is an isosceles triangle with $AB = BC$.

Work out the size of the angle BCA.

Give a reason for each step
of your working.

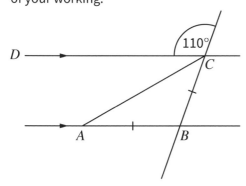

EXAM TIP

Mark the angle you want
to find on the diagram to
help you.

[3 marks]

30.12 There are 400 counters in a box.

The counters are blue or white or green.

$\frac{2}{5}$ of the counters are blue.

35 of the counters are white.

What percentage of the counters are green?　　　　**[4 marks]**

Knowledge

31 Scatter graphs

Scatter graphs, correlation, and causation

Scatter graphs show the relationship between two sets of quantitative data (or variables), such as the age and height of a group of children. In this example, each point represents one child.

Correlation describes how data may be related. It can be positive or negative, and range from strong to weak:

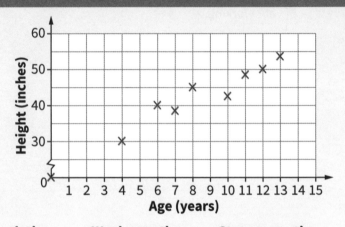

Strong, positive

Weak positive

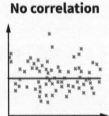

No correlation

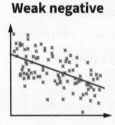

Weak negative

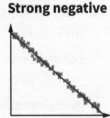

Strong negative

Correlation does not always mean that one variable **causes** the other. For example, this data shows the number of shoes and siblings that a group of people have.

The two are positively correlated, but the number of siblings that someone has does not cause a person to have more shoes. There is correlation, but not **causation**.

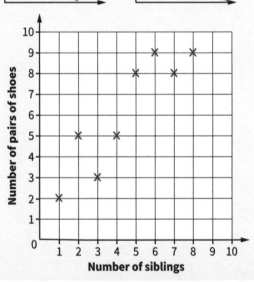

Plotting scatter graphs

A **line of best fit:**

- allows you to see the trend more clearly
- ignores **outliers**, and goes through as many points as possible
- does not need to go through the origin

- goes to the edge of the data and not outside it
- can be used to estimate a value (**interpolation**) within the line of best fit
- should not be used to predict results outside the line of best fit (**extrapolation**).

Key terms Make sure you can write a definition for these key terms

causation   correlation   extrapolation   interpolation
line of best fit   outliers   scatter graph

Plotting scatter graphs

Worked example

The data shows the age of 11 chickens and the number of eggs each one laid in a month.

Age (years)	1	2	2	3	3	4	4	4	5	5	6
Eggs per month	22	18	24	16	20	15	17	19	16	19	5

1. Plot a scatter graph to show this information.

2. Add a line of best fit.

3. Use interpolation to suggest how many eggs a 2-year-old hen would lay.

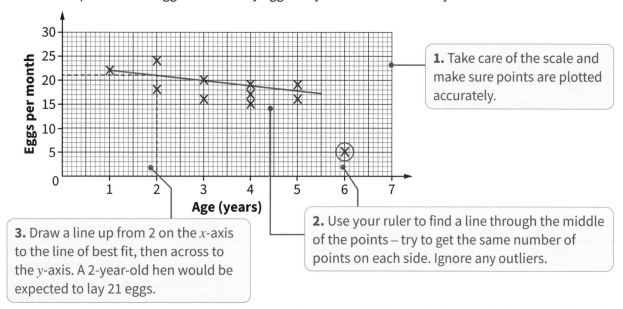

1. Take care of the scale and make sure points are plotted accurately.

2. Use your ruler to find a line through the middle of the points – try to get the same number of points on each side. Ignore any outliers.

3. Draw a line up from 2 on the x-axis to the line of best fit, then across to the y-axis. A 2-year-old hen would be expected to lay 21 eggs.

Worked example

1. Estimate the speed of texting for a 40-year-old.

   22 words per minute.

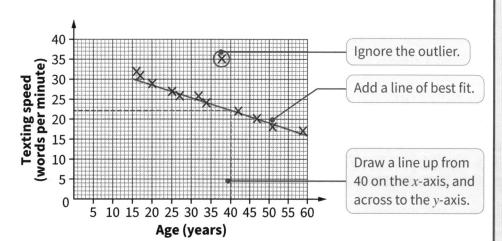

Ignore the outlier.

Add a line of best fit.

Draw a line up from 40 on the x-axis, and across to the y-axis.

2. Millie claims that the graph shows that a 5-year-old will be able to text approximately 34 words per minute.

   Comment on Millie's claim.

   You don't have any data for people under 16, so Millie is using extrapolation and her estimate is unreliable (and seems unlikely).

31 Scatter graphs

Learn the answers to the questions below, then cover the answers column with a piece of paper and write as many as you can. Check and repeat.

	Questions	Answers
1	What is correlation?	A relationship between two sets of data.
2	What is a line of best fit?	A line which follows the trend of the data.
3	What are the types of correlation?	Positive and negative (and strong/weak).
4	What is interpolation?	Using the line of best fit to estimate a value within the range of the data.
5	What is extrapolation?	Making predictions outside the range of data.
6	Why do we need to be careful when extrapolating data?	It is not reliable. The relationship between the variables might not hold for values outside the data.
7	Does correlation mean causation?	No.
8	What does a strong positive correlation look like?	All points are close together and follow a positive gradient.
9	If a scatter graph has no correlation, what does this mean?	There is no relationship between the two sets of data.
10	How do you draw a line of best fit?	Use a ruler to find a line through the middle of the points, trying to get the same number of points on each side. The line of best fit should only go to the edge of the data and not outside it. Ignore outliers.
11	Describe a weak correlation.	Points that are roughly following an upward or downward line but are fairly spread out.
12	What type of data can be plotted on a scatter graph?	Quantitative data (numerical values).

Put paper here

Previous questions

Now go back and use these questions to check your knowledge of previous topics.

	Questions	Answers
1	What is the mode of a set of data?	The most common value or group.
2	What is qualitative data?	Non-numerical data (such as hair colour).
3	If an event is certain, what is its probability?	1
4	What shape is the locus of points that are a fixed distance from a point?	A circle.
5	What is the value of sin 90?	1

Put paper here

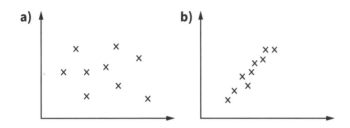

31.1 State whether these scatter graphs show correlation.

When there is correlation, state the type.

a)

b)

[3 marks]

31.2 Write the type of correlation, if any, you would expect between

(a) the number of hours listening to music, and shoe size   [1 mark]

(b) the number of builders, and time taken to build a house   [1 mark]

(c) the length of a fish, and its mass.   [1 mark]

31.3 The scatter graph shows information about ages and heights of children.

It shows the age and height of each child.

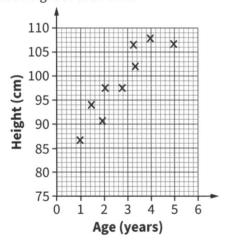

(a) A child is 20 months old.

Estimate the height of this child.   [1 mark]

(b) Estimate the height of a child aged 36 months.   [1 mark]

Exam-style questions

31.4 Farid records each student's number of absences and exam mark.

The table shows his results.

Number of absences	0	2	5	10	17	20	25	30	35	40
Exam mark	90	85	76	75	75	50	35	80	40	20

(a) Draw a scatter diagram for this information.

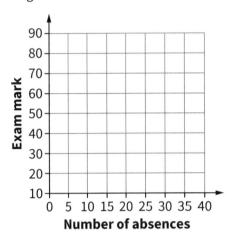

[2 marks]

(b) One of the points is an outlier.

Circle the outlier on your graph. [1 mark]

(c) Write down the type of correlation. [1 mark]

31.5 The scatter graph shows information about bus journeys.

It shows the time of each bus journey and the number of times the bus stopped.

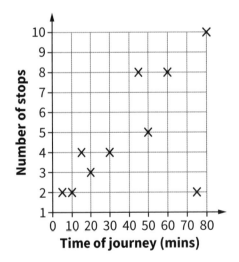

(a) Describe the correlation between the time of a bus journey and the number of stops. [1 mark]

(b) Write down the coordinates of the outlier. [1 mark]

31.6 Trevor draws a scatter graph of number of sandcastles on a beach and number of electric fans sold.

His scatter graph shows positive correlation.

Trevor says that an increase in the number of sandcastles causes an increase in the number of electric fans sold.

Explain why Trevor is wrong. **[1 mark]**

31.7 The scatter graph shows information about cycling up hills.

It shows cycling speeds on hills with different uphill gradients.

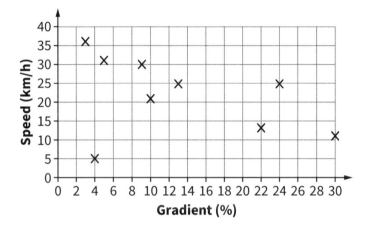

(a) Ignoring the outlier, draw a line of best fit on the scatter graph. **[1 mark]**

(b) A cyclist's speed is 15km/h.

Estimate the gradient of the hill she is cycling up. **[1 mark]**

(c) Marta estimates that a cyclist on a hill with 40% gradient will have a speed of 5 km/h.

Is Marta correct? Explain your answer. **[1 mark]**

> **EXAM TIP**
> Remember an outlier does not follow the same trend as the rest of the data.

Questions referring to previous content

31.8 The area of a rectangle is $4x + 10xy$.

(a) Fully factorise the expression for the area. **[2 marks]**

(b) Use your answer to part (a) to write a possible length and a width for the rectangle, in terms of x and y. **[1 mark]**

Great Clarendon Street, Oxford, OX2 6DP, United Kingdom

Oxford University Press is a department of the University of Oxford. It furthers the University's objective of excellence in research, scholarship, and education by publishing worldwide. Oxford is a registered trade mark of Oxford University Press in the UK and in certain other countries.

© Oxford University Press 2023

Written by Naomi Bartholomew-Millar, Paul Hunt and Victoria Trumper

The moral rights of the authors have been asserted

The publisher would also like to thank Katie Wood and Jemma Sherwood for their work on the first edition of Edexcel GCSE Maths Foundation Revision Guide (978-138-200649-1) and Revision Workbook (978-138-200650-7) on which this revision guide is based.

First published in 2023

British Library Cataloguing in Publication Data
Data available

978-1-382-03984-0

10 9 8 7 6 5 4 3 2 1

The manufacturing process conforms to the environmental regulations of the country of origin.

Printed in the UK by Bell and Bain Ltd, Glasgow

Acknowledgements

Artworks: QBS Learning

The publisher would also like to thank Deb Friis and Katherine Pate for sharing their expertise and feedback in the development of this resource.

Although we have made every effort to trace and contact all copyright holders before publication this has not been possible in all cases. If notified, the publisher will rectify any errors or omissions at the earliest opportunity.

Links to third party websites are provided by Oxford in good faith and for information only. Oxford disclaims any responsibility for the materials contained in any third party website referenced in this work.